The Display of Archaeology in Museums of Northern Greece

The Socio-Politics and Poetics of Museum Narratives

Archondia Polyzoudi

The Display of Archaeology in Museums of Northern Greece

The Socio-Politics and Poetics of Museum Narratives

Archondia Polyzoudi

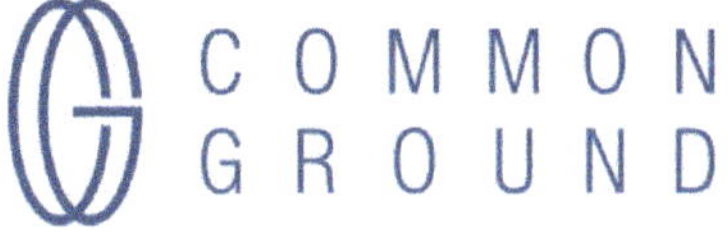

First published in 2020
as part of the Inclusive Museum Book Imprint
http://doi.org/ 10.18848/978-1-86335-185-0/CGP (Full Book)

Common Ground Research Networks
2001 South First Street, Suite 202
University of Illinois Research Park
Champaign, IL
61820

Library of Congress Cataloging-in-Publication Data

Names: Polyzoudi, Archondia, author.
Title: The display of archaeology in museums of northern Greece : the socio-politics and poetics of museum narratives / Archondia Polyzoudi.
Description: Champaign, IL : Common Ground, 2020. | Includes bibliographical references. | Summary: "This study takes an interest in exploring Greek museum representations of the past in relation to the intellectual histories of the archaeological accounts involved in the investigation of material culture. It is argued within this work that museum is place of power and a forum in which the knowledge of the past is created, interpreted and presented to the public and re-presented and re-interpreted due to the multiple narratives created by multiple recipients and heritage consumers. Also, this study is concerned with a thorough discussion examining how and by whom the action of 'making meaning', 'story-telling' or 'narrating past histories' is produced in archaeological discourses and museum representations; and what kinds of relationships and networkings are created by this process. The critical analysis of the museum exhibitions of case studies is carried out by examining the museum as institution, as architecture and as narrative, as a way of seeking to understand its multiple roles, educational, historical, symbolic, in modern society, which serve as social formulations of socio-cultural knowledge"-- Provided by publisher.
Identifiers: LCCN 2019045442 (print) | LCCN 2019045443 (ebook) | ISBN 9781863351836 (hardback) | ISBN 9781863351843 (paperback) | ISBN 9781863351850 (pdf)
Subjects: LCSH: Archaeological museums and collections--Greece. | Antiquities--Interpretive programs--Greece. | Material culture--Greece. | Museums--Social aspects--Greece. | Cultural property--Greece.
Classification: LCC DF11.2 .P65 2020 (print) | LCC DF11.2 (ebook) | DDC 949.50074/4956--dc23
LC record available at https://lccn.loc.gov/2019045442
LC ebook record available at https://lccn.loc.gov/2019045443

Cover Photo Credit: Phillip Kalantzis-Cope/CGRN

Table of Contents

List of Abbreviations

AMT	Archaeological Museum of Thessaloniki
CAC	Central Archaeological Council
CSVPA	Cultural and Spiritual Values of Protected Areas
DMEEP	Department of Museums, Exhibitions and Educational Programmes
DASMR	Department of Archaeological Sites, Monuments and Research
DDRPA	Department of Documentation, Registration and Publications of Antiquities
DC	Department of Conservation
EBA	Ephorate of Byzantine Antiquities
EFF	European Funding Framework
EU	European Union
EC	European Council
EPCA	Ephorate of Prehistoric and Classical Antiquities
EMT	Ethnological Museum of Thrace (Alexandroupolis)
FEMMT	Folk life and Ethnological Museum of Macedonia-Thrace
ICOM	International Council of Museums
ICOMOS	International Council Monuments and Sites
IUCN	International Union for Conservation of Nature
KEDKE	Central Union of Municipalities and Communities of Greece (CUMCG)
MBC	Museum of Byzantine Culture
MD	Ministerial Decree
MoCT	Ministry of Culture and Tourism
NAM	National Archaeological Museum
PD	Presidential Decree
UNESCO	United Nations Educational, Scientific and Cultural Organization

CHAPTER 1

Introduction

I. INTRODUCTION TO THE STUDY

This study aims to explore the museum's institutional potential in relation to archaeological scholarship engaged in the interpretation of material culture. It discusses the diverse nature of the archaeological museum as a space for creating and constructing meanings by examining the potentialities of presenting and exhibiting the past in a museum context. The archaeological museum, as a medium and as an instrument of archaeological discourse, has influenced theoretical and practical thinking as to how the material culture of past societies should be presented and interpreted. It constitutes a dynamic location where representational practices and interpretive means can have a fundamental impact on the way in which the past is perceived and 'translated' by the public. Through the involvement of different agencies in the meaning-making process and the multiplicity of approaches that the museum or museum-like contexts can adopt in the creation of representational narratives, the museum as a field has come to acquire an interdisciplinary character, crucial for its critical theorizing.

It can be noted that the archaeological museum can take multiple forms, depending on the socio-political, cultural, and economic values placed on past remains and the way in which these values are manifested in the museum context. In this way, the museum as a 'modern' institution determinately defines and influences the framework in which an understanding of the past is formed by the public. The narratives as produced in the museum environment can further play a decisively active role in the formation of archaeological discourse insofar as they participate in forming interpretations of the archaeological material that will be the subject of investigation of this dissertation.

Within this framework, this investigation takes into consideration the theoretical accounts and readings of the material culture and the museum field which have put at the centre of the discourse of the past their multifaceted approaches to the interpretation of both tangible and intangible heritage. In this way, a new direction is given not so much to the content but to the way in which something is written or told and the social and historical conditions surrounding the writing and telling. So, it can be argued that in a museum context what is really stressed is not the material evidence of past societies but mainly how these traces invoke multiple readings and invite multiple approaches. Following these aspects, the emphasis in this work is placed on investigating how the heritage is used, interpreted and presented to the public; which 'agents' define these processes; and by which mechanisms trajectories of communication are created. Reflecting on this approach, it is interesting to consider a museum as a medium or instrument of archaeological discourse, since 'any discourse, particularly when it is promoted by bodies of 'experts', state-sanctioned agencies and international bodies...carries power' (Smith, 2006:299), and it is mainly that attribute that makes the museum one of the most effective political means of communication in the first decade of the twenty-first century.

The 'power' of the museum rests on a diversity of potentials of 'museum materialities' (Dudley 2010) that take as a starting point, and as a key focus for the exploration of museum narratives, the role of the object in a dialectical relation with the agents that produce and consume meanings in a museum context. Archaeology as a discipline constructs its past objects through the workings of a discourse that can be treated as a set of heterogeneous networkings; technologies of cultural production which provide the conditions within which statements may be made, texts constituted, interpretations made, even people constituted as subjectivities (Shanks and Hodder 1995:24). Contrastingly, the museum is part of the above discourse and generates a new spatial-temporal framework within which new aspects and facets of narratives of the material culture of the past are illuminated, creating a nexus of interpretive tools and 'languages.' Within and through this nexus, the objects as 'signatures' of the past (Appadurai 2010) and the audience as consumers and producers of the same past are engaged through a communicative active mechanism that is promoted by the museum context. Prompted by these observations, this study aims to shed light on the theoretical and practical complexities that have arisen in the research and study of the museum as an institution in the meaning-making process and in the construction of communicative channels of meanings in a wider sense. Questions of how to explain and understand the archaeological material remains of the past, how to interpret them, write about them and present them to the public create a number of interesting and challenging dilemmas which are encountered by archaeologists and heritage practitioners, causing them to produce and adopt different rhetorical strategies of narrating the past. These questions have significant implications in the study of the museum 'phenomenon' and create multiple interpretation 'channels' and museum-methods concerned with power, authority and their relationships with their audiences (Dudley 2010; Hooper-Greenhill 2004; Karp and Lavine 1991; Karp, Kreamer and Lavine 1992; Macdonald and Fyfe 1996; Macdonald 1998; Merriman 2000; Waterton and Watson 2010).

The above considerations and pursuits have found fertile ground in my investigation of the vast and enthralling treasury of antiquities existing within Greek territory, based on which the museum as *institution*, as *architecture,* and as *narrative* is being 'de-constructed'. By adopting a broad and interdisciplinary framework for studying and managing the past and conducting an exploration into the 'philosophy' of museum representations, the 'museum materialities' are re-evaluated. The Greek museum in this study represented an interesting and stimulating working space for research, allowing us to investigate the multiple and changing character of the museum as a place for telling stories about the past. This multi-variant nature, formed by different interpretations and approaches to archaeological material, is reflected in the multiple 'pasts'[1] of the Greek context, which in turn create a 'palimpsestal' present. Traces and remains of the past are seen and read through the lenses of the present, creating a dynamic relation with the future. This relation can be revealed and approached by the research theories of archaeologists, anthropologists and museologists, building the story-telling framework within which museum narratives and heritage meanings will be expressed. And here lies the challenging spectrum of the archaeological interpretations and museum representations in Greece, which encompass all the historical, political and social foundations upon which the archaeological practices and museum discourses have been built over decades.

New discoveries of archaeological sites in northern Greece have come to light within the past few decades giving new directions to our understanding of the past and a new stimulus for the creation of a considerable number of exhibition spaces, which are ready to house a plethora of artefacts, along with their ideologies, politics and poetics—in other words, their biographies (Kopytoff 1986). Archaeological sites, open-air museums, state and private museums and collections, cultural institutions, and foundations have emerged to engage with the past. It could be argued that the Greek remains of the past are approached by a) *seeing* an object or monument through the process of visual experience, b) *being* in a place, through the act of communication and of making and experiencing meaning, and c) *acting* in the present: that is, by interpreting, writing and presenting the Greek past to the public, a process that is taking place in the present. In a series of writings and theoretical accounts produced during the 1980s and 1990s, Greek academics, professional archaeologists, and museum practitioners have developed their own theories regarding the historical, ideological, social, and epistemological role of the archaeological museums in modern Greek society (Kotsakis 1991, 1998). Their approaches have given new stimulus to the development of a framework in which archaeology as a discipline and the museum as a cultural process have become embedded in a given social-cultural context.

The concern of this study, as will be described in the next section, is to challenge these archaeological heritage and museum considerations, perceived as traditional, and to provide a new way of thinking by theorizing about heritage and museums in a different framework of study, using case studies from Greece where many pasts and many stories are made to be told.

II. Research Purpose

The purpose of this study was to provide a critical approach to the development of Greek Museums in northern Greece in post-modern times and to investigate the way in which Greek archaeology is approached, written, and presented in museums. My intention was to investigate how the discursive nature of archaeology was expressed

[1] With the phrase 'multiple pasts' the author is referring to the chronological classification of the discipline of archaeology as formulated by the Greek Archaeological Law and as used by the archaeological community. So, there is Prehistoric, Classical, Byzantine...archaeology, each with a distinct 'past'.

and reflected in museum writings and their readings of the past and to what extent these two fields are interacting or have become identical in their primary functions, i.e. in their attempt to interpret, reconstruct, and manage the past. The museum was examined as the object of study; as such, the main attempt of the study was to uncover the reasons why the nature of an institution has constantly changed in recent years and to what extent it is being affected by ideological and political constructions and perceptions of the representations of the past. The perspectives from which we see it and from which we critically theorize the museum are multiple, and they are drawn from different fields, such as archaeology, anthropology, philosophy, sociology, and linguistics, reflecting the dynamic and active role of the museum as a social institution in modern or post-modern societies. It is argued within this work that museums are places of power and political arenas in which the understanding of the past is created, formulated, and disseminated to the public, becoming re-presented and re-interpreted due to the multiple narratives created by multiple recipients and heritage consumers. Exactly how that power is generated and expressed, and what socio-political implications arise from museum practices, the poetics, and the rhetoric of museum strategies was examined through this study.

In aiming to reveal the poetics and politics of museum representations of the past, that is, 'the structures, rituals and procedures by which the relations between objects, bodies of knowledge and processes of ideological persuasion are enacted' (Sherman and Rogoff 1994(x)), this study essentially tried to shed light on the discourse of the northern Greek museums and their archaeological exhibitions. My interest in these subjects was engendered by these questions: what kind of attitudes, state or private, towards the archaeological past and its material remains can be located and identified in Greece? To what extent do museums in northern Greece address the theories of archaeological practice? Taking into account on the one hand the impact of the theorization of Greek antiquity, as undertaken and perceived in Western Europe following the creation of the Greek state, and, on the other, how Greek antiquity (ruins, monuments, objects) dominated the intellectual and political existence of the new state of modern Greeks, it is first necessary for us to analyze the attitudes and perceptions of modern Greeks to the archaeological past and its remains.

This thesis seeks to contribute to both heritage and material studies as well as to museum studies. One can easily recognize that these fields are characterized by multiple and interdisciplinary approaches, creating room for further research and study. Finding new ground for thought and reflection is always a stimulating opportunity, especially when the case studies are rooted in such rich material and such varied perceptions of the past as exist in the Greek context. And, on the other side, the museum as a research field constitutes a place that can beget manifold and multi-faceted insights and approaches that, in turn, can induce and stimulate creative and academically effective research.

The problems addressed by this thesis were discussed within a theoretical and practical framework of analysis. The former was informed by a long theoretical tradition, which was created in related disciplines (as mentioned above), and the latter was grounded in the application of various forms of methodologies that have been put into practice in heritage and museum policy-making strategies, in trying to reveal the dynamics of the so-called museum phenomenon during the last few decades.

III. Studying Archaeology and Museums: Theoretical Reflections and Methodological Tools

The focus of this chapter was the theoretical framework within which museums' narratives and their constructions of the past are created. First, considerations of the past and of the heritage arising from the discipline of archaeology are a matter of concern. The discussion then turns to the theoretical approaches generated within the disciplines of anthropology and museology and discusses the function that the theoretical background could have in the investigation of Greek museum displays. In that direction, concepts and approaches from other disciplines, such as history, art history, and heritage and cultural research management, have been taken into consideration. One of the primary concerns of this section was to formulate a background theoretical approach to encourage the critical analysis of the museum context, leading to a new and challenging perspective on the projects presented. Definitions of the main terms that appear in the study are provided. The section ends with the presentation of the sources, the case studies, and the methodological tools used in the research.

Approaching the Museum

This sub-section first illustrates the theoretical approaches related to museum analysis, then moves on to discuss how these theoretical perspectives have given new impetus to the development of the critical analysis of the museum.

1. Archaeological Theoretical Approaches to the Museum

Some of the theoretical approaches that shed light on some initial parts of this study are those introduced by Shanks and Tilley (Shanks and Tilley 1992) in which they conceive the museum as an ideological institution which intervenes in the past as it conserves, preserves and presents artefacts which originated in the past to the public. They argue that museum exhibitions are rhetorical performances which encourage persuasive intention and meaning (Shanks and Tilley 1992:68-99). In the different types of museums that they analysed, they proposed that a redemptive aesthetic could exist through the recognition of the fragmentary nature of the past and the placing of emphasis on the multidimensional character of meaning (ibid: 97-99). Also, of great concern in their work is to show how political content could influence the form of some conventional displays, thus manipulating and misrepresenting the past for present purposes. Influenced by these differently grounded viewpoints, this study attempted to go deeper and to produce new reflective channels, for example those referring to the rhetorical and persuasive mechanisms used by the museum to communicate meanings (the case studies in chapters III, IV, V, and VI).

Other theoretical contributions examined the writing of the past and presented it as invoking a plurality of interpretations of the past (Bender 2002; Saunders 2002; Tilley 2002, 2006). Archaeology is an interpretive practice which has to do with meanings, making sense of things, doing, and acting (Dudley 2010; Merriman 1995; Olsen 2010; Shanks and Hodder 1995 etc.). This is the claim of research in post-processual or interpretive archaeology, in which archaeology is conceived as a material practice in the present, making things from the traces of past constructions which are no less real, truthful, or authentic due to being constructed (Shank and Hodder 1995:3-28). The main elements of interpretive archaeology are founded on the interpretation discourses involved in making sense of the past, such as dialogue, narratives, poetics, and rhetoric of the fragmented designed pasts. This approach influences the critical aspect of this study, examining the museum as a narrative construction of meanings. In that sense, one could argue that the concept of the museum process could be considered as identical to the archaeological one, where the polysemic nature of the archaeological interpretation of the past meets the multivocal character of the museum narratives. The main feature of the interpretive approach is its empowering ability to transform the reader, the audience, from a passive recipient of prepared and closed texts and narratives into an active and dynamic creator of meanings, producing judgments and viewpoints and engaged in a productive, critical and creative dialogue with the workings of a written text.

Additionally, taking into account that Greek archaeology (and generally the discipline of archaeology) is significantly grounded in the study of and research into the abundant material traces (objects, buildings, houses, cities etc.) of past cultures, focusing mostly on the typological and functional features of things, this study pays attention to accounts and writings related to the importance of objects and materialities (Olsen 2003, 2010, Dudley 2010) and their roles in our perception of the past. In recent years, there has been a re-examination of the primary role of things, especially in material culture studies, causing archaeologists to return to fundamental patterns and norms of theorizing past cultures under the prism of modern and advanced methodologies. This shift is examined in the book by Olsen, 2010, *In Defence of Things*, where the things, the material traces of the world, 'possess their nonverbal qualities and are involved in their own material and historical processes' (Olsen 2010:172) and recognizing their durability and their 'in-place-ness' (ibid:173) has become one of the key aspects of our understanding of the world. Informed by these viewpoints, this study examined the discursive role of archaeology and the museum's representational mission; it puts these material traces at the forefront of the analysis and explores their passive or active contribution to the public perception of tangible and intangible Greek heritage.

2. The Museum as a Space and the Place as a Museum

Theoretical approaches that examine the museum as space and the sense of place have been introduced by many disciplines in which the museum is considered as a 'unique' place to exhibit the past. Accordingly, the place, archaeological or historical, in its own right is considered as a 'container' of the material traces of the past, which is socially constructed, and which can also be conceived as a museum which exhibits its own material potential and provides experience of the past. This study was informed by the approaches of heritage and museum studies as illustrated in a series of writings in recent years which aim to unmask, first, the architectonics of the museum as a space (Bal 1996; Duncan 2005; Knell 2007; Merriman 2000; Silverstone 1994; Ritchie 1994) and, second, the archaeological place or landscape as a 'living' museum in the broader sense (Ashmore and Knapp 1999; Bender 1993, 1998; Daniels and Cosgrove 1988; Schofield and Szymanski 2011; Stroulia and Sutton 2010; Tilley 1994; Waterton and Watson 2010) which were examined in the later chapters.

This study received thought-provoking impetus from one of the initial accounts of the sense of place in the book *Representation of the Past*, by Walsh 1992, in which he attempts to define the framework in which a sense of place can be provided by interpreting the past. For Walsh, developing a sense of place is crucial if people are to perceive their own past localities (Walsh 1992:148-175). He suggests that the perspective which sees the museum of the future as a *facilitator of the sense of place* (emphasis added) will be the main task of museum practices (Walsh 1992). After examining various different examples of eco-museums, he stresses the importance of the appreciation of the linkages of the material remains with the spaces which generated them in the articulations of the interpretation of the past. The main argument, according to Walsh, for developing a sense of place emphasizes the role of diachrony, and the temporal depth of places (ibid: 151). In recent writings, such as those in the edited volumes *Local Heritage, Global Context* (Schofield and Szymanski 2011) and *Archaeology in Situ* (Stroulia and Sutton 2010), it has been observed that there has been a shift towards engaging in interpretation and in working and understanding in more local contexts and taking into account what local people value about their local environment, thus defining its local distinctiveness (Clifford 2011). These trends contributed to my thinking within a changing framework; they are of crucial concern for this study because they provided a critical framework for the museum to be seen as an active space engaging in the creation of new forms of reading the past, combining the narratives provided by the multilayered historical-archaeological landscape and those provided by the museum as a communicator and creator of messages.

Other readings[2] which stress the active role of the place in the praxis of the interpretation of the past are included in Smith's, 2006 work on *Uses of Heritage*, where she attempts to define a framework within which the 'sense of place' is used and which communicates with the public. She argues that 'places or artefacts are cultural tools in the heritage process and as such can and do become integral to the heritage process, and can and do have their own effect, creating an important inter-relationship' (Smith 2006:305). The 'power' of that effect relies also 'on the power

[2] The concept of the sense of place has been a topic of study by many works, some of which include Uzzell and Ballantyne 1998; Low and Lawrence-Zuniga 2003; Lowenthal 2005; Carman 2002; MacLeod 2005; Silverstone 1994; and so on. This study has been influenced by a broad range of theoretical approaches which demonstrate the inter-disciplinary nature of heritage and museum studies.

given to them in heritage discourses, and the way they are conceived and valued as items of desire, status, or simply as possessing innate values and properties' (ibid:306).

3. Using Theoretical Approaches from Museology and Anthropology

Aspects of representation, ownership, ideology, and political issues have always been of great concern for those working in the field of anthropology and other social fields (Baxandall 1991, Walsh 1992, Uzzel and Ballantyne 1998, Merriman 2000). It should be noted that the majority of these studies situates the museum as a contested terrain, a symbolic place, and an important instrument for articulating national identity (Karp and Lavine 1991; Duncan 1991). The nature of the museum as a socially constructed institution in which the academic community can meet the broader public communities makes it one of the most powerful means of mediating information. 'Exhibitions like monographs have been given over to the representation of multiple perspectives, to the voices of the previously "spoken for" or ignored, to the acknowledgement of ambivalence, uncertainty and objectivity, to irony and the disruption of established form, and to self-reflection' (Macdonald 1996:7). The multivocality of the stories that are told in museum representations has been articulated as central to the discourse of the museum, whether this refers to the intrinsic features of the artefacts, the presumptions of the narrated stories of the curator or the active visitor.

> 'All exhibitions are inevitably organized on the basis of assumptions about the intent of the objects' producers, the cultural skills and qualifications of the audience, the claims to authoritativeness made by the exhibition, and judgments of the aesthetic merit or authenticity of the objects or settings exhibited' (Karp and Lavine 1991:11).

On the curator's role and that of curatorial ability in creating exhibition stories, many accounts from museum studies have been presented focusing on the powerful and catalytic role of the interpreter. The curators are perceived as 'the catalysts who determine the way relationships are established between publicly seen artifacts and consumers' (Gathercole 1989:75). Their role is decisive in defining the contents of these relationships but also in creating room for new insight and the way that communication channels are created through which this experience is disseminated to the consumers. An important aspect of the growing awareness of the nature of exhibitions is that the curatorial monopoly over exhibition space and narrative has tended to be re-examined. This study attempted to investigate how technological innovations facilitated the new desire for more interactive audience participation, encouraged by changing curatorial agendas and a wider range of interpretive strategies challenging in that way the dominance of the curator's voice.

In addition to the above, there has been an effort to define the framework within which the museum is conceived as a ritual (Duncan 2005). By emphasizing the 'museum experience as a monumental creation', Duncan argues that the museum 'is not the neutral and transparent sheltering space that it is often claimed to be'. It is a place full of intended messages designed to be reserved for 'a particular kind of contemplation and learning experience' (Duncan 2005:78-88). These issues were brought to the forefront in this study in order to understand how meaning is made and negotiated in a 'living' museum

Definitions

This sub-section examines concepts that were central to this study. The definitions were provided to show how these notions were used in the overall context of the analysis and to elucidate some alternative aspects of these notions.

1. Poetics

One concept that appears frequently in this work is the term poetics. Influenced by Aristotle's work *Poetics*, whose main scope is the art of poetry and its styles and techniques, the study attempted to approach 'the art of creating the meaning of the past' (Anagnostopoulos 2009). In a general way, the concept of poetics refers to the linguistic influence that the discipline of archaeology has received, grounded in its ability to create stories and interpretations of the past. The uncovered material and the traces of the past have to be written and told using a communicative language and subsequently, as Tilley initially put it, 'it involves a problematization of the entire project of archaeology as traditionally conceived, focusing attention on the forms in which written archaeological texts are constructed and interpreted' (Tilley 1993:11).

Among the aims of this thesis was the investigation of the technique and style archaeology uses to design and present its past and the analysis of museum exhibitions as vehicles for the transmission of these stories through the written texts and the way that the messages produced within a museum communicate effectively with the public. To put it another way, the aim is the deconstruction of past constructions created within the exhibitions in the museums studied here. That presupposes the acceptance of the assumption that 'museums' exhibitions are texts' (Silverstone, 1994:166) and as such they have their own structure and are ruled by their own principles or technologies.

Archaeologists construct the stories of the past by interpreting its traces in the present and using the tools and the means of language through their texts. That gives them the power to change, to re-write these texts, to re-interpret the past in a way as such that this past can be conceived and approached by the public. That is a key point in motivating our attention not so much on the content of an exhibition or the setting of material remains but to the way that something is written, presented, or told, and the social and historical conditions surrounding the writing and telling (Shanks and Hodder 1995).

> '...the time for the archaeologist is a *poetic time*...the archaeologist [as excavator] of the ground and of the time is transformed into a real creator [artist], like a poet. He/she brings to life whatever has died, a lost memory, using only his/her scientific knowledge equipment. So, doesn't the poet do

> the same, as another *excavator of the human soul* [psyche]?' (Σακελλαράκης 2003:69, emphasis added).

Archaeology and museums, as modern practices, use the material remains of the past to support their own interpretations, which are the writing and telling of 'texts', and are means to diffuse messages. What the mechanisms of that process are and to what extent they could have an effect on public instruction, entertainment, and involvement in experiencing the past: that is the poetics of the work, along with the concepts of rhetoric and representation, some of whose definitive elements were analysed in the following sections.

2. Rhetoric

If poetics has to do with the 'the aesthetic strategies of display, those intended to bring pleasure', then rhetoric focuses 'on the mechanisms of persuasion, those intended to instruct' (Macdonald 1998:5). In this realm of definitions stands the concept of rhetoric as it was used in this work. This is not just conceived as a way to tell a fascinating story about the past within the boundaries defined by the discipline of archaeology and within the limitations of the museum, but a quite far-reaching process which aims to tell the intended messages in a way that can persuade the public that this is how those messages should be told and written. It is a process that depends on the belief that the exhibition settings and interpretation stories not only instruct and attract people's interest but impact strongly on the way that the audience can accept or reject the presented ideas and messages and, in some cases, be encouraged in the maintenance of current mentalities and stereotypes.

It can be argued that the study and analysis of the museum's constructions of the past and of the archaeological representations should consider the above practices as a language system of their own, which combines objects of all kinds, labels, texts, graphics, hardware etc., all put together in a specific form (Coxal, 1991:93). From this perspective, the present work investigated the entire museum-methodological mechanisms of exhibition-making, consisting of written texts, graphics, catalogues, reports, information panels and so on, which are used to establish unquestionable statements about the past.

Influenced by ideas referred to in Aristotle's thought-provoking work *Rhetoric* (Anagnostopoulos 2009), this work took the museum as a form of public speech (chapter VI), focusing on and stressing the social and democratic role that the museum has or should have in modern society, promoting dialogue and interaction with and among people and the material traces of past in present societies.

It is of crucial concern for this study to unmask the underlying aims of the exhibition itself, the choices made in selecting, the criteria that guided these choices, and the intentions of the exhibition makers and curators, exploring the ways in which the transition from ideas and theoretical considerations to practical implications and complexities is achieved. Further critical issues for this work are the way that design strategies are implemented and the purpose and intent behind these decisions.

3. Representations

The word representation has multiple flexible meanings, many of which can be related to the museum context. It applies to the mission and primary goal of the museum, which is to represent or reconstruct original things or ideas and theories through objects and the evidence of the past. There is long-established literature in sociological writing that elaborates representation as a key element and a starting point of meaning-making construction, influencing cultural, communication and tourism studies, archaeology, and anthropology (Moira and Smith 2006; Evans and Hall 1999; Schirato and Webb 2004, Smiles and Moser 2005; Rose 2007). According to the Oxford Dictionary of Sociology, representation refers to 'the way in which images and texts reconstruct the original sources they represent' (Marshall 1998:565). The definition stresses the fact that 'it is important to examine what lies behind the image and the text: who constructed it, where and when, for what purpose and for which audience's gaze' (ibid). Based on the guidance of that definition, it is important to recognize the agents involved in the construction of the museum's representations: the curator, the displayed objects, the audience, and the dynamic relationships created among them.

Also, representation is closely connected to the way that the tangibility of the material culture is seen, or visuality, communicated and understood and the meanings that are produced by these relationships (Watson and Waterton 2010). Material culture in museums and open archaeological sites is a visual culture which in a museum context can become representational through the objects and their dynamics in their relation to and connection with other socio-cultural and spatial contexts. So, the objects are voiced, and they play a critical role in the representation practices of the museum, which in the case of Greece means that this role is empowered and reinforced not only by the abundance of movable and immovable antiquities but also by the dominance of the aesthetics of Classical archaeology. All these issues were examined at various points in this thesis in an attempt to unmask the complexities and implications of these relations.

Another point on which this thesis will place great emphasis is the role of the place in the creation of the museum's representations: that is, how the sense of place and the notion of sitedness can not only affect the messages' reception by the public but also show alternative interpretations to the story-maker in directing the sense-making process, from a static and single aspect approach to more holistic attempts at past representations. That is an aspect that will be discussed in the following sections. 'Any museum or exhibition is, in effect, a statement of a position. It is a theory: a suggested way of seeing the world. And, like any theory, it might offer insight and illumination' (Macdonald 1996:14). By recognising the implications of that statement, this study showed how their dynamics and their changing character could allow us to see these museum practices in terms of their potentialities to create present stories about the past. In that sense, it was argued that the museum is a representational process wherein the narratives, values, and cultural and social meanings that empower certain identities are assessed and legitimized.

Case Studies

This section introduces the case studies, which function as sources through which the main issues and reflections of this thesis were explored and developed.

The first group of museums under study was the Archaeological Museum of Thessaloniki, the Museum of Byzantine Culture in Thessaloniki, and the Ethnological Museum of Thessaloniki. This choice was based on the current work's attempt firstly to investigate more decentralised museological and archaeological practices in the representation of the past in Greece, seeking alternative writings and readings of museum narratives, which challenge the dominant perspectives; secondly, to examine the influence of state and private sector by discussing differences and similarities in terms of their authority, management practices and museum technologies, searching for conflicting interests and claims over the past; and, thirdly, to cover chronologically all periods from Prehistory to modern times. The three state museums of Thessaloniki are of great interest because they are representatives which can be used to explore the museum policies and practices in Greece. Also, they provide important information on the history of the archaeological discipline in northern Greece, as they were the repositories of the antiquities of northern Greece, and they first produced decentralised and innovative practices and directions in the museum representation of the past.

The second group of museums consists of two museums which are considered to be archaeological site museums: the Museum of Vergina (or, more correctly, the museum of the Royal Tombs of Aigai) and the museum of Mount Athos, as an example of a living museum. These two archaeological places, or landscapes, are of great significance in terms of their archaeological and historical value. The current study will highlight some of the main issues in relation to the interpretation of the material remains of the past, taking into account the importance of the sense of place for our attempts to approach, interpret, and experience the past. These case studies were stimulating for the purpose of challenging the traditional museum narratives and introducing new thinking into the theoretical investigation of the museums as institutions.

The third and final case study is that of the Ethnological Museum of Thrace, Alexandroupoli, northern Greece. It is a private museum based on collections of the recent past from the 18th, 19th, and early 20th centuries and consisting mostly of objects of daily life and from the rural economy. The choice of that museum was based on the criteria of exploring and defining the private collecting policies adopted in Greece and to what extent the public, communities, and locals are engaged in the creation of museum narratives and the construction of identities. Specifically, the chapter's concerns were to investigate the potentialities of the presentation of and approach to a recent past and to unmask the challenges related to full public engagement in the interpretation of not-so-remote facets of Greek history. This pursuit gave us the opportunity to expand the strict traditional boundaries of the institutionalised Greek archaeology and to start discussing and reconsidering more inclusive analytical methods of managing and interpreting the past.

It should be noted that the case studies mentioned above have been selected on the basis of the need to highlight different aspects of and perspectives on the museums and on heritage management as expressions of state and private practices in Greece. Some of the issues that were brought to the fore are very different, but the case studies still have the same aim: to stimulate investigation of the nature of museum narratives.

Methodological Tools and Processes

For the case studies, various methodological tools and techniques were used in data collection. The use of these tools and techniques revealed various strengths and weaknesses with theoretical and practical implications for investigating the museum phenomenon. The methods that follow were those applied in structuring my research and my visits to the museums under study (and others).

1. Fieldwork was carried out in order to collect the material needed for the de-constructions of the museum exhibitions. The aim was to look at the founding of these museums, their collection policies, their classification systems, and the design and planning of their exhibitions. To achieve this, my attempts were concentrated mainly on the following: first, observing the exterior and interior architecture, the physical evidence of the museums, such as the buildings, the organisation of space, the addition or removal of structures, and the architectural history of the buildings and their meanings as traced through the architectural elements, transformations, rehabilitations, and reuses of old buildings. These observations were relevant in attempting to reveal the purposes and intentions behind the museum as a building and as an institution within the society and how the concept of the museum changed through time, following either the theoretical trends and the academic thinking of the era or covering the urgent needs of the plethora of antiquities that saw the light after long- and short-term excavation projects. Second, the study of the museums' architectural history was supported by the detailed collection of the architectural plans found in catalogues, leaflets, and scripts, but the most important sources proved to be the archival material of the museological reports (initial and final), the working notes and feasibility studies of the planning of exhibitions, when these existed and were available. In this material I found useful information on the thinking behind the museum architecture and the purposes that it would serve as an institution. Detailed architectural plans allowed me to trace the spatial syntax of the exhibitions in order to focus my investigation on the hidden messages of the scenario that the curator wanted the visitors to pass through. Locating the micro and macro spaces of the organization of the museum exhibitions, my research explored what artefacts were exhibited, the installations, texts, graphics, and labels. For that purpose, my visits were numerous and meticulous photographic recordings were carried out.

2. A further source for this study was the literature produced by the museums themselves: brochures, guidebooks, annual reports, and professional and popular journals and newspapers. In these accounts, information on the history of the museum, the periods exhibited, the aims and future plans, and projects (research and

educational) were provided, giving me insight into the functioning role of the museum and the mission of its exhibitions.

3. A detailed observation and examination of the exhibition panels was carried out in order to conduct an investigation into the textuality and inter-textuality of the intended messages. The language used played an important role in the way that ideas and concepts, as constructed in the museum context, are presented and disseminated. The observation of different types of writing strategies for narrating the scenario, as decided by the exhibition working team, gave me the opportunity to locate the linguistic and poetic patterns with which the information about the periods, objects, and socio-cultural relationships of past societies was presented and contextualized for the education and entertainment of the recipient. Through that process I had the chance to consider which objects and ideas were ascribed more or less importance and significance; how the written information was transformed into a communication in the form of a written text which could be more or less attractive and encouraging to the visitors' interest; and the relationship between the texts and the displayed objects or the whole structures—the buildings and archaeological landscapes—in the construction of educational and authentic images of the past. These examinations were carried out on the site museums, especially in the Museum of the Royal Tombs of Aegai, where I sought to explore the interactivity among the traces-buildings; the objects of the past; the exhibition story as a written text in panels and the audience. The entire process was carried out by transcribing the introductory or thematic panels and labels and taking photos for further examination, aiming to discover the communication elements and rhetorical strategies that facilitate the circulation of messages and the creation of multiple meanings.

4. In the above attempts at analysis, the I produced data-recording sheets for my research, which proved useful for the organization of the collected material. One sheet was developed following the main axes on the basis of which the exhibitions were organized (periods, content, objects, themes) giving me the chance to proceed with some observations and comparisons of the importance and significance of the displayed objects and the role of the museum. Another sheet was developed to record the interviews with people from the archaeology and museum worlds in order to collect supplementary information on different issues, such as legal or administrative issues, or comments on museological plans and reports and the importance of the development of museological projects within a new strategy of museum policy in Greece.

5. Interviews were conducted with the directors of the Ephorates working on projects (such as the archaeological site of Vergina) in the museums under study, with heads of departments of the official state service (Ministry of Culture), with leading archaeologists operating in international institutions such as ICOM (Greek department), and with academics and managers involved in projects of archaeological management and museums. The interviews were based on an unstructured style that allowed me to produce a more freely flowing conversation with spontaneous questions, in which I tried to elicit information and critical comments on the discussed issues rather than just descriptions and statements.

Decisions concerning whom to interview were based on criteria related to the construction of the museum exhibitions, the shaping of official archaeological and museum policy in Greece, the role of the private sector in the museological process as expressed in Greek museums, and the investigation of the new role that Greek archaeologists are called to play in interpreting and presenting the Greek past.

6. Finally, newspaper material was used to illustrate an indirect public view and reading of the Greek past, and this proved to be invaluable in relation to the considerations and aspects discussed as a way of questioning and challenging the prevailing thinking and authorship involved in museum practices. The translation of that material was undertaken by the author.

Complexities and Challenges of Conducting Research

While undertaking this research, I worked as an active archaeologist in the Ministry of Culture, 10th Ephorate of Byzantine Antiquities (Thessaloniki, Northern Greece). I saw it as a challenge to produce a critical and analytical work that would broaden my spectrum by achieving a better understanding of the museum as a phenomenon and the practice of archaeology as a contemporary discipline. There were many opportunities that made me recognize the complex and changing nature of the museum field and revise my view of many of the traditional aspects that governed Greek archaeology. My research and my work in museums and on archaeological projects challenged me to move constantly between study, reflection and writing and the implementation of theoretical frameworks in everyday practical work.

As an active insider archaeologist and one who had been working within the field for years, I was privileged to conduct a deeper analysis of museums involving multi-faceted approaches to the investigation of invisible meanings and intentions. Especially in the site museums, in the cases of Vergina or the historical place of Mount Athos, where the archaeological landscapes and the history of the archaeological excavations in these areas are involved in the perception and presentation of the places, I managed to transfer not only the official image but also the 'inside' picture of the research and study carried out by the experts and their multiple impacts on the audience's thinking about these sites. Although Mount Athos seemed bound to be a problematic site for access, my position in the related Ephorate gave me the chance to collect the data required for the specific analysis and investigation. Also, access to the archival material of the Ministry was given without obstacles and delays following the required procedures of permission. That completeness to my research in terms of data collection and avoided the danger of missing important documents and reports revealing the goals and intentions of the decision-making processes.

Many times in the process of my research, I was taking the role of the 'outsider', or the visitor, in order to adopt a different perspective and approach to the material under study and to acquire a better understanding of what I was seeing (in my museum visits) or to pose questions and pursue quarries that would change my direction of thinking. However, what was stimulating in my position as someone working in the field was the fact that always I had to challenge my preconceptions and investigate critically, moving the research away from standardized limitations and traditional borders. That was not an easy task and I faced many difficulties that I managed to overcome by pursuing this form of research that enabled me to more fully explore the potential of the museums.

The Use of Greek

A large part of the data, the source information material, and the bibliographic references are in Greek and their rendering in an understandable style was a problem in this work. In order to be consistent but at the same time readable, some Greek texts or references within the text, where necessary for the purpose of better understanding, were translated, while some others were left in Greek. Place names were written in Latin or English form, as established widely for the correct recognition of international sites. The Greek bibliographic references were left in Greek, while a substantial translation of legislation rules and official documents is given.

IV. Outline of the Study

This chapter provided an outline of the structure of the thesis and gave a brief summary of each chapter.

In Chapter II, an attempt was made to define the framework in which archaeological practice and museums operate in Greece and to pursue a discussion of the socio-politics of museum reconstructions of the past. That consisted of an account of the historical development of the museums in Greece and the examination of the theoretical framework within which the ideological and social attitudes and perceptions towards the Greek past were formulated. Questions arose such as: why and how are the presented objects subjected to different valuations? By whom and how are these values recognised? An inquiry into these subjects was carried out with the aim of exploring the uses and abuses of the archaeological heritage in Northern Greece. There was also an exploration of recent approaches to archaeological heritage management in Greece. It was of great concern to underline the legislative[3] and administrative framework within which authorship and regulation are expressed and the decision-making process agenda is set. In this way, a critical analysis of the new archaeological law and the new administrative rules were brought to the fore in order to discuss the new reality for archaeological heritage practice as it is taking shape under the two (or three) European Funding Framework Programs. Based on the above, the chapter moved to discuss further the

[3] It should be noted that the examination of legislation will be done mainly in terms of the museums. But what it is important to stress here is that in Greece archaeological practice is tightly related to museum and exhibition constructions, and an indication of that is that the majority of museums are based on objects of archaeological excavations (I am not referring here to early modern ethnological objects). Also, the archaeologists who work or who used to work in an Ephorate could also work in a museum. That framework illuminates some interesting aspects, as will be discussed in later chapters, of archaeology as a discipline and the museum as a practice in Greece.

displaying of archaeology in Greek museums in general by attempting to explore the implicit and explicit dimensions of their museum exhibition practices in the last few years. This discussion mainly consisted of a review of the museum concept in Greece. The chapter concluded with a summary of the main points of the framework within which a critical analysis of Greek museums' reality was undertaken.

Chapter III discussed the first of the three case studies, where the three museums of Thessaloniki, Northern Greece, were considered. The intention of this chapter was to investigate the narratives of Greek archaeological museums by trying to deconstruct their exhibitions. The museums under study were examined in terms of the following aspects: a) Their founding, and the process of the decision making in the creation of the museums and their exhibitions; why they were created and what role they were designed to play; and with reference to the history of the museums and their exhibitions, how they were created; b) their collection policies: the concept of their exhibitions, their interpretive methods, their tools and their perspectives and attitudes towards the museum's and the exhibitions' goals; c) their classification systems: the design and planning of their exhibitions as expressions of the 'writing' of the past. It should be noted that the museums under study were regarded as institutions, as spaces (buildings, architectural features), and as narratives (poetics and rhetoric of exhibition strategies). Also, the current chapter raised some conflicting interests which were examined as expressions of the ideological and political role that museums could play.

Chapter IV examined the second group of case studies and attempted to explore the alternative practices of the reconstructions of the past and to produce a discussion of the two site museums as symbols and places of reference. The museum was seen and examined here as a living space which fully interacts with the exhibited remains of the past. The historical and archaeological landscape imposes its ideological and social character which is involved decisively in the interpretation process. In dealing with the above issues, a new term was introduced in order to elucidate our critical thought on representation practices and to challenge the traditional image of the museum. The term 'museumscape', a synthesis of the words 'museum' and 'landscape', reflects the reciprocal relationships created between the museum and the landscape as containers of material remains and the values of the past that the two case studies evoke. Through the analysis, a new alternative way of viewing the past was suggested and a new way of thinking, which was more holistic, was proposed, reflecting the need for a broadening of theoretical approaches to the past.

In Chapter V, an attempt was made to structure on a step-by-step basis a kind of thought that will enable an understanding of private museum policies within a general intellectual, social, historical and museological context. It seeks to investigate how cultural diversities and identities are expressed through private museum policies and to explore the interpretive tools involved in making histories and alternative identities in museum exhibitions. By focusing on management practices, as these are operative in the decision-making process, it tried to reveal the potential of private collections for empowering cultural diversity and intercultural dialogue.

Chapter VI acknowledged the changes and shifts in heritage and museum practices that have occurred in the last decades. New directions in theoretical approaches have been adopted and new initiatives to develop inclusive practices encouraging the diversity of heritage and museum experience are discussed. Focusing on the multivocality of the past remains, the plurality of interpretations and the potentiality of the archaeological landscape, this chapter stressed the changing and challenging role of the contemporary museum, reflecting in that way its active nature in creating and constructing meaning. A brief summary of the thesis and its aims was provided, discussing the main issues raised by this research concerning the presentation of the Greek past within Greek museum discourse. Informed by the new research advanced in museum, archaeological and cultural studies, this work attempts to contribute a new kind of thinking to the way of seeing and interpreting the material culture of the Greek past. Finally, concluding remarks concern past and current writing in archaeology in the context of the Greek museum, and this work concluded by proposing some reflections on future theoretical and practical developments in museology in Greece and beyond.

CHAPTER 2

Archaeological Heritage Management and Museums in Greece: The Socio-Politics of Museums

I. INTRODUCTION

This chapter sketches the framework within which archaeological practice and museums operate in Greece. That consists, firstly, of tracing briefly the historical development of museums in Greece and, secondly, defining the recent approaches to archaeological heritage management. This chapter also aims to formulate a theoretical framework within which the ideological and social attitudes and perceptions towards the Greek past will be examined. Thus, the chapter begins with a brief historical review of the protection of antiquities in Greece before and after its independence as a country and the creation of the first museums. It is of great importance for the purpose of the current study to have a clear view of the first attempts of the Greek state to protect and preserve its past remains, ascribing to them a considerable ideological value as symbolic and national emblems, and how the concept of the museum was that of a temple (naos, ναός), where art treasures are kept as tokens of a glorious ancestry. Furthermore, the present study took into consideration the socio-political context within which archaeological and museum practices in Greece were originally formed (and are still being formed). It discussed the use of Greek archaeology in the creation of a national identity during the nineteenth and twentieth centuries and examined of the socio-political context within which the concept of the ideological continuity of the Greek past was created and promoted by the state. It further examined recent examples of this use of the past and how this is reflected in museum decision-making policy.

The chapter then moves to more recent approaches to archaeological heritage management in Greece, aiming to shed some light on this and to explore the legislative and administrative framework within which authorship and regulation are expressed and which sets the decision-making process agenda. In this way, a critical analysis of the new archaeological law and the new administrative rules is brought to the fore as we consider the new reality of archaeological heritage practice as it takes shape under the new funding conditions. The chapter then further discusses the display of archaeology in Greek museums in general by exploring the implicit and explicit dimensions of their exhibitions and how multiple narratives about the past gain expression through museum practice in recent years. In the conclusion of the chapter, the outcome of the above exploration was framed as part of a critical analysis of the issues under investigation in the following chapters.

II. THE PROTECTION OF ANTIQUITIES IN GREECE: THE FIRST MUSEUMS AND THE CREATION OF THE NATION[4]

The first attempts at the protection and safeguarding of the antiquities of Greece can be traced back to the pre-revolutionary years of the country[5], when the eminent scholar of the Greek Enlightenment Adamantios Koraes reacted to the exporting of Greek antiquities by foreign 'observers' of the Greek landscape[6]. He suggested the creation of the 'Greek Museum', in 1807, aiming at housing and keeping safe all the antiquities: '...in that place should be gathered all the antiquities...after their registration in a catalogue...' (quoted in Κόκκου 1977:28-31). His views were very pertinent for that time, considering the dominant pre-revolutionary circumstances, where the demand for an independent Greek nation had been increasingly growing and the ideological attachment to the glorious ancestry of Greece would have been a vehicle for that accomplishment. So, the creation of a place (*mouseion*) in which all the vestiges of the past would be collected would underscore the ideological continuity of the present Greek nation. This direction was pursued in the attempt of the Filomousos Etaireia in Athens in 1813 to create a museum where '...the antiquities were collected in a place, called Mouseion, with the purpose of being viewed by their lovers' (Πρωτοψάλτης 1967:12). In 1824, the Etaireia's efforts continued with its declaration of the foundation of a museum in Erechtion where '...all the remaining vestiges were to be gathered open for all to see them' (Πρωτοψάλτης 1967:13) but unfortunately its plans never came to fruition. During the Revolution (1821), interest in the ancient traces of the past was growing and an emotional attachment to their past remains was expressed by many of those involved in the country's national independence[7].

In 1829, the governor Ioannes Kapodistrias declared the creation of the first museum of Greece, called the National Museum, on the Greek island of Aegina, and as the director-curator of the museum there Ioannes Moustoksides was appointed, the first museum curator of the country. The museum was primarily conceived as a shelter for the antiquities and, in one of his documents, Kappodistrias called for all Greeks to respect and take care of the past remains, because '...these are the remains of your ancestors' glory...[which]...are sacred...it is your duty to protect them for your honour and respect...' (Πρωτοψάλτης 1967:107 no 82)[8]. That museum became a receiver of antiquities from all over the country, and it constituted the main source for the collections of later museums such as the National Archaeological Museum and the Epigraphic Museum in Athens. Despite

[4] For an analytical study of the creation of the first museums see: Κόκκου 1977; Βουδούρη 2003.

[5] The Greek Revolution started in 1821.

[6] 'Even before the independence of Greece had been recognised, the acting Greek Government had prevented a party of Frenchmen from excavating Olympia. It came as an incredible shock to Europeans when one of the first laws of the Kingdom of Greece in 1832 forbade the export of ancient remains from Greece' (quoted in Prott and Keefe 1984:36, emphasis added).

[7] The incident is well known where one of the main defenders of the Greek Revolution, Makriyannis, said to some soldiers who were trying to sell two statues '...these [statues] even for ten thousand talara you cannot take these statues out of the country. We fought for them' (Βλαχογιάννης 1947).

[8] See some extracts from the original document no 82 in the appendix III (in Greek).

the fact that the museum was not created on the basis of modern museographical standards and it would be considered as a depository or a storage room rather than as a museum, it was Greece's first attempt, as a nation, to preserve its past remains and to stimulate public awareness towards the safeguarding of antiquities (Γκαζή 1999:43).

Following the creation of the museum, the first effort to establish a legal framework was made with the first law of 10/22 May 1834 *'Concerning the scientific and technological collections and the retrieval and conservation of antiquities and their use'* (Government Gazette No. 22, 16 June 1834). That law set the first legal framework for the overall protection of the cultural heritage. It was projecting the spirit of its age in that it mainly showed a concern for classical antiquities, an attitude which was already prevalent all-around Europe (Ζέπος 1966). Nevertheless, that law provided a legal text in which museum issues were defined systematically along with those of antiquities and public services (Βουδούρη 2003:23). It was in force until 1899 when it was replaced by the law ΒΧΜΣΤ' 'On Antiquities' (Government Gazette No. 158A, July 27, 1899). In that law, the ownership of the antiquities was established and the exclusive role of the state as the regulator and as the entity responsible for the protection of past remains was clearly defined. '[A]ll the antiquities, wherever they are located, whether movable or immovable, from the most ancient times and afterwards, are the property of the state' (Art. 1 of the 1899 law).

The laws mentioned above foreshadow the law which was until recently enforced, i.e. law 5351/1932, which used to be the main legal tool[9] for the archaeologists of the archaeological service of the state to deal with issues such as property, protection, illicit trafficking of antiquities, excavations, conservation, and safeguarding of the past remains of all periods until 1830 (i.e. the establishment of the Greek nation)[10].

A significant role in the uncovering of remains, their study, and the creation of the first museums was played by the Archaeological Society (Etaireia) established in 1837[11]. According to its first administrative organization, its aims consisted of 'contributing to the discovering, uncovering and complementary researching of antiquities in Greece' (art.2) and it was noted that '...the finds are the property of the State Museum, but in the museum's catalogues [the finds] are to be registered as finds under the Archaeological Society's expenses' (art. 2) (quoted in Βουδούρη 2003:30). The activities of the Archaeological Society have proved to be of very great importance in the preservation of antiquities and the creation of museums in Athens and in other parts of the country. In 1846/47 it organised a number of activities related to the housing of antiquities such as the placement of models of the Parthenon sculptures in a Turkish bath of the 17th century in the Roman agora, the

---

9 That law was in force until 2002, when the recent law 3028/2002 was passed which covered all the legal issues of archaeological heritage management in Greece (that law will be analysed in the next section)

10 For a detailed analysis of the archaeological laws, see Παπαπετρόπουλος 2006; Βουδούρη 2003; Voudouri 2010; Τροβά 2004; Χριστοφιλόπουλος 2005.

11 For the history of the Archaeological Society see Καββαδίας 1900; Πετράκος, 1987.

displaying of its collections in galleries at the University, Varvakeio Lykeion and Polytechneion, in which some of the Mycenean antiquities found by Schlieman were also placed (Κόκου 1977). These efforts proved to be revolutionary for that period and gave rise to the 'first museums' which were '...open to all', in which museum equipment (cases, etc.) were used for the first time (Γκαζή 1999:49), and whereby the museum, as an institution, took its initial steps, along with the national attempts to preserve and manage its national heritage.

Accordingly, concerning the construction of museums during that period and under the above laws, one could argue that from the beginning of the establishment of the Greek state an almost complete system consisting of operational regulations and principles defining the establishment and function of the museums had emerged. However, few of those guidelines were enforced, and the finds of the first large-scale excavations were gathered and stored within ancient monuments, churches, schools and other public buildings in Athens and in the regional areas of the country. The museum of the Akropolis, the National Archaeological Museum, the Numismatic Museum, and some other museums on the periphery of the Greek state were first constructed on the basis of organised displays at the end of the 19th century and were the forerunners of a growing number of museums which were established later, during the 20th century, in an attempt to formulate the museum policy of the country within an overall legislation system that was struggling to confront the demanding preservation requirements of the excavation finds that had come to light.

The evolution of Greek museums during the 20th century and until today[12], following a route of increasing development, reflects the growing archaeological activity of long- and short-term excavations that have taken place all over the country, and takes place within a framework of establishing (in the first museums) an ideological continuity, a chronological linear representation of the history of the Greek nation, and secondly providing a systematic-based representation and interpretation of the Greek past. In discussing the character of the first museums and the first legal principles of the protection of antiquities in Greece, the following sub-sections summarise and capture their three essential roles.

The Museum as a State Institution

One of the primary regulations of the first laws was establishing a definition of all antiquities (as I have mentioned earlier in the section) and museums as state property, whose objects came exclusively from excavations and not from private collections and donations. The state had full responsibility and control over all past remains, excavation, study, research, presentation, conservation, and the formulation of the museum policy of the country. The democratic role of museums was established from the very beginning, as they were open to all who came to admire the traces of the past, legitimising their existence as descendants anchored in

[12] It is not one of the purposes of this study to explore analytically the evolution of museums in Greece, but rather to discuss the creation of the first museums and the first legal protection system in order to create a basic framework within which the subsequent issues can be investigated.

a glorious past full of works of art. The museum objects were seen mainly as masterpieces and unique works, following the German scholarly tradition of the 18th century which considered the discipline of archaeology as part of the history of art. On the other hand, the modern Greek public perception of the Greek past was exclusively based on a belief in its ideological continuity and the creation of a national identity rooted in this glorious classical past. As a consequence, the state museum used to consist, in the majority of cases, only of antiquities of the Classical period. However, with the law of 1899, the antiquities of other periods, Byzantine or post-Byzantine, came under protection and that was clearly expressed by the creation of the first Byzantine museum in the country, that of the Byzantine-Christian Museum in Athens in 1914. That resulted in empowering the prevailing sense of Greek identity grounded on a diachronic representation of the Greek past and establishing Byzantium as the middle link in the unbroken chain of historical continuity. The same framework of an historical diachronic representation of the Greek past also grounded the founding of other newly-established museums with historical and ethnological content during that period in Athens. This purpose has been (and still is) one of the main motivations and features of museums' construction in Greece.

The Museum as Instructor

The educational role of the Greek museum has been expressed from its initial attempts to instruct the wide public and show it the glorious achievements of its ancestors. Also, the gathering of ancient remains in schools gave the teachers the role of guardians and museum curators and equipped them with the immediate means (i.e. the antiquities consisting of statues, ceramics, columns and other remains) to instruct and diffuse information of the ancient past, 'so that each school will gradually have its own museum…a most necessary thing…for knowing the abilities of our ancestors' (Κόκκου 1977:41). Furthermore, the museum was defined also as an open place for researchers and the public who wished to acquire a more profound insight of antiquity and to pursue further study of past remains, and especially those of the classical antiquities, which were seen mostly as highly accomplished works of art, a view influenced by the established Western theoretical tradition of archaeology and history of art.

The Museum as Depository

The depository role and the gathering mission of the first Greek museum defined its existence. The ancient remains were collected from all parts of the country and were deposited in a safe place, i.e. a museum, whose mission was to preserve and protect them. 'A museum is the name of a place where antiquities are deposited and cared for. Antiquities are old things, i.e. those which were made by our ancestors' (Πρωτοψάλτης 1967:107, no. 82). Despite the huge number of objects coming into museums, a basic system of cataloguing was created to be applied to them (as was demanded by the first laws), thus constituting the first attempt to create the necessary organized registration principles to coordinate the traffic and provenance of antiquities. Given the limitations and the lack of basic knowledge in these matters, those efforts proved the willingness and determination of the Greek state to control and protect its antiquities by establishing the first regulations and creating archaeological legislative regulations from its very earliest existence.

Based on the above considerations it is interesting to point out that many features of the museum as a socio-political and democratic vehicle of expression of ideology and cultural and social values have been formed and expressed in the first museums in Greece and continue to define their main character through the years until today.

III. The Ideological Use of the Greek Past. Bridging the Past and the Present

> 'Ancient heritage: real bridges, destroyed and rebuilt. Between the ancient and the new Hellenism there was flowing, and there still flows, a...river of whose sources we are not aware...On the two banks of the river, there are some traces of bridges which are documented historically—which I call real [bridges]. There are also some other bridges created by our ideological passion which we have attached to Greek antiquity...' (Μαρωνίτης 2002:13-24)[13]

In a conference held in 2000 in Athens on the uses of heritage by modern Greeks, a number of interesting and stimulating papers were presented to open and pursue a discussion (almost for the first time) on the socio-politics of antiquity and its impact on modern Greek society and, more broadly, on the role of history and archaeology in the formation of the idea of 'Greekness' and public perceptions towards the past. The study of the ideological use of Greek archaeology and the antiquities in general has preoccupied scholars in Greece over the last few decades and a discussion and analysis has started to raise awareness of the socio-politics of the representation of the past (Hammilakis 2007; Kotsakis 1991, 1998, 2003; Κωτσάκης 1997; Χουρμουζιάδης 1990, 1999, 2002; Plantzos 2008; Yalouri 2000, 2010). Greece constitutes a remarkable case study, where the wealth of its remains derived from multiple layers of time and sanctioned and studied by institutionalized archaeologies (Prehistory, Classical, Byzantine and so on) provides us with fertile ground on which to reflect on the political nature of archeology and its representations of the past in the way that it produces, re-produces, and mediates meaning through a dynamic interplay of intentions and interests (Macdonald 1998:2-5).

Inspired by Maronites' paper (Μαρωνίτης 2002), in which he considers the ancient Greek past and the present as being like the two banks of a river and likewise the bridges as being either built or else re-established by 'us' (the scholars, the public, the non-archaeologists) in order to communicate with the past

---

[13] My translation

(Μαρωνίτης 2002:16), this section discusses how the Greek antiquities have been used in the creation of national identity and the building of the ideological continuity of the Greek past, by attempting to bridge the gap between the past and the present. This analysis sheds some light on our understanding of the way in which, firstly, archaeology as discipline operates in a socio-political context in which specific and selected aspects of the past are used to legitimize nation-statehood and to reinforce an ideological continuity and a sense of rootedness, especially in the Mediterranean countries (Silberman 1989); and secondly to highlight some aspects of the way in which the public can become emotionally attached to the archaeological remains by transforming them into symbols and national emblems.

As we have seen in the previous section, the archaeological remains in Greek territory, through a number of state-institutionalized protection regulations, played a very significant role in the formation of the Greek nation and the reinforcement of Greek identity during the nineteenth century. Archaeology as a discipline, attached to history and the classics, provided it with the tools needed to stress those elements of the archaeological resources that serve to constitute a Greek past that is coherent and unbroken from the glorious ages to the present. 'It was first and foremost an expression of the role and the obligations of archaeology as a discipline within the particular social context' (Kotsakis 2003:56), in which many countries in Europe at that time were struggling to legitimize their sense of nationhood by attaching themselves to their past (Anderson 1991; Diaz-Andreu and Champion 1996; Kohl and Fawcett 1995). The development of the concept of nationalism has been associated with the discipline which studied and protected the valuable remains of the glorious past, in the case of Greece, in order to enable the people to prove their direct links with their ancestors. However, it should be noted that this national interest in and ideological attachment to the Greek past should be considered not only as a local phenomenon but rather as part of a wider development of a Western European identity, which identified Greece as its idealized ancestor (Friedman 1992). Consequently, based on this identification and the increasing interest of foreigners in archaeology, the ideological attachment of the Greeks to their past, of which they were the physical descendants, and specifically to the classical past, '...became the embodiment of European identity, the only way to separate Greece from the oriental other of Europe' (Kotsakis, 2003:58). The search for the Hellenic identity was extensively reflected in the monumental work of the 'History of the Greek Nation' by Konstantinos Paparigopoulos in 1925 (Kotsakis 1998), in which an attempt was made to present an unbroken continuity; this had a profound impact on social and historical thought in Greece. That sense of continuity and the obsession with historical unity has also been expressed in a series of more recent writings such as those by the leading researcher of folk culture theory in Greece, Kyriakidou-Nestoros, (Κυριακίδου-Νέστορος 1978) and also in the 'History of the Greek World' published in the early 1970s (Χριστόπουλος et al. 1970) and in 'Macedonia, 4000 years of Greek History' (Σακελλαρίου 1982). Central to these writings is the development of narratives based on the unified image of Greece and its origins and on the concept of an historical continuity which is researched and documented through the archaeological remains and historical evidence.

It is quite interesting to note, given the prevailing attitudes towards the cultural diachronia of the Greek past and their attachment to the classics, the position of prehistoric archaeology in Greece during that period, that, despite its influence due to the introduction of the New Archaeology, it had little impact on Greek archaeology, except for those scientific fields which were engaged in studying Minoan and Mycenaean civilization. However, Greek prehistorian archaeologists, such as Professor of Prehistory D. Theocharis, exerted influence on Neolithic studies, making a considerable effort to establish a close relation between this field and later historical periods, and thus contributing to extending the origins of modern Greek society back to Prehistory. As Theocharis stated:

> 'The continuous march of man on the Greek land through millennia, from the first settlements of the Stone Age up to the present day, is followed by the history of the Greek Nation. It presents the documented continuity of the Greek World, its cultural unity and the internal integrity of Greek culture... Just as today the annexation of the Creto-Mycenean World to Greek History is considered natural, so tomorrow everyone will accept the truth which is already visible that the basic roots of the Greek nation and the main components of the Greek spirit are laid down in Prehistory' (Χριστόπουλος et al. 1970:9, quoted in Kotsakis 2003:61).

In considering the above observations, mention should also be made of the Byzantine past and Byzantine antiquities as part of the authentication and legitimization of Greek cultural continuity. Within the socio-political context of Western culture of the nineteenth century, a great interest was expressed in the classical heritage of the country and this was adopted by Greek archaeology, creating images of cultural perfection and resulting in the underestimation of the Byzantine past. That preference had a considerable political content, demonstrating a constructed orientalism of Greek culture and philosophy that relates to the creation of the ideological spectrum of the Greek Enlightenment (Κιτρομηλίδης 1996 quoted in Kotsakis 2003). The deprecation of the Byzantine period during the nineteenth century by the West scholarship has resulted in a less researched and studied field in the rest of Europe and the destruction of a great number of related monuments (Κόκκου 1977). With the establishment of the Greek state, and when the Byzantine monuments could play an integral part in the restored Greek national narrative through the selection and the documentation and identification of the Byzantine archaeological centres of the country, an appreciation and a growing interest in Byzantine studies started to emerge[14].

Having considered all the above conditions which prevailed during the nineteenth century, one can recognize the tight link that existed between the discipline of archaeology as a practice and politics. As Silberman insists,

[14] In contemporary times, there are a plethora of centres, universities and institutions for Byzantine studies, among which a leading one is that in Dumbarton Oaks in Washington DC.

archaeology may always be an unavoidably political enterprise (Silberman 1989) which produces and re-produces national and ideologically endowed narratives to be used and consumed by past consumers and past clients. That brings us to a recognition of a defenceless past (Sørensen 1996) and its openness to uses and abuses depending on socio-political needs. In the Greek case—and given the socio-cultural conditions of the era—archaeology as a discipline and its narratives were used to support the national identity and ideological continuity of the country by building a bridge between the past and the present of the Greeks. However, in recent times, Greek archaeology, to some extent unexpectedly (Kotsakis 2003), has found itself having to defend its scientific basis and its professionalism by being called upon to provide the scientific background for the so-called Macedonian issue. Though it is not one of the purposes of this study to engage in an analytical investigation of that issue, a brief account of the main points and how they are related to the politics of the past was given in the later section on the uses and abuses of the Greek past.

In the light of the above considerations it could be noted that if the past often serves as a source for national virtues and for glorification of the nation and pride in the ancestors, then it could have a significant impact on the way people experience the past through the present. A prevailing sense of monumentalization of the past could affect the public's perception and this could be moved from a national level to a local one, reinforcing a sense of locality and claims over the antiquities as vehicles that are used to authenticate the local past, all of which were issues that were discussed in a later section.

IV. Recent Approaches to Archaeological Heritage Management (AHM) in Greece: A New Reality for Greek Archaeology

> 'Law gives archaeological material a publicly recognised value' (Carman 1996:22)

This section seeks to illustrate the recent approaches to archaeological heritage management and to develop a critical analysis of the relationship between archaeology and the law, focusing not on the law itself but on the effect of legal and administrative policy on archaeological material and especially on the museum practices.

The Recent Archaeological Law 3028/2002 'On the Protection of Antiquities and Cultural Heritage in General'

The rapid changes which have been taking place in modern times have placed Greek heritage in danger and the need for a consistent legal system has been the main concern of the government and the archaeologists. The previous law 5351/1932, which was still in force until recently, has proven to be the linchpin of the Greek legislation regarding heritage protection, as it provided the basic legal framework, with the main principles and definitions concerning the ownership of antiquities, excavations, collections, import and export of movable antiquities, and other regulations that proved crucial for the preservation of Greek heritage (Βουδούρη 2003; Δωρής 1985; Πετράκος 1982). Moreover, the importance of the cultural patrimony in Greece is reflected also in its Constitution (Greek Constitution 1975, articles 24 and 18), according to which the protection of the natural and cultural environment constitutes an obligation of the State which it must fulfil by taking all necessary measures, both preventative and remedial.

However, the protection of antiquities was not completely ensured and new developments at the international level relating to heritage protection (produced through UNESCO, Council of Europe, Charters and Acts) have forced the Greek archaeological community and the government to realize the need for an updated legal system to cover more efficiently the new issues which have arisen in relation to archaeological heritage management, embracing new principles and overarching regulations for the care, study and promotion of the Greek past[15].

The new archaeological legislation framework consists of the new archaeological law[16] 3028/ 2002 bearing the name 'On the protection of antiquities and cultural heritage in general'. The law's intention to promote a networking of legal regulations which would broaden the protection as sanctioned practice, extend the chronological limits of protected antiquities, and be more inclusive, was initially made apparent by the choice of its title (Παπαπετρόπουλος 2006:31-34). Also, a great effort was made to identify the main terms of cultural heritage and to explicitly provide the definitions involved in the shaping of the legal protection framework. It should be noted that one of the most innovative points of the new law was the introduction of legal principles covering the intangible heritage, consisting of '...legends, customs, oral traditions, dances, songs...abilities which constitute witnesses of traditional, folk and literary culture (3028/ 2002, art. 2, 'On

[15] There have also been supplementary laws according to which new regulations have been introduced in terms of the museum as an institution. These were firstly the law 2557/1997 Government Gazette No. 271, 24 December, 1997 'Institutions, measures and actions' by which, among other regulations, a Council of Museum Policy has been created for the first time, and the main principles defined for the implementation and supervision of museum projects by the Ministry of Culture (art. 6) This regulation was first put into force recently (law 2002 art. 52), and extends the power of the Museum Council giving it the authority to design and regulate the museum policy of the country (this will be discussed in the relevant section); by the same law, museums as special administrative institutions have been created (as will be analysed later in the section). Another law which introduced new regulations was that of 5081/1931 'On the foundation of City Museums' Government Gazette No. 186/A' July 7, 1931 which legislated for the creation of a museum in every big regional city of the country whose aim would be '...the enforcement of the spiritual and artistic life of the regional cities' (art. 1 par. 2). That regulation would prove to be very advanced for that period, but also prophetic, as the main aim of the contemporary museum policy of the Directorate of Museums and of the Ministry, according to the Director Dr Kalamara, archaeologist, 'is to create a museum in every regional capital of the country' (personal interview 22/05/2009, MoCT, Athens). See also the related official documents from the archive of the Directorate of Museums ΥΠΠΟ/ΓΔΑΠΚ/ΑΡΧ/Γ1/Φ21-ΓΕΝ/99931/1388/23.10.2007 and ΥΠΠΟ/ΓΔΑΠΚ/ΔΜΕΕΠ/Γ1/Φ21-ΓΕΝ/99797/1387/23.10.2007

[16] For a detailed analysis of the archaeological law, see Παπαπετρόπουλος 2006; Βουδούρη 2003; Voudouri 2010; Τροβά 2004.

Definitions'). The introduction of the idea of an intangible heritage has been made for the first time, legally, following the international principles of the Convention for the Safeguarding of Intangible Cultural Heritage (UNESCO 2003). This reveals the intention and determination of the law creators to widen the protection spectrum and for this to be harmonized with legal developments at the international level.

Of great interest are the regulations that were put in force applying to the museums' functions and operations. The law introduced a new system of principles for all the museums to follow in order to fulfil their mission while following the international standards (Παπαπετρόπουλος 2006). Based on the traditional definition of the museum grounded in the origins of the term *mouseion* as the place of the Muses (the guardians of the arts), and in the definition of the ICOM, the law defines a museum as follows:

> '...a non-profit service or organization...which acquires, receives, safeguards, conserves, catalogues, documents, interprets, researches, and mainly exhibits and displays to the public collections consisting of archaeological, artistic, ethnological or other material remains of humans and their environment, aiming at study, education and entertainment. Services or organizations could be also considered as museums which have related aims and functions, such as open-air museums.' (3028/ 2002 art. 45, par.1).

The social role of the museum is dominant in the legal text and this is influenced by the definition provided by ICOM, and through its Greek department established in 1983, placing the needs of the public at the heart of museum practice. Analyzing the legal articles on museums, one could argue that they have provided a more organized system in which museums and exhibitions could constitute separate autonomous areas of study, management and further research. A number of categories of museum are provided for by the administrative imperative based upon the content of the collections on the basis of which the museum management is practiced and the museum exhibitions are constructed. Thus, according to the law, the Greek museums are divided into state and non-state museums, and the state museums are in turn divided in those which are incorporated (controlled by) into Ephorates (which means that the museological and museographical program of the museum's exhibitions are carried out and implemented by the team and the director of the related Ephorate) and those that are considered as special administrative institutions (two categories analyzed later in the section).

The museums are also categorized on the basis of chronological criteria as Archaeological, Byzantine[17] and post-Byzantine and of Early Modern Culture. Of great concern is the designing of diachronic museums in which objects from all periods of time (from Prehistory to Modernity) are displayed in an attempt to create a cultural sequence and an historical and linear representation of the past. This is the

[17] A division which was not very successful as the Byzantine museum is also an archaeological museum. It was suggested that they should be called the Museums of Prehistory and Classical Antiquity and the Museums of Byzantine Antiquities (Παπαπετρόπουλος 2006:192)

case for the diachronic museum at Larissa (central Greece) where displayed objects derived from Prehistory to post-Byzantine times are used to highlight the past of the region. Moreover, based on my personal involvement in the construction of museum exhibitions, my aim when I was responsible for the management of a museum project in Ouranoupolis Byzantine Tower, Chalkidiki (Northern Greece)[18], was the diachronic presentation of the past of the local area under study grounded in the provided finds, thus leading to a better understanding of the history and culture of the region. The suggested exhibition policy had a very positive impact on the locals, and many of them expressed their willingness to get involved in the protection and preservation of the tangible and intangible culture of the wider area (Πολυζούδη 2004). The multidisciplinary character of those museums means that these constitute a very interesting category, providing an opportunity to include more facets of the Greek past which can be presented in a museum. That practice seems to be expressed and followed mostly in decentralized museums, showcasing a new approach which adopts more holistic attitudes to the past, developed within a regional administrative framework of archaeological practice which is detached from the strict directions of the state's central museum policy (this issue discussed in a later chapter).

Furthermore, a framework has been created to allow a collection or a group of registered objects to be credited and recognised as a museum on the basis of the features introduced by the definition of a museum.

> 'Based on the Ministerial Decision (MD) issued after the proposal of the [Museum] Council the recognition of a museum is possible if the aims and goals of the par.1 [definition] are ensured...the function of the recognized museum is under the supervision of the Minister of Culture' (art.3, 4).

To move in that direction, a number of museological and museographical feasibility studies need to be submitted to the responsible service of the Ministry, and a responsible existing museum needs to be defined in order to be entrusted with the management and sustainability of the proposed museum. That sort of accreditation was a decisive step towards controlling and monitoring the growing number of museums in the country and creating some standards on exhibition policy and museum practice, aiming to foster the educational role of the museums in Greece. The necessity of this measure and its urgent implementation was based on the so far uncontrolled creation of small-scale museums, particularly those following a museum method and strategy not directed by an overall and integrated museum policy, but often involving less scientific standards of documentation for the cultural period they represent.

Another division of great importance is that of non-state museums, which are divided into ecclesiastical museums, constructed and operated on the basis of article 45 of the Law 540/1977 of the Constitutional Charter of the Greek Church, and

[18] Archival material: Reports on Management and Museum Study of the Byzantine Tower on Ouranoupolis Chalkidiki, Archive of 10th Ephorate of Byzantine Antiquities, Ministry of Culture. Funded by the 3rd European Framework, submitted by A. Polyzoudi.

private museums (supervised by the state), which in their turn are divided into those recognised by the state and those which are not recognised[19]. The recognised museums are funded partly by the state and enjoy some of the privileges of the state museums, such as being preferred after the state museums, and being able to acquire objects from collectors (as defined by the law) and to make use of tax exemptions (as defined by the law art. 47).

What is apparent and worth being analysed in relation to the above principles is the need to define a network of management rules of sustainability of museum institutions as social constructs. The museum is seen as an operational and valued vehicle empowered with abilities to influence and have a great impact on the public's perception of the past. It has been shown that a number of canonized rules and requirements operating within a framework could make a museum able to function as a mass media instructor controlled and fully supervised by the state. Under such a system, only those who are accredited by the state are eligible to conduct archaeological and museum work, while in contrast any activity undertaken by others (not accredited by the state) is commonly considered to be a 'criminal' one. Furthermore, the way in which the new law, by introducing new standards and principles, covers important issues of museum efficacy and museums' roles in Greek society, illustrates the determination of the legislators to change the scenery of the Greek museum as an institution and to pursue new ways of challenging the traditional formalities of museum representations of the past. However, 'further things need to be done in terms of museums' operation as attached services to the Ephorates' in the view of Professor B. Labrinoudakis, one of the participants in the Preparatory Committee for the new Law, and an eminent academic as Professor of Classical Archaeology at the University of Athens[20].

The need for that shift in thinking has been expressed by the whole body of the archaeological community[21] in recent years and has constituted the main concern of the planning of the new legislative and administrative framework on which the protection and promotion of the Greek past has been based. The shift in the way that the practitioners perceive the management needs of the protection of the past has also been followed also by the changing and growing interest of the public towards the Greek museum 'as a means for the protection and the management of its cultural heritage which is recognised as the main factor which creates culture and is considered to be a source of great economic capital' according to archaeologist Dr P. Kalamara, former director of the sub-department of state museums within the Directorate of Museums[22].

[19] The recognised museums have some duties defined by the law (2002), such as to provide access to the public and researchers (par. 5), and to operate in accordance with internal regulations (par. 6), in terms of their collections, their storage and their provenance. Concerning the latter, specific regulations are set by the law to control the policy of acquiring objects within those museums, and in the case of objects whose provenance is doubtful due to the illicit movement of antiquities or illegal excavations, there is a requirement for them to be investigated (par. 8, 9 and 11).

[20] Personal interview with the Professor B. Labrinoudakis 10/6/2009, Athens.

[21] See Conference Proceedings of the Association of Greek Archaeologists, held in 2000 and 2006 where extended debates have occurred on the present and the future aims of the Archaeological Service

[22] Personal interview with Dr Kalamara 22.05.2009, Athens

Also influencing the above discussion is the Greek department of the ICOM, created in 1983, which by its presence managed to establish a new reality in museum practice (according to Dr A. Kokkou)[23] by fostering the exchange of aspects and ideas on museum theory and practice and encouraging the inter-relationships of archaeologists of the countries' members. Within this framework a number of conferences have been organized in Greece with the aim of consciously involving 'traditional' archaeologists in archaeological heritage management and museums and getting them to start producing an overall way of thinking about how to protect the Greek past and present it to the public. Thus, one could argue that the modern discussion of the roles of the museums in Greece had its roots in the conference held in Athens in 1984, bearing the name of the 1st Meeting of Museology, under the auspices of the Greek ICOM's organizing committee. During the opening talk by the committee president, the changing role and the opening up of Greek archaeologists to new trends and practices used in other countries was for the first time expressed, by declaring 'the museum cannot be any more a cold place, let's say, the grave of past beauty, but rather a place of spiritual stimulation and processing' (Πάλλας 1987:21). That statement would prove to be the initial impetus for the realization of the need to take a number of important actions to improve the principles and the standards of museum policy in Greece. Similar meetings and conferences followed in the subsequent years (1993 and in 1997), and many outcomes followed, such as the creation of journals whose central topic is that of museums' practices and exhibitions like Τετράδια Μουσειολογίας (Cahiers of Museology), Μουσειολογία (a digital Museology journal launched by the Department of Cultural Technology and Communication of the Aegean University[24], and To Μουσείο (the Museum) launched by the University of Athens. Moreover, the growing interest in museum practice is illustrated also in the initiative of the Ministry of Education to create MA courses in universities in Greece, in which academic scholarship would be provided concerning museum issues. That action has been welcomed with some caution by the archaeologists but has proved beneficial in changing attitudes towards the designing of exhibitions, as new museum thinking has been provided based on exhibition strategies, educational programmes and communication practices. But, on the other hand, one could argue that these courses have not yet achieved the goal of formulating a fully-developed theoretical background against which Greek museum and heritage management, as overall practices, can be explored and analyzed in order to challenge and introduce new directions of thinking[25].

The above initiatives contributed to the formation of a deeper theoretical framework, leading archaeologists to the adoption of new management practices and more effective regulations for the preservation and presentation of the Greek

[23] Personal interview with Dr Kokkou 10/6/2009, Athens. Dr Kokou is an archaeologist and one of the founding members of the ICOM. She is trying to make ICOM's voice more widely heard in the planning of museum policy. (This is an aspect which is also shared by the president of the ICOM, Dr. Chadjinicolaou, an archaeologist, the director of the Directorate of Modern Cultural Heritage of the Ministry of Culture. Personal interview with Dr Chadjinicolaou 4/6/2009, MoCT, Athens)

[24] Available at www.aegean.gr/culturaltec/museology.

[25] These remarks are derived from discussions with archaeologists and museum curators.

heritage[26], as manifested in the new archaeological Law (3028/2002) and the administrative Presidential Decree 191/2003, analyzed in the next section.

The Administrative Framework: Who Sets the Agenda?

The organisation of archaeology in Greece, in administrative terms, is quite complex, with a large number of separate branches associated with different sectors of administration. The Ministry of Culture bears full responsibility for the preservation, conservation, restoration, protection, and presentation of the antiquities, as well as for the listing and planning control of historical and archaeological sites and museums.

An extensive network of central and regional archaeological services provides a complicated administrative structure, by means of which decisions and legal regulations are implemented[27]. According to the new Organisation of the Ministry of Culture, Presidential Decree 191/2003 (Government Gazette 146 June 13, 2003) the central structure of the Ministry follows in general the same divisions as originally set out, but the number of the regional divisions and departments covering the geographical divisions of the country has been increased, aiming to achieve a greater decentralization of management processes and decision-making practices (as will be shown later in the section). Thus, the main structure of the Archaeological Service within the Ministry of Culture could be represented as illustrated in table 1.

[26] The recent creation of an MA course on archaeological heritage management at the Department of Archaeology in Athens is an effort of great interest on the part of academic archaeologists, showing the need to produce further insight on these issues (interview with Dr Lambrinoudakis, 10/6/2009, Athens)
[27] This study focuses mainly on the analysis of the administrative structure of museums, but first an overall view of the administrative structure of the Ministry is considered.

Table 1: The administrative structure of the Archaeological Service of MoCT

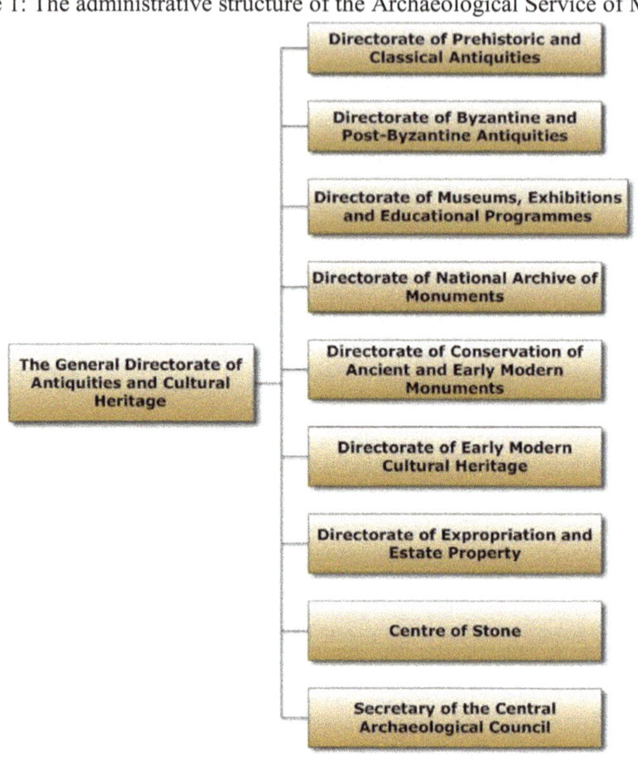

All the above are central services, and they exercise a controlling and approval role over the archaeological projects issued by the archaeological services of the periphery and designed to further the basic principles of the protection, conservation and museum policy of the country. The aim of the new structure was mainly to provide a more decentralized organisation and for that reason the further division of the central directorates into departments has been followed also by the regional Ephorates all over the country. Thus, each central Directorate of Antiquities, for instance, that of Museums, Exhibitions and Educational Programmes, consists accordingly, of several departments as illustrated in Table 2.

Table 2: The administrative structure of a Directorate of the Archaeological Service of MoCT

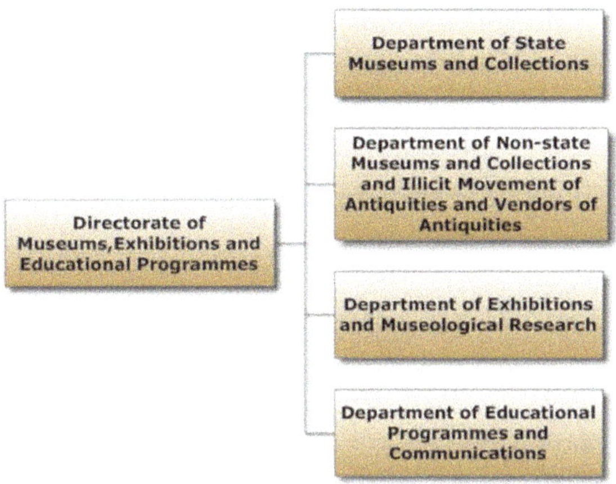

The above division was an innovation for the central services as, until recently, the museums' museological and museographical plan-studies and directions used to be arranged by the museum section within each central directorate[28], resulting in museum workings and exhibition planning being less well researched, as the rescue and preservation management practice of sites and antiquities always came first in the priorities of the central directorates. The newly-created Central Departments of Museums and Exhibitions is intended to be more flexible and more effective in designing and planning large-scale museum and exhibition projects, conducting a more complete museum policy by introducing new exhibition and educational projects, and reinforcing the cooperation and active involvement of the Ephorates of the periphery in interrelated activities. That was the case, for example, of a project introduced by the Directorate of Museums under the title 'The Tree of Life', which called on all the Ephorates (Prehistoric-Classical, Byzantine and Modern Culture) and museums of the country to present and organize small-scale exhibitions and events on the central topic, consisting of monuments, settings, and tangible and intangible objects. Based on my personal involvement in the above project, as the archaeologist responsible for selecting the related objects and accompanying texts (as suggested by the Ephorate) I found it a useful experience, providing me with the opportunity to share the plethora of interpretations and meanings of the proposed subject diachronically and to acquire material for further study. The project was a great success because it managed not only to coordinate and bring together all the state and private services (museums and Ephorates) but also to encourage a multidisciplinary approach to a facet of the past that is apparent from the publications that resulted from this project and were made available to the public[29].

[28] The directorates of Prehistoric-Classical and Byzantine Antiquities used to be sections within the departments of archaeological sites, museums, restoration and technical works and other divisions, according to the previous Organization of the MoC (PD 941/1977) which resulted in the accumulation of a large number of reports to be approved by a limited number of skilled employees, thus leading to delays and bureaucratic complexities.

[29] Archival material: Directorate of Museums, Exhibitions and Collections. 2008. 'The Tree of Life', Ministry of Culture. Athens.

A further administrative division that we need to consider pertains to the peripheral (regional) archaeological services, the Ephorates. In the recent reorganization their number has been extended[30], aiming to cover properly and adequately all the regions (Nomarchies[31]) of the country, thus facilitating the archaeologists' protection and preservation work. The above regulation has had a great impact on the practice of museums and exhibitions, as the state museums of the periphery are administered by the related Ephorate and every museum and exhibition project is managed and controlled by the 'mother' Ephorate. How that could affect museum practice and its role within society, and what the implicit and explicit effects are on the decision-making management process within the implementation of a museum project, are some of the issues that will be discussed later in the section. The further division of the Ephorate into departments is one of the innovative features of the current administrative system. Thus, each Ephorate is divided as illustrated in table 3.

Table 3: The administrative structure of an Ephorate of the Archaeological Service of MoCT

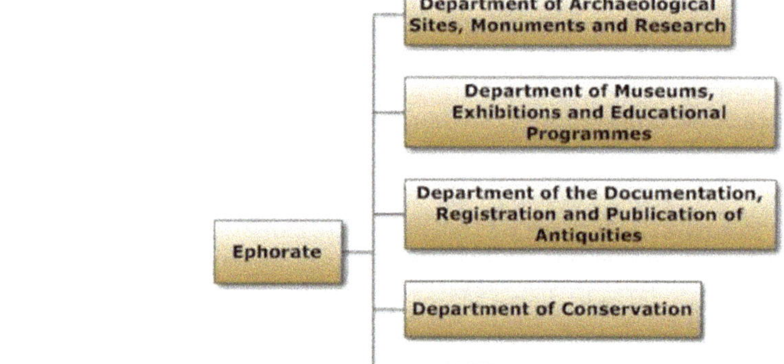

The DASMR's responsibility lies in the management of archaeological sites and monuments, excavations, protection preservation, restoration and rehabilitation works of the monuments and their environment, and also the supervision of the research of Greek and foreign scientific, research and education services. The DMEEP's main aims are the creation and implementation of museological and museographical studies, the management of museum and exhibition projects, the control of the illicit movement of objects, the planning (in cooperation with central

[30] From 25 to 39 Ephorates of Prehistoric and Classical Antiquities and from 14 to 28 Ephorates of Byzantine and Post-Byzantine Antiquities.
[31] Administrative departments (counties) which cover geographically all the country.

service) of permanent and temporary exhibitions, the planning and implementation of educational programs and public information on issues of cultural heritage. The DDRPA's responsibilities include the creation of records of all excavation and research fieldwork reports, digital registration of movable and immovable antiquities, digital archiving of photographs, chart and plans, declaration and archiving of antiquity owner information, and so on. Among the responsibilities of the DC are the conservation of antiquities for the support of the permanent and temporary exhibitions.

It should be noted here that the above re-structuring of the Ephorates has been made in pursuit of the decentralization of state services and the effectiveness of the development of the periphery in general. The function of the local councils of monuments, whose responsibility is to provide decisions on archaeological and cultural heritage matters of the related region of responsibility, was also moved in the same direction[32]. The local councils constitute one of the areas of collaboration between archaeology as an authorized discipline and the public in the form of local representatives of local-state services[33] who are involved in the decision-making process on antiquities protection (rescue) or conservation projects. That sort of 'collaboration' might be a starting point and a stimulus to raise locals' awareness of the preservation of their past and to have a voice in relation to the formative and safeguarding role of archaeology and museums on the periphery. These concerns are shared among many archaeologists working in the regional Ephorates of the country along with the need to grasp properly the problems and the new directions opened to cultural development, and to encourage decentralized activities and initiatives targeting the empowerment of the locality, of local memory, of the local communities and their environment (Παπαθανασίου 2002; Γκότσης, Λέκκα, Σακαλή 2002). However, at the level of the operation of local councils, given their severe decision-making character, their issuing of decisions sometimes seems to be considered as dysfunctional. This is due to the lack of the required skilled persons among the external representatives of the local authorities, which makes the above process and the integration of voices quite problematic, leading to delays and one-sided decisions or the forwarding of the responsibility of making a decision to the central authorities (Δούλκερη-Ιντζεσίλογλου 1987). In order for the local authorities to have a voice, firstly, in the preservation and protection of their past and, secondly, in the further economic and touristic development of their environment, they should put their houses in order by ensuring the appointment of specialized persons who are able to pursue the sustainability of the cultural heritage of their region.

The above discussion has been grounded in the belief that public involvement and engagement is essential, according to the organization of the MoCT and of the archaeological law through the local councils, in the preservation practices of the heritage of the country. This measure constitutes a step forward for the discipline of Greek archaeology, which used to be considered very traditional and extremely

[32] However large-scale projects and works demanding thorough examination and study are forwarded, accompanied with the report of the local Ephorate, to the Central Archaeological Council of the Ministry.
[33] KEDKE that is a sort of County representatives

strict in the implementation of the legal regulations, trying to maintain tight connections of the cultural heritage management process with state authority and regulations. Furthermore, the above argument can be applied also in the realm of museum practice with respect to the local museum councils[34] (as specified in the current archaeological law). However, in this case, public involvement is considerably limited and is focused mostly on the educational practices and on the experiencing of the past through the creation of museum exhibitions (permanent and temporary), educational programmes and cultural events designed and launched by the local Ephorates, which have full responsibility for the study of the antiquities and the running of the museums which house them.

What implications arising from the relationship of the Ephorate to the museum, and to what extent the role and the mission of the museum are adequately fulfilled, are some of the issues that were raised in the following discussion.

The Archaeological Museums and the Ephorates

The incorporation of museums into the administrative structure of the Ephorates, resulting in the lack of any kind of independent or autonomous decision-making management, have had a considerable impact on the museums' character, function and role. In administrative terms, the responsibility for the function of the Ephorate and its museum is placed upon the Ephorate's Director who is responsible for all the issues arising in the realm of archaeological practice, such as excavations, protection, project funding management, administration employees' management and so on. Considering the complexity of these matters and the decision-making process related to archaeological and museum practices, the attempts of the Ephorate archaeologists to control and set out an effective management plan prove very difficult. As Professor M. Andronikos[35] argued concerning the management of Greek museums and their administration by the directors of each Ephorate:

> 'it means that the museum constitutes only a small part of the Director's duties of the overall burden of everyday work which expands most of the time over more than two administrative prefectures. So, it is often perfectly possible for a director to be responsible for more than one or two museums and archaeological places. It is quite self-evidently the case that the archaeologists are unable to focus on defining adequately a strategy compatible with the good functioning of museums, which should not constitute only places which exhibit good looking objects' (To Vima 1990)[36].

Moreover, the archaeologists engaged in the organisation and supervision of the related museums are very limited in surplus capacity and are unable to develop

[34] For a detailed analysis and discussion of the subject, see Βουδούρη 2003:347

[35] M. Andronikos has been a professor of Classical Archaeology at the University of Thessaloniki and the director of the excavation project at Vergina

[36] Daily newspaper *Το Βήμα* [To Vima]. 1 and 8 July 1990.

exclusively any museum management project, as they are also involved in other archaeological projects of the Ephorate[37]. On the other hand, one could argue that the above remark is twofold in its implications and that it is challenging at the same time, as it illustrates, first, the need for the specialization of the discipline and the expertise required to develop more advanced working plans and, secondly, how the traditional archaeologist who specializes academically in an archaeological topic (e.g. Byzantine painting of the 14th c.) is called upon to experience other working practices within archaeology and to develop a more holistic approach to archaeological heritage practice. But, even though these positive aspects could arise from that sort of administrative dependence of the museums on the Ephorates, still in the light of the above one could argue that their operation is hindered by the lack of specialized persons skilled and dedicated only to their museum duties, the limited funding (exclusively from the Ephorates' projects budget), and the lack of directors or heads (other than the Ephorate director) to undertake full studies of the functioning and sustainability of those museums.[38]

The Legal Imperative for the Establishing of Museums Detached from the Local Ephorate (2557/1997 Law, Art. 7, Par. 28)

The necessity for a legal imperative, which would consider some of the big city museums, in terms of their geographical and administrative conditions, as separate services with their own directors and museum-skilled scientific personnel and recognize the educational role of museums as public institutions, was expressed at a very early stage during the conference of the Greek archaeologists in 1967 and by other eminent archaeologists and academics, such as Professor M. Andronikos. These concerns led to the adoption of the legal principles contained in the law 2557/1997 'Institutions, measures and actions of cultural development' which define museums as special administrative institutions of the Ministry of Culture, issued by Presidential Decree (PD), and require the appointment of museum-skilled directors and personnel. Also, the administrative framework of museums' organization and operations has been defined together with the relationships of the new museums to their mother-Ephorate[39]. It is quite interesting that the above regulation has not been welcomed by a large part of the community of Greek archaeologists, who argue that the above separation would cause further problems due to the enrichment of the new museums with antiquities derived exclusively from the Ephorate's excavations. Also, they consider that these museums are integral parts of the Ephorates and that only some exceptions could work in cases

[37] That is one of the major problems of the archaeological service which has been encountered by the author (being an active archaeologist) in the practice and management of archaeology. Due to the shortage of new archaeologists entering the service in recent years, a very limited number of current archaeologists are being called on to work upon all the tasks of an Ephorate, experiencing most of the time all the facets of archaeological work, excavation, survey, cataloguing, project management, exhibition designing, educational programmes, and so on.

[38] According to the Organization of the Ministry, positions have only recently been created for heads of museum departments within the Ephorates; a regulation which is still in 'on paper' in many Ephorates.

[39] That issue is of great importance for the sustainability of these museums, as we will discuss later.

where there exist complete collections of antiquities forming overall groups and where responsibility for these and their management are placed upon the new museums.[40]

In the light of the above, one could argue that the proposal would favor the Ephorates, since part of the work would be moved to the new institutions and it would be necessary to appoint a considerable number of personnel skilled in museum practice. But, on the other hand, the reaction of the archaeologists was based on the dominant and well-grounded views and attitudes which were formed during the years of traditional archaeology, which viewed organizing the museum as a second-rate task among others of the Ephorate, or as simply the placement of objects in storage waiting to be studied and published on[41].

Archaeological Museums as Special Administrative Institutions

According to the Organization of the Ministry of Culture (art. 39-43 PD 941/1977) some of the museums of the country have become special administrative institutions in which antiquities of great importance are gathered from all over the country and exhibited on the basis of the museological attitudes and conditions as well as according to the main principles of the great museums of Western countries. These museums are the National Archaeological Museum, the Numismatic, the Epigraphic, the Byzantine and Christian Museums in Athens, and later (with the law 557/1997) the Archaeological Museum of Thessaloniki, the Museum of Asian Art in Corfu, the Museum of Byzantine Culture in Thessaloniki, and the Archaeological Museum in Herakleio.

That group of museums could be considered to have an independent and autonomous status in that the administrative regulations provide them with the ability to design their own management plans; to pursue exhibition projects; and to conduct their own education policy based on the personnel appointed by the Ministry and committed only to the tasks of the museum. Nevertheless, one could argue that this autonomous status has proved to be superficial in a sense because the basic museum activities are controlled by the central administration; the decisions concerning donations or sponsorships are approved by the central decision-making process; and their (state) budget is not dependent on their competence as museum institutions. However, what is worth noting is the realization of a step forward which has been made by the MoCT in the realm of museum practice in the country, the understanding of the impact that these regulations could have on the creation of

---

[40] See Conference Proceedings of the Association of Archaeologists of Greece 2002, Athens, where many archaeologists expressed their opposition to the related regulation. However, some of them (mostly directors of museums) were more open to flexible administrative principles applying to museums.

[41] The issue of publication is one of the greatest issues within the archaeological service and always has been the major topic in the Conferences held by the Association of Archaeologists of Greece. What is remarkable and closely related to our study is the fact that the above conditions have a tremendous impact on the sustainability of the new museums and the creation of new temporary or permanent exhibitions, as the publication rights on the objects belong to the Ephorate (the excavator). These issues will be analysed in the relevant chapter (IV).

a national museum policy, and the preparation of the ground for future challenging initiatives and transformations in museum practice.

Archaeological Heritage Project Management or 'Rocking the Boat'

One condition that is worth examining further is the project management undertaken by the Ministry of Culture within the last two decades in receipt of European funding, the second and third European Funding Frameworks (EFF) and their effect on the practice of archaeological and museum work in the country.

The expression 'rocking the boat', borrowed by the insightful article of T. Nixon (Nixon 1995:216-223), is introduced as appropriate to the case of archaeology as practiced in Greece, with reference to the new directions grounded in new funding conditions. It applies in the sense that management strategy as conceived in Western countries is a brand new field in Greece and is revolutionary for a country in which the tradition of archaeology as a discipline is rooted in strict and limited regulations and in which any strategy which can be translated into economic terms has no room for implementation within its realm of practice.

However, as seen earlier in the chapter, a number of regulations and guidelines have come into force in recent years addressing these changes in order to deal with new conditions of preservation, protection and presentation of the past dictated by international bodies, pursuing in that way a more complete and interdisciplinary framework for the safeguarding of world heritage. In the case of Greece, archaeology is a discipline with 'unlimited potential and limited resources' (Nixon 1995:217). The opportunity to conduct complete project management of archaeological and museum works was given with the 2nd and 3rd European Funding projects, which created a new reality and presented the archaeological service with challenging issues to consider.

The sub-project 'Culture' of the 2nd EFF (1994-1999) integrated within the project 'Tourism-Culture' constituted the first attempt to establish a co-funded project between the EU and the country, as a reality in the culture sector on the national stage. The larger part of the funding has been invested in building infrastructure, such as the construction of new museums and cultural centres, and another part had been used on archaeological works, such as the restoration of monuments and the rehabilitation of archaeological sites. In the course of the implementation of this project, the archaeological service, bearing its traditional status, encountered the world of the technocratic mechanisms of management with all their implications. It is interesting to mention here that both sides had the same goal, which was the proper implementation of the project in the very best way. For the archaeologists, this would involve the gathering of all the data provided and their assessment, and the respect for the historicity of the monuments, at any expense in terms of duration and project cost. On the other hand, for the management specialists, the implementation of the projects depended on strict regulations of funding, deadlines and the completeness of the suggested project. The different language of the two worlds was apparent from the very beginning and a new tool of management, whose responsibility would have lain fully on the MoCT and its services, began development in order for the archaeological service to be able to create works of great importance and scale for the protection and the presentation of the cultural heritage. The design of those managerial tools and the creation of a basic framework were the tasks given to an external project management company[42] whose main task was to familiarize the archaeologists with management strategies, as required by the principles of the European funding projects. It should be noted that according to the law any archaeological work must be carried out by the archaeological service (central or regional)[43] involving the provided staff (skilled or not) and the provided technical equipment.

Given the demanding requirements of the suggested projects, in terms of management principles and technical organization, the traditional base of the archaeological service was unprepared to absorb and understand all the economic and management terms which had come to 'rock its boat' and its way of thinking and practicing. Working with the only legal and administrative tool[44] of the Ministry, the external management group managed to set the main principles[45] (economic and administrative) of the archaeological heritage management and the archaeological service to successfully complete large-scale projects and to ensure the approval of a second stage of European funding, that of the 3rd EFF.

The presentation and analysis of the main features of the 3rd EFF relies on the fact that it is more engaged in the issue of museums, as many museums and exhibitions took place during its implementation process. The aim of the 3rd European Project (2000-2006) 'Culture' was set forth in the prologue of the European Union Regulation:

> '...cultural development, the quality of the natural and the man-made environment, the qualitative and cultural dimension of life and the development of tourism contribute to making regions economically and socially more attractive in so far as they encourage the creation of sustainable employment' (Regulation (EC) 1260/1999, preface, no. 6).

A new opportunity for Greece appeared to put forward and implement a number of ambitious archaeological works projects which this time focused more on the periphery development and on decentralized initiatives. In this framework, many museum displays and re-displays have been carried out (such as the re-display of permanent exhibitions of the Archaeological Museum of Thessaloniki, as will be discussed later) and new initiatives for the construction of small-scale museums

---

[42] STADION Company (www.stadion.com.gr).

[43] At least for the purely archaeological works the construction responsibility lay with the directorates and Ephorates of the archaeological service, whereas the technical works could be undertaken by external collaborators under the supervision and control of the related Ephorate.

[44] Law of 1958/1991 by which '...archaeological works...are carried out by the Service due to their scientific and artistic nature and their exceptional delicateness' (art. 81, par. 1). That law has been extended with the Presidential Decree 99/1992 bearing the name 'Study and implementation of archaeological works in general' which is currently in force.

[45] For detailed charts and figures showing the development of the works carried out by the Ministry see Μαστραντώνης 2008.

have been undertaken, resulting in a stimulating dynamic of designing a changing museum and exhibition policy (as will be discussed in the next section). The archaeological service, with its new experience, showed a considerable maturity (Μαστραντώνης 2008:101) in the management of the current projects, a task that was not easily accomplished[46] but was the outcome of many meetings and seminars involving the external companies who were responsible and the directors and responsible secretaries of the Ministry. For that reason, a new administrative body has been formed in the central service, the Central Management Office, aiming to provide the control, supervision and consultancy required for the proper implementation of the integrated projects. Due to the fact that a large number of integrated projects had to be implemented at the regional level, the burden of the management and administration fell on the local directors as 'the scientists responsible' according to the dictated regulations. For a very traditional and earth-bound archaeological practice in an Ephorate on the periphery, distanced from the more organized administrative central service, to meet that challenge, was a major task and required great efforts for the Ephorate's staff to show their potential and abilities to adapt. Based on my personal experience as one of those responsible for one of the projects (museum exhibition) I have to admit that the project's bureaucratic demands were often so technical and economically founded that they engendered confused reactions and expressions of doubt at the end, even relating to the initial goal and its implications for the nature of archaeology as a practice. I could argue that my colleagues and I felt like accountants who had been appointed to quantify and assess in economic terms the value and the significance of an archaeological project or a museum work which for us used to be a purely scientific process. That was a challenging process which provided us with new thinking and new possibilities to explore[47]. Moreover, these efforts were becoming even more demanding and difficult for the new Ephorates, established with the new Organization (PD 191/13 June 2003) as they were unprepared for the tricky mechanism of new funding conditions due to the lack of staff with the required training[48].

Concerning the museum and exhibition projects, a complete management planning strategy was set up related to the museological and museographical preliminary and feasibility studies. A number of detailed and well-researched reports referring to the suggested museum or exhibition project had to be compiled. This consisted first of a target and sustainability study, which would contain all the

[46] According to the STADION Company's director, the familiarization of the archaeologists with their new role and management tools yielded many reactions and contradictions which sometimes hindered the regular development of the projects. 'It needed a lot of patience, adapting and flexible attitudes and close collaboration from both sides to move on' Personal interview with Dr Mastrantonis, director of STADION Consultancy Company, consultant collaborator with the Ministry of Culture, Athens 26/10/2010.

[47] For more details on the projects see archival material: Ministry of Culture, 10th Ephorate of Byzantine Antiquities, 3rd European Funding Framework, 2000-2006.

[48] That was the case for the 17th Ephorate of Byzantine Antiquities in Kozani: the only archaeologist running the service was the director, who was facing the numerous bureaucratic implications of filing applications and writing reports in order to meet the requirements as dictated by the central services. Personal interview with the director Dr Tsiapali 28/3/2009, Kozani.

elements linked to the cultural development of the region: public measurement studies; analysis of the economic and administrative impacts of the project; and a SWOT analysis (Strengths/Weaknesses/Opportunities/Threats) based on thorough research and an understanding of the nature and the main goals of the museum or exhibition. Secondly, it included a preliminary research and design of the museological project consisting of a thorough object documentation, assessment and photographic archiving of the collection under study and, finally, complete museological and museographical plan-studies[49]. That was the first step in transforming the exhibition and museum construction policy in Greece, aiming at a well-organized and researched examination of the potentialities of the museums' roles. Based on the above principles, the museum as an institution, which used to be viewed as a storage house of objects and a repository of the material culture of the past, and as having a secondary place in the Ephorate's priorities, is now seen by the official policy rather as a place which conducts research, and which pursues a social and educational role in the society within which it operates. It is, also, seen as a place which through frameworks and principles can function as the producer of diverse expressions and negotiations of powers as generated in museum practice. So, the museum redefined its place first in the archaeological community by making archaeologists realize the necessity of openness to the discipline, using the museum as a vehicle to identify or re-identify the goals of archaeology with those of the museum, which are the interpretation and representation of the past; and, secondly, by being recognized by Greek society in general not only as a means of legitimizing national identity and as a sacred distanced place but also as an educator and mediator of messages, stories and narratives that are socially constructed.

In the light of the above and considering that project management means change (Nixon 1995:216) one could argue that the case of Greece verified these considerations and compelled the archaeological society to become aware of the changing and flexible nature of the discipline in order to accommodate new principles, to adopt new rules for efficiently protecting and preserving its cultural recourses, and to pursue a new way of thinking about the representation practices of the past by 'rocking the boat', as discussed in the following chapter.

V. Displaying Archaeology in Greek Museums: Challenging the Archaeological Interpretation Process in Greece

Having discussed the legal and administrative practicalities of the discipline of archaeology and the museum as an institutionalised place, the discussion now moves on to explore to what extent the above measures and initiatives had an impact on museum exhibition policy in Greek museums in general, as a practice, and the form of the theoretical discussion produced within the museums concerning the interpretation process and their approach to the Greek past.

[49] Archive of the Ministry of Culture, General Directorate of Antiquities and Cultural Heritage, Guidelines Book, Section B', Specifications of Archaeological Works Studies, 2009, where detailed reports and guidelines were distributed in all Ephorates conducting this type of project.

In the last two decades, an increasing awareness among Greek archaeologists[50] of the theoretical and methodological challenges facing archaeological research in Greece has come to the fore (Kotsakis 1991; Κωτσάκης 2001; Χουρμουζιάδης 1990). New directions and trends in the study and interpretation of past material, as recognized by the discipline of archaeology in Western countries, have had a great impact on Greek theoretical archaeologists, i.e. academics who were seeking new interpretative methods to approach the huge amount of material coming to light during a considerable number of systematic and rescue excavation projects taking place all over the country and especially in Northern Greece (Kotsakis 1991, 2005). That progress of new thinking in archaeological approaches towards the past was, however, not followed by a comparable advance in theoretical thinking in the realm of museology and the study of museums in general.

The first attempts at a systematic discussion of the theoretical issues concerning the museum process as a praxis were made by the professor of Prehistoric and Theoretical Archaeology at the University of Thessaloniki, Dr. G. Chourmouziadis[51], with two articles in 1980 and 1984 in which an analytical framework was proposed to examine and discuss the nature and character of museums, focusing on their social and ideological role (Χουρμουζιάδης 1980, 1995). In his articles, the analysis was highly influenced by a Marxist approach and his suggestions were more directed towards the social order and the hierarchy of things and classes than to museum challenges and perspectives. It was only after the museology conferences held in Athens and Thessaloniki[52] in 1984 and 1997, respectively, and that of the Greek Archaeologists' Society[53] in 2000, that the question of museums began to find a place among the academic and scientific theoretical issues that needed to be explored. The most common views of the museum people in the above meetings concerned the need for the Greek museum to change and for its curators to discover new ways of presenting and communicating the past. The concept of the traditional Greek museum as a sacred place that presented the great examples of ancient art and was seen as a repository of the excavation finds of the Ephorates was unable any longer to meet the needs and the demands of modern society and should be re-evaluated and reassessed. The above views were tightly connected not only with the lack of museum studies and of theoretical thinking but also with the limited financial resources and a lack of funding projects that would allow the archaeologists to implement more complete museum exhibition strategies (Αρχοντίδου 2001).

In considering the above, what is remarkable is the fact that, in the case of Greece, any research on the theoretical and practical implications for museums

[50] This was mainly expressed by the archaeologists working on Prehistory, though the discussion has focused on archaeology's problems as a whole.

[51] It must be noted that Professor Chourmouziadis (now retired) was one of the pioneers (along with, later, Dr Kotsakis) in introducing the study of theoretical archaeology as a specifically taught course at the University of Thessaloniki, in the Department of Archaeology, when in the other departments of the country (such as the one in Athens) the focus was mainly on the study of archaeology seen as part of the history of art.

[52] ICOM 1984, Athens (as we saw earlier) and ICOM-ICMAH 1997, Thesssaloniki

[53] See Conference Proceedings of the Archaeological Society of Greece 2002, Athens

seemed to be approached as an exploration of a brand new field, and as the pursuit of a 'foreign country', borrowing Lowenthal's (1985) assertion about the past, rather than as a creative multidisciplinary field which could constitute a meeting place for many specialists to discuss alternative approaches to the role of the Greek museum in modern society.

Local Heritage/Museums versus National Heritage/Museums: Conflicting Interests over Selected Pasts

Taking into account the above considerations and remembering, on the one hand, the wealth of the Greek past in terms of movable and immovable antiquities and, on the other, the prevailing administrative framework in which local authorities, Ephorates, and museums operate to protect and manage these multiple pasts, as discussed in the previous section, it could be argued that in recent years a considerable shift to more regional (local) and theoretical pursuits has started to emerge. That understanding has manifested in many ways, particularly in the creation of new museums in the periphery (regional museums), in which we can recognize an attempt to localize the past by attributing to remains and to archaeological places and monuments symbolic and ideological associations, raising in that way the public's awareness of their local past. On the other hand, through these considerations the role of the museum as a place of multiplicity and shelter to many voices and socio-political articulations is also recognized.

In the case of the Byzantine museum of Thessaloniki (further discussed in chapter III), that sense of locality has been expressed in the form of claims over antiquities which took the form of national repatriation with significant impact on the public's engagement in the protection of antiquities. This issue has arisen where antiquities have initially been removed from their original place (Thessaloniki and other parts of Northern Greece) in order to be kept within the Christian and Byzantine Museum of Athens. The return of the antiquities (from Athens to Thessaloniki) has been symbolic and has acquired a strongly local character which mobilized different public aspects on the role that a museum should play in a local society. Thus, the creation of the Byzantine Museum of Thessaloniki has been directly connected with the repatriation of a lost local heritage, and it was among the founding priorities of the newly-built Byzantine Museum that it would attribute to the town its appropriate symbolic value and authenticate its Byzantine past (as it used to be the second city of the Byzantine Empire, after Constantinople). The determination of the archaeologists to restore the Byzantine character of the city, based on the richness of the monuments and groups of antiquities, is apparent in the following twofold goal: on the one hand, they wanted to create an ideal museum to house the antiquities found in Thessaloniki and in other places in Northern Greece, and on the other, they wanted to celebrate the Byzantine past of the city. These aims constituted the cornerstones of the museological plan and scenario studies which were prepared and signed by the archaeologists of the related Ephorate (9th Ephorate of Byzantine Antiquities) and sent to the central services of the Ministry of Culture to be approved. According to Dr E. Kourkoutidou-Nikolaidou, archaeologist and former director of the 9th Ephorate of Byzantine Antiquities:

> '...an issue of great importance related to the current [museological] study is the return of almost 1000 antiquities removed to Athens seventy years ago and kept in the Byzantine Museum of the capital [Athens]...With the establishment today in Thessaloniki of a Museum specializing in Byzantine Culture, we think that the moment for the antiquities to be returned to the city has come and in that way a demand of the intellectuals and the people [of Thessaloniki] needs to be satisfied' (Kourkoutidou-Nikolaidou 1993. Archive of DMEEP, MoCT)

The claims of the antiquities to be returned were based primarily on the fragmentality of the objects that were transferred to Athens along with other antiquities; that is, the claim that they did not constitute an overall scientifically interpreted group and that therefore their return is necessary for the sake of their proper interpretation and identification. Secondly, some of these antiquities constituted parts of the main Byzantine monuments of Thessaloniki, such as the sculptures of St. Demetrius Basilica, and their return would enable their immediate association with the monument and their better understanding by the public. Thirdly, the association of the artistic production of Byzantine art in Thessaloniki and the glorious still-standing Byzantine monuments would enhance the representation of the Byzantine identity of the city. Finally, the planning and the implementation of the new museum, according to the latest developments in museum building construction, aimed to create a globally unique entity, a Museum of Byzantine Culture built in the originally Byzantine city of Thessaloniki. '...It is our ethical, scientific and national duty to help in the realization of that goal' (Kourkoutidou-Nikolaidou ibid).

Within the above discourse, the socio-political role of archaeology as an agent regulator is embedded in the way that its practices are seen as focusing on a politics of recovery and rehabilitation of a past by re-unifying and re-interpreting its remains in terms of its own origins. The archaeological remains of the past, the objects, become symbols and ideological means which carry the messages and evoke both individual and collective memory, contributing to the building of local pasts. It is the 'symbolic capital' (Hamilakis and Yalouri 1996) invested in those mechanisms that forms a local base for the national structures and imperatives of the idea of the cultural continuity of the Greeks. On the other side, the socio-political role of the museum as an institution which has the authority and the power to accommodate the multiple voices and changing aspirations of a wider public is expressed through its practices and identifies the interrelationships that exist between the socio-politics of the past, the intellectual developments, and the changes in archaeological legislation and museum practice in Greece.

Nevertheless, the concern on the part of archaeologists for the proper restitution and scientific identification of some facets of the past (as in the case of Museum of Byzantine Culture in Thessaloniki) has had a considerable impact on the public perception of their past and contributed to their developing automatically and more fiercely that sense of locality, that emotive attachment to the local antiquities and their ownership. In the case of Greece, the plethora of archaeologically significant places discovered all over the Greek territory and the large amount of discovered objects have created the conditions for the construction of numerous archaeological museums in the main cities of the periphery but also near the archeological sites, providing in that way an immediate viewing experience and association with the ancient place. Thus, in these local antiquities, local communities find those attributes and values that evoke a strong and tight sense of place, allowing any claim on these ancient objects, which have been removed and kept in some other place, to be expressed in the form of a local claim. This is the case with the Museum of Byzantine Culture (MBC), as was mentioned above, where the daily and Sunday press, expressing the hopes of the public in a broader sense, tried to present the event of the return of local antiquities as 'a war' between the 'Northerners' (people of Thessaloniki) and the 'Southerners' (people of Athens)' or as 'a war of Byzantine icons'[54]. Additionally, according to the accounts, the return of the Byzantine antiquities caused among Greek archaeologists' sentiments and reactions which are indicative of the nature of archaeology as a discipline. Their emotive attachment to museum objects, as witnessed in the above case, may lead us to adopt more multifaceted practices and approaches towards interpreting, managing and presenting the past to the public: '...she receives the CAC's decision almost crying—the director of the Athenian Byzantine Museum...' according to the daily press[55].

That tendency has also been manifested in many other cases in Greece in an even more local and community-based sphere in which the sense of locality, strongly voiced and expressed, has contributed decisively to the management decision process concerning antiquities. I refer to my own experience as an archaeologist participating in the excavation of Ancient Stageira (known as Aristotle's birth place) in Northern Greece in 1993, during which significant remains of the ancient town came to light and were identified with the ancient Stageira of the Classical era, according to the archaeological evidence. Conflicting interests started to emerge among the locals relating to claims about the position of a modern statue of the philosopher identified with his birthplace. It should be noted that before the excavation project, in a nearby modern village called Stageira, a statue had been established years before and adopted by the locals as a result of the false identification of some post-Byzantine remains (towers and parts of mural structures) with the philosopher's birthplace. The archaeologists were very well aware of the place of the classical city, based on written sources and topographical observations of surveys which had been made in the area. The excavation project[56] was carried out by the IST' Ephorate of Prehistoric and Classical Antiquities of Thessaloniki and provided rich archaeological evidence which 'puts things in

---

[54] *Ελευθεροτυπία [Eleutherotypia]*, 24/6/1993 and 21/7/1993, *Καθημερινή [Kathimerini]*, 17/7/1993, *Θεσσαλονίκη [Thessaloniki]* 20/7/1993 and 21/7/1993, *Τα Νέα [Ta Nea]* 21/7/1993.
[55] *Ελευθεροτυπία [Eleutherotypia]* 21/7/1993 and *Τα Νέα [Ta Nea]* 21/7/1993.
[56] On the excavation project of Ancient Stageira see Σισμανίδης 1993-1994-1995 (multiple volumes)

order'. But the locals (from the modern village), attributing economic and symbolic values to the archaeological traces, and seeing them as vehicles of development and for the mobilization of tourism, made claims about their local past ignoring the imperative of experts.

Based on the above examples it is interesting to note that the public's perception of the past is crucially dependent on the way that significance and socio-political values are ascribed to past remains in the present by people (locals) who further connect them with economic values in order to bolster the sustainability of their place. This practice can result in the strengthening of the sense of locality, which form new approaches and channels of re-theorizing and re-considering the Greek past. This aspect is reflected in many Greek cases, such as this of the discoveries of the Tombs of Aigae (Vergina), discussed in chapter IV.

Valuing Archaeology and Museums as Signatures of the Visible

A discussion of the socio-politics of the past should recognize those mechanisms and practices which are produced by attributing values and meanings to the remains as constructed entities in the present. Based on this recognition, one could argue that archaeology as a practice and the museum as an institution are those agencies through which these meanings and narratives are produced and re-produced to form, as Appadurai has thoughtfully put it, the 'signatures' of the visible which are required to serve national imaginations and global heritages (Appadurai 2010:215).

This section discusses the socio-politics of valuing museums and archaeology and the narratives that are produced within these fields, and it shows how the interpretation of the past relies on the process of ascribing values to monuments, sites and objects, thus producing significance and appreciation. The plurality of the pasts which have existed in Greek territory provides challenging grounds for developing and pursuing a discussion of the conflicting and debated socio-political uses of the past, thus explicitly demonstrating the discursive nature of archaeology and the multiple roles of museums in the shaping and re-shaping of history within modern societies.

The importance of objects and the significance of archaeological places depend on a complex range of codes or signs that are created by the context. The role of the archaeologists is to read the codes and to translate these signs by projecting them into the present and re-shaping and reconstructing a past interpreted environment through the creation of museum space. So, the past remains are transferred into a new context as new entities bearing this new information in the form of messages which are ready to be disseminated through museum exhibition practices or other means. Objects, once removed from their original context, may take on significance and value beyond that of their use and evoke a symbolic meaning which may be derived from their historical associations (Hodder 1994:12). As Shanks and Tilley put it, the objects '...are used as vehicles to a story of the past, as signs in the present carrying information to the visitor. They are given an explicit communicative function' (Shanks and Tilley 1992:77). And it is exactly this process of telling stories, creating narratives of past lives and interpreting and re-interpreting the material remains by ascribing to them symbolic, economic, aesthetic and informational values (Lipe 1984:1-11) that the politics of the past relies upon. This analysis recognizes the subjective nature of the creation of meaning and the political nature of archaeology as a discipline and the museum as a practice.

Based on the above, one could argue that archaeology, at every stage, through the process of excavating, processing, studying, and reading the material culture, produces values which are legitimized within the museum as an institution. This is apparent in the process of the selection of the objects, monuments or places to be excavated, studied and eventually displayed, preserved or listed, respectively, and managed in order to be approached, viewed, and consumed by the public. The recognition of the above mechanisms requires us to undertake a critical appraisal of our involvement in studying and managing the past and to seek a better understanding of the pluralistic approaches to multiple pasts.

Multiple Pasts, Selected Pasts, Re-Constructed Pasts

Archaeologists in Greece very often encounter the complexities derived from the discursive nature of archaeology as a discipline in their attempt to reveal some facets of the Greek pasts, and they interpret their material evidence through the technologies of the museum exhibition. This is the case when multiple layers of the past come to light during an excavation project and a decision-making process of preservation has to be made. The process of selecting (and the concept of selectiveness) used in assessing past remains is, in its own right, a political praxis endowed with the subjectivity of the process based on who is authorized to make the selections and what criteria we should use to develop a decision-making process. One reason that is primarily and widely accepted is that archaeologists possess expertise and they are appointed to study the past and to establish its material evidence by safeguarding it from any further destruction, taking into account the alarming rate of its loss. However, the answer is more complicated when you are facing a multifaceted past consisting of objects or buildings of different periods and part of an ongoing rescue archaeological project, when a network of public works needs to be carried out for the benefit of the development of a city or a village community. This is one of the challenges of the Greek territory, which is rich in antiquities and archaeologists as experts are called on to evaluate and to define (or re-define) the future of these antiquities. Especially in the case of large-scale projects, such as the Athens metro and, very recently, Thessaloniki's underground and Egnatia motorway[57], remains of Prehistoric, Classical, Roman, Byzantine, and post-Byzantine periods coexist in many parts of these archaeological excavations. Equally, in projects such as the Unification of Archaeological Sites in

[57] This is the national motorway which connects the Eastern part with the Western part of Northern Greece. During this construction a considerable number of archaeological projects have been carried out mainly by the related Ephorates and the University of Thessaloniki, contributing in that way to the discovery of many archaeological sites which were hitherto unknown. For details, see the archaeological reports in Αρχαιολογικό Έργο στη Μακεδονία και Θράκη (The Archaeological Work in Macedonia and Thrace) Ministry of Culture and Aristotle University of Thessaloniki [in different volumes] and Εγνατία [Egnatia].

Athens, one of whose main goals is to rehabilitate and to promote the various archaeological pasts within the modern built environment by constructing what is essentially an archaeological promenade under the shadow of the holy rock of the Akropolis which is accessible for the public, the process of evaluation and assessment of the built heritage should follow certain criteria and standards[58].

The relevance of the values attributed to the material of the past becomes greater when this material is transformed into an archive from which we select some elements to reconstruct fragmented images of the past within the rooms of a museum. The objects become signs and symbols carrying messages, and their importance depends on a variety of codes that are created by the context. In recent years there has been an increasing awareness of museum practice which recognizes the subjective position of the creator's message and thus the political nature of the process and the inclusive role of the message recipient in the interpretation and understanding of the past (Crooke 2011; Hooper-Greenhill 2004; Fyfe 2011; Mason 2005; Macdonald 2005, 2011).

Building on the recognition that the past is valued as a product of the present, it is important to see how it is valued and how the objects within the museum could create a 'valuable past'. In the case of Greek museums, the role of aesthetic and historical values has prevailed in the selection of the objects to be presented to the public, since the aesthetics of the classics formed a defined typology for labelling things and places according to their visual qualities. So, well-made and well-preserved objects with specific and unique decorations which indicate the art of the era and the relevant historical associations and meanings are selected in order to offer a contextualised story to the visitor. It should be stressed that aesthetic value has a strong impact on the public's perception of past objects, and this can be consumed as a form of entertainment and surely provides a way for the visitor to experience the pleasant facets of the past. Also, the historical meanings that selected objects convey stimulate the public's appetite for learning by making the museum effectively a social institution. Moving in that direction, displays in Greek museums have made extensive use of reconstructions of groups of objects, such as in the Museum of Byzantine Culture in Thessaloniki (as discussed in chapter III) in order to educate the public by providing an overall image of an authentic but fragmented past. Related to the historical values are the religious values which are attributed to sacred objects displayed in museums in order to stimulate the public's interest. Of great importance in that category of objects has been the settings of objects derived from the Byzantine Monasteries for display purposes, such as in the exhibition 'The Treasures of Mount Athos,' held at the Museum of Byzantine Culture in Thessaloniki in 1997,[59] which had great public appeal (as discussed in a later

[58] For more details on the subject see Ενοποίηση Αρχαιολογικών Χώρων, Υπουργείο Πολιτισμού [Unification of Archaeological Sites, Ministry of Culture] www.culture.gr.

[59] The exhibition was held due to Thessaloniki's celebration of its status as Cultural Capital of Europe 1997 and a number of exhibitions were organized under the auspices of the Ministry of Culture and the Organization of the Cultural Capital of Europe. On the exhibition mentioned above see the Exhibition's guide 'The Treasures of Mount Athos' Thessaloniki 21 June 31 December 1997, Holy Community of Mount Athos, Ministry of Culture-Museum of Byzantine Culture, Organization of the Cultural Capital of Europe.

chapter). In that case, the museum objects are endowed with the sacredness of the place from which they derived and have acquired religiously intended messages which evoke respect and admiration. Apart from their artistic and historic values, attributed to them by their fitness for archaeological study and research, they have also intrinsic values consisting of their being '...artefacts of [religious] belief, expressions of admiration and sacred offerings to God...they constitute a shared spiritual heritage...' according to the introductory text of the exhibition guide[60].

In the light of the above, one could say that since the museums continue actively collecting and serving as repositories for ongoing archaeological fieldwork, the information offered to the public is promoted according to how the past is valued and assessed in the present, using the material of the past as signatures to legitimize the museum narratives which lead to the creation of a defenceless past open to both uses and abuses. Another aspect of the above consideration is to recognize the process through which the political praxis of selectiveness and ascribing values is authored within the museum practice, which shows the power inherent to the museum environment which has a considerable impact on how people perceive and understand the past. That authorship of Greek museums is decisively connected with the legislative and administrative structure and management of Greek archaeological heritage which creates various conditions of generating powers upon the material remains of the past.

The Dominance of the Classical Archaeology Tradition in Greece

Classical archaeological practice in Greece has prevailed for many years in the excavation projects and has created a 'great tradition'[61] among the scholars who have studied the Greek past. Relying on the written sources, in which classical texts (drama, philosophy, literature) constituted the core of a proper education, classical archaeology has long been established as a major component of humanistic studies[62]. German scholars gave a specific form to this tradition with their emphasis on texts and on philological sources. The text-aided nature of classical archaeology in Greece was expressed in the extensive use of Pausanias as a guide to excavation, directed mainly to big cities, palaces and sanctuaries, resulting in classical archaeologists focusing for a very long time on large urban centres and monumental complexes such as Athens, Corinth or Delphi, and Olympia.

The museum exhibitions created by these large-scale excavations were intended to show the grandiose treasures and the high-level objects of art which represented exclusively the highest social rank of ancient society. Thus, the national museum and other museums on the periphery of the country were used to gather and display the masterpieces of ancient art, which were identified with the most famous centres or the most famous sculptors or architects of antiquity, derived from the excavations over the years and were to be disposed to the public's gaze. Consequently, the

[60] See the Exhibition's guide 'The Treasures of Mount Athos'(ibid)

[61] Classical archaeology constitutes what some call a Great Tradition (Renfrew 1980)

[62] For a detailed discussion of the development of classical archaeology see Morris 1994; Snodgrass 1987.

Greek museum was seeking to identify itself through the acquisition of the most splendid art treasures among the findings and to create glorious stories to tell to the people within a place that was intentionally constructed as an ancient temple. It can be argued that the Greek museum under the shadow of the scholarship of classical archaeology acquired a monolithic and one-sided perception of the interpretation of the past, leaving no room for alternatives and multiplicity in museum narratives.

Rethinking the Museums and Exhibitions in Greece: The Museum Powers

What we might call the transformative and revolutionary era for Greek museum policy coincides with and is related to the funding opportunities from the EU, the undertaking of the 2004 Olympics by the Greek Ministry of Culture and Tourism (MoCT), and the legal and administrative re-organisation of the Greek Archaeological Service. Moreover, parallel to the athletic event of the Olympics a massive initiative was taken on the part of the MoCT with the Cultural Olympiad (2001-2004), where a huge number of cultural works and events and constructions took place in many parts of the country. The role of that was not, according to the former Minister of Culture of Greece E. Venizelos, '...supplementary and supportive to the athletic event but rather it is for us the perene [core] of that preparation...and [moreover] it is a message sent to the world: the need for an establishment of "a culture of civilization".' (Βενιζέλος 2002:14).

Given the above conditions, a large number of displays, re-displays, and re-organizations of old and new museums and exhibitions took place all over the country, focusing mainly on decentralized activities. According to the official policy, among the new aims of the 'new' museums are the upgrading of the educational and entertainment role of the exhibitions through the reinforcement of alternative ways of interpretation and approaches to the material past; the encouragement of the use of communicative tools in the dissemination of messages; the introduction of new technologies; and the encouragement of the involvement of the visitor in the exhibition process (Καπελώνη και Καλαμαρά 2008)[63]. Moreover, the openness of the museum to society is a central new pursuit of the museum policy, providing and planning temporary exhibitions, educational programmes, special days dedicated to Cultural Heritage (such as International Museum Day, European Days of Cultural Heritage, and so on), conferences, websites, and marketing within the museums.[64] Also, a great deal of care was to make the Greek museums more accessible by establishing new infrastructures in every new and old museum building in order to create an inclusive place for all members of society[65]. Furthermore, new planning for the digital management of collections and

[63] Also, personal interview with Dr Kalamara 22/05/2009, MoCT, Athens

[64] See ibid.

[65] Archive of the Ministry of Culture, General Directorate of Antiquities and Cultural Heritage, Guidelines Book, Section B', Specifications of Archaeological Works Studies, 2009

excavations and of objects and sites have come to the fore[66] in order to make the archaeologists' life easier, and new measures are being taken for the storage rooms of museums and Ephorates, providing better working conditions for the conservators and the museum people.

Taking into account all the above considerations and directions taken by official policy within the last few years, one can see in a positive light the changes in operation and the approaches of the representation process of many of the contemporary museums in Greece compared with those of the earlier years. For instance, we could mention the Byzantine Museum of Athens, the recently built New Akropolis Museums, and the decentralized examples of the Archaeological Museum and the Museum of Byzantine Culture in Thessaloniki (as discussed in a later chapter). In the state museums, the objects are not seen only as works of art and within the framework of aesthetics, as they used to be seen for years due to the dominant archaeological theoretical trends, but they are part of a contextualized environment pre-designed to receive the material remains and to reconstruct new relations with the public by telling them their stories. In order to achieve the new thematic divisions discussed above, new classifications, new supportive exhibition techniques and also new interpretative approaches have been brought to the fore which have contributed to the radical change in the character of the museum as an institution attempting to represent the past, issues discussed further in the relevant chapter.

Additionally, apart from the big city museums, where collections of antiquities are gathered to constitute entities and create stories, there is a large category of museums where a challenging interpretation process is taking place: namely, the archaeological site museums. These museums are widely represented in other countries as they are in Greece (mostly in the Mediterranean countries, e.g. Italy and the Middle Eastern countries), where the plethora of ancient remains participates and interacts with everyday life (a further discussion of this will be produced in the relevant chapter IV). A site museum engages with the public and facilitates that dialogue. So, these museums, which are incorporated into the Ephorates museums in administrative terms, have the potential to direct a new way of thinking about the representation of the past.

Furthermore, another category should be mentioned which challenges the image and the role of museums by making them more involved and interactive places: the 'metro-exhibitions' which have been created by the large-scale public underground works construction in Athens[67]. It was a demanding task for the Greek archaeologists to carry out the relevant policy in a multifaceted manner, pursuing not only the rescue and documentation of the remains but also creating 'exhibition

[66] Within the European Funding project called 'Information Society', a considerable number of digitization projects relating to cultural objects, collections and sites have been implemented and are currently still being implemented under the 4th European Funding Framework.

[67] For a detailed analysis, see the catalogue of the exhibition 'Η Πόλη κάτω από την Πόλη' [the City under the City] held at the Cycladic Art Museum February 2000 December 2001 under the auspices of MoCT and of the Cycladic Art Museum in Athens.

corners'[68] aimed to communicate the past in relation to the present life of the Athenians. That initiative had a great impact on the public's perception of the museums and their role, because the past intervened in a way in the people's life and could be experienced in multiple ways based on the interpretation tools and approaches to the discovered material remains, on the one hand, and the receiver's meanings and values ascribed to the past traces, on the other, resulting in a more entertaining and interactive type of museum and exhibition space.

However, if the success of the museums' effectiveness is related to their accountability to their visitors, then one could promptly argue that, according to the statistical figures, the Greek museum had a considerable visiting decline within the last few years[69]. Despite the established changes mentioned above, the new intentions adopted and implemented by the practitioners, and the expertise of the museums in their attempts to introduce a 'new museology', museums are less frequented than archaeological sites. Public research on the profile of current or possible visitors would be useful for archaeologists to uncover the reasons for that decline and help them to reevaluate and assess their museums policy, but unfortunately these sorts of research tools are lacking at the moment in Greek museum studies[70] and only a few museums, mainly the central ones, are starting to introduce evaluation practices and planning assessment reports on exhibitions and educational activities[71].

Building on the above, one could note that in searching for new alternatives in the representation of the past, museums have offered the opportunity and the power for multiple narratives and new interpretive ways to be expressed and tested. Due to the administrative re-organization, the newly-constituted (by the new law) category of Greek archaeologists-museologists have been called to introduce new thinking in the re-exhibition and redisplaying of large and small museum collections all over the country. But that necessity has created a new framework of tensions and classes within the museum environment which is related to the 'authorship' or to 'who has the authority to display, to interpret or to represent'. Based on my experience of participating in many archaeological and museum projects, little room is left to the new generation of museologists in the implementation of new tendencies of museology and conflicts emerge between traditional archaeologists and archaeologists-museologists. This was apparent in different stages of planning and implementing the museum-scenario study, transforming the museum into a 'scene' or an 'arena of powers' within which museologists' main aim is to be voiced and

[68] There are other examples of that kind but in smaller scale such as that in The Hague's tram station, Netherlands (personal visit during the EAA 2010 conference). See the related presentation at the conference available at www.eaa2010.nl

[69] Numerous articles in daily and weekend newspapers have referred to the decline of the figures of visitors, stressing the contradictory situation of the large amounts of money spent on the restoration and museums' works on the one hand and the low level of museum visiting on the other. See indicatively Καθημερινή (Kathimerini), 2/3/2008, 12/4/2009, 24/1/2010 and Επενδυτής (Ependytis), 10/5/2008, where interesting views are expressed on the reasons for that decline.

[70] According to Dr. Kalamara. Personal interview 22/05/2009, MoCT, Athens.

[71] See the Museum of Byzantine Culture and the Archaeological Museum of Thessaloniki, as well as the major museums of Athens.

heard. It is very interesting for the contemporary archaeologist or museologist to realise the power of the modern museum to create those conditions and channels through which multiple and differently grounded views could be expressed and promoted aiming at the understanding and representing past societies, but at the same time reflecting the socio-cultural framework of the present.

VI. Uses and Abuses of the Greek Past

Building on the belief that the impact of past objects and places relies on the power given to them within heritage and museum discourses and the way they are valued as items of symbolism, status, or as a way of acquiring intrinsic values and qualities (Smith 2006), we argue that places and objects are becoming commoditized and that they acquire a usable value according to which they are vulnerable to being used, misused or abused. To what extent that quality of past objects and sites acquired in the present can be controlled, and what the role is of the practitioners in defining limits to the use of the past in order to safeguard its archaeological integrity within the cultural environment, has been one of the main issues of the socio-politics of the past within the last few years.

In Greece in recent years, a large number of large-scale reconstruction projects have been carried out, revealing the intention of the dominant official policy to make the heritage sites and monuments more readable and accessible to the public, based on their educational and instructive features but also on the emotional engagement with the remains of the past. Thus, many scholars who are excavating extended cities or sanctuaries are trying to apply the idea that the monuments and the archaeological sites are preserved properly through their use. 'If you leave the monuments without any use they will collapse' or 'we dig on purpose to restore' states Professor Themelis[72], one of the most eminent archaeologists, in a daily newspaper[73]. This idea tends to be shared by many archaeologists whom have many doubts about the conditions under which any site or monument should be used for any purpose, transforming the past remains into packaged and commoditized products for sale. That was (and still is) the case regarding the use of ancient theatres for modern performances and meetings, where a number of strict conditions have to be met in order for the theatres to be made available for modern use (Polyzoudi 1999). For example, according to the CAC, any cultural programme that is staged should be pertinent to the historical site and should ensure the quality of the spectacle, or the number of the people should be limited and they should follow the regulations in terms of spectators' behaviour towards the vulnerable stones. In this context, in some theatres, like that of Epidauros, only performances of ancient drama, tragedy, and comedy, are allowed to take place, thus contributing to the continuity of the spirit and the character of the theatre. However, there have been cases where '...priority is given to utilitarian values at the expense of artistic, environmental and other values, of which each monument constitutes the vehicle'

---

[72] Professor Themelis has been excavating for many years in the area of Messene (Southern Greece) and has initiated many restoration projects in the archaeological site of Messene.

[73] Daily newspaper Καθημερινή [Kathimerini], supplement on Arts and Letters 26/10/2008 p.4

(Bouras 1995:7). That is where the abuse of the remains of the past starts, since they are seen as a means for commercial profit and the pursuit of economic advantages, raising many conflicts among practitioners and non-experts, leading both sides towards monolithic and inflexible approaches and also away from more applicable strategies (Polyzoudi 1999:34-39). These strategies would be able to balance the contradictory interests and would open the road to a more interdisciplinary experience of the various Greek pasts. The commercial uses and abuses receive fierce opposition from the whole body of Greek archaeologists and practitioners who work on monument restoration and who immediately try to evoke their own professional but at the same time emotional attachment to these remains which are experienced as sacred and precious.

> '...I always feel fear in front of them [the monuments]...as I worked for a long time on the Akropolis and, even though I was often very tired, I have never touched the wall with my body, nor have I ever seated myself on ancient marble...I thought it would be a shame'

This was stated by Professor M. Korres[74] in an interview with a daily newspaper, thus expressing his belief that only through public education can the monuments have a proper and effective protection[75]. The same views were shared also by other eminent archaeologists and architects who have been working for years as part of Greek conservation and restoration projects, explaining the lack of care for the sites and monuments on the basis of the lack of wider education and the attitude of the Greek people towards their ancient heritage, which is often left to commercial and economic abuses. Thinking about Professor Ch. Doumas'[76] statement that 'every exploitation [of monuments], apart from the promotion of their value as historical witnesses, undermines them and undervalues them'[77], one could self-consciously argue that the inherent historical values of the past evidence are self-evident and they are the only ones that should be expressed and promoted in order for the past material to be experienced in the present as proof and evidence of the past for future generations. However, public perception of and engagement with the past consist of different images of the past, not only projecting onto it an emotional attachment and seeing it as an emblem of the pride and glory of their ancestors as a cultural and historical resource but also seeing it as an economically profitable resource in the present, playing a crucial role in the local, national, and international industry of tourism. The last aspect raises many debates on the issue of the engagement of local communities and in general of the public in the process of knowledge production through the study of past evidence, artefacts, monuments and sites for which archaeology as a field, at least in Greece, is privileged to stand as the only authorized interpreter and regulator of the construction of meanings and narratives

---

[74] M. Korres is a professor of Architecture at the University of Athens [Εθνικό Μετσόβιο Πολυτεχνείο] and he has been responsible for the great project of the Parthenon restoration.

[75] Daily newspaper *Καθημερινή [Kathimerini]* 27/6/2010, supplement Arts and Letters p.1

[76] Ch. Doumas has been a professor of Prehistoric archaeology at the University of Athens.

[77] The daily newspaper *Καθημερινή [Kathimerini]* 29/3/2009, supplement on Arts and Letters p.15

for the present and future generations (Stroulia and Buck Sutton 2010). This duality of the heritage as an economic resource and as socio-cultural capital reveals the subjective nature of the study of the past and leads our understanding towards not what heritage is documented, saved or protected, but rather to how the heritage is used, valued, interpreted and presented within modern societies.

Additionally, and taking into account the multiple uses of past remains, we argue that uses and abuses of the past could occur in every expression of the social life of people, of a community or a nation, due to the capacity of the past to validate the present and legitimize social actions through material evidence. So, in cases when heritage constitutes a cultural product and a political resource, reactions, conflicts and debates could be raised on the way of interpreting and studying the past so as to contribute to historical and cultural scholarship.

In the Greek case, this emerged recently with the so-called Macedonian issue, making the Greek scholars feel as though they were defending their territory from distortion and misinterpretation of the archaeological research evidence (Kotsakis 1998). We were able to observe the way in which the past is abused and distorted in order to serve political power and national legitimization. It should be noted that when the eminent Greek archaeologist Professor M. Andronikos was discovering historically and scientifically significant settings of buildings and objects in Vergina in 1977, his primary concern was with their protection and proper conservation, and he did not realise that so much concern and interest would be expressed in relation to the political and commercial qualities of the use and abuse of these discoveries rather than on the historical ones on which this new understanding should be based.

> '...we have never imagined that kind of unconceived image; with religious respect and reverence we were standing in front of this 'sacred' relic, like a Christian standing in front of a Saint's relics'...'I think that I have never experienced in my life that feeling and I will never have it again. I felt that my eyes were clouded with tears...just for one time I felt really happy because of the dream I was experiencing at high noon...' (Ανδρόνικος 2006:142,143)

As an archaeologist devoted to his science and to the search for historical truths and scientific affirmations and one who was overwhelmed by his new discovery, Andronikos' duty was to make known and to publish the new knowledge over the coming years in order for it to be accessed by a much wider public, an aspect which was used to encourage very warmly the opening of the monuments to the public.

> '...and I remember once more my teacher K.A. Romaios[78] saying that "we, as archaeologists, are responsible for approaching all the Greeks, to show them the richness of their heritage"...what I realized is that these discoveries were not only significant and important for the archaeologists but that they touch all the people, make them want to go to the museums

[78] K. Romaios has been a professor of Archaeology at the University of Thessaloniki.

> and to look at and read about them and their significance.' (Ανδρόνικος 2006:201)

To the present time, the successor archaeologists[79] excavating in the area of Vergina, who have been supporting scholarly the ongoing research and realising the political and economic uses that archaeology could have as a field, are called upon to defend the historical and systematic-based nature of their discipline based not only on its ability to produce knowledge but also to present it and disseminate to the wider public. So, a considerable number of exhibitions have been made, some of which are ongoing, and new museums have been constructed or planned in order for the public to experience the newly acquired historical understanding. At the same time, new directions are going to be undertaken in the research as part of the ongoing projects in Northern Greece engaged in mapping the archaeological time and place of the wider area.

Based on the above considerations, one could argue, also taking into consideration the impact that this site has had on the public, that the Vergina case can be compared to the Akropolis (Hamilakis and Yalouri 1996; Yalouri 2001; Yalouri 2010). It has been used in many forms in the heritage and tourism industry and it has been sold as a very popular cultural product conveying symbolic and powerful messages which could persuade people of their validity. However, '...the monuments are not scenes providing decoration for the tourism offices...' as Professor St. Drougou states, implying that the official policy strategies and the decision-making of heritage management should rely more on scholarship and on practitioners and consultancy rather than on the directives of the economic and political powers.

VII. Conclusions

This chapter discussed the main trends and tendencies of archaeological and museum management in Greece. Focusing on museums, a brief history of the creation of the first museums was provided in order to explore the origins and the roots of the museum practice of the country and in order to highlight the ideological values ascribed to antiquities since the country's independence. A discussion of the socio-politics of the Greek past then led to the formulation of a theoretical framework in terms of which ideological and social attitudes and perceptions are formed which influence archaeological and museum practice. Having considered the ideological use of Greek remains as symbolic and national emblems and their contribution to the formation of national narratives for the newly established Greek State, the chapter has focused on the examination of recent examples of using the past and how this process is reflected in the museums' decision-making policy.

In considering the above, the discussion moved to define the recent legislative and administrative framework within which Greek archaeology operates and which

[79] On the part of the Ministry of Culture and Tourism Dr. Kottaridi and on the part of the Aristotle University of Thessaloniki Professors St. Drougou and Prof. Chr. Paliadeli

forms its protection and promotion strategies and guidelines. The state as regulator and constructor of the main legal system has set principles and provided the basic framework for the archaeological service and the archaeologists in order to meet the requirements of a considerable number of archaeological and museums projects funded by the EU. This has resulted in the adoption of new management strategies and standards and the pursuit of new ways of thinking about archaeological heritage management in general and the perception of the Greek past in particular. Such thinking has caused changes in the administrative structure of the main body of the archaeological services and allowed a reconsideration of the role of the museum and its curators in contemporary Greek society. In the light of the above considerations, the chapter considered the display of archaeology in Greek museums and the prevailing tendencies within museum theory and practice. Despite the traditional dominance of Classics within archaeology as a discipline in Greece, it seems that the theoretical trends, as formed within Western scholarship, mainly in the Prehistory field, have had a considerable impact on the representation of the past and the perception of the role of the museum in recent years (as discussed in later chapters).

Having discussed the museum conditions and the archaeological heritage management framework, what needs to be stressed is that a new reality is under way and the wind of modernization is blowing through the realm of museum and heritage studies in Greece, which provides us with a stimulating basis for us to pursue further study on the way that the past is written and told in museums' narratives and how these have changed and are changing. Greece offers a rich potential field of archaeological research, challenging the way that the past could be reconsidered through the multifaceted approaches and potentialities that are provided by the nature and the social character of archaeology and of museums.

It was argued that objects (and places) have biographies which are interconnected with human biographies (Kopytoff 1986; Hoskins 1998). Objects and heritage sites are not passive markers, nor are they solely containers conveying only their inherent values and meanings. They also are carriers and producers of new meanings and messages according to which values and uses are attributed to them in the present socio-cultural and political context. This study considered the places and objects of the past as active and not as passive markers, having a tremendous power and transformative energy which is acquired under specific socio-political conditions. They are able to constitute expressions of locality, emotional attachment and contestation and to create a nexus of powerful ideological and social interrelationships among the people of the society. Furthermore, this chapter recognized the impact of the social context on the practice of archaeology and the formation of museums and it has considered how archaeology and museum objects can represent symbolic meanings and how they have created associations to legitimize and authenticate stories and narratives about the past, as discussed in the upcoming chapter.

CHAPTER 3

Investigating the Narratives of Archaeological Museums and Exhibitions in Northern Greece

The statues are in the museum. Goodnight.
No, they pursue you, why can't you see it?
I mean with their broken limbs,
With their shape from another time,
A shape you don't recognize
Yet know

Seferis, 1946, 'Sensual Elpenor', Thrush
(Keeley E. and P. Sherrard 1982)

I. INTRODUCTION

After illustrating the framework (theoretical, legislative and administrative) within which Greek museums operate, this chapter examines the first of the three case studies and considers the three museums of Thessaloniki in Northern Greece. The intention of this chapter was to provide a detailed description and analysis of the narratives of Greek archaeological museums by trying to 'deconstruct' their exhibitions. The museums under study were examined in terms of: a) their founding, i.e. the process of the decision making involved in the creation of the museums and their exhibitions, why they were created, what role they were to play, their history, and in particular their exhibitions and how they were created; b) their collection policies, which means we were concerned with the concept of the exhibitions, their interpretive methods, tools, and other aspects and their attitudes towards the museum's and the exhibitions' goals; and c) their classification systems and the designing and planning of exhibitions as expressions of the writings of the past. This structure reveals that the museums under study are regarded as institutions, as spaces (buildings, architectural features) and as narratives (the poetics and rhetoric of exhibition strategies). So, more specifically, this account of their foundation history, their goals and roles, and their ideological aims as educational and social vehicles at local, national and international levels will be couched in terms of their institutional status (as defined by legislative and administrative regulations and principles, discussed in chapter II). The museum as an architectural space was examined in terms of its building-making values as a container of valuable things, and we considered how that image could have an impact on the public's perception of the museum as a keeper of antiquities (the traditional view) or as an open place for entertainment and social interaction. We discussed the architectonics of the internal museum space and the exhibition technologies and strategies which have been adopted as new strategies to foster the public's interest and to encourage more inclusive approaches. Lastly, the museum was analyzed as a creator of narratives and a storyteller by examining the poetics and rhetoric of its narration of 'past' stories to present audiences. Issues of multiple interpretations and meanings due to the plethora of extended written texts (exhibition panels, leaflets and guides or book-length monographs) are examined in order to explore hidden mechanisms that and the role of the narrators of the stories, the curators, in the understanding of the past, setting the theoretical directions that will enable us to explore the museums under study.

II. Investigating Museum Exhibitions

The need for an interdisciplinary approach to the analysis and investigation of the roles and practices of the museum at the present time has been recognized over recent years by many scholars and researchers (Bal 1996; Corsane 2005; Knell 2007; MacDonald 2006; Pearce 1990); the aims have been to locate the museum as a social and cultural institution within post-modern societies. The potential roles that museums can play, from being guardians of precious and rare things, as they used to be, to being places of inclusion and of multiple interpretations and interactions, mean that a museum is automatically an active and dynamic place that will always be at the forefront of research into its potential roles and impacts. The museum depends on its theatrical character which makes it socially and culturally attractive to members of society. Seen from that perspective, the investigation of the museum's goals and aims is a challenging task that requires a multidisciplinary approach to reveal the hidden strategies and meanings of the museum as a creator of institutionalized narratives.

The museum's sequenced spaces and arrangements and the setting of objects, architectural details and lighting features create a stage and a script, a scenario, where the performers are the objects themselves. And, as Tilley put it insightfully, the theatre consists of different parts and spaces: one, inside the 'theatre-museum', which is a physical and social space, a second which is the gap between the stage and the audience, and thirdly the backstage space where all the theatrical machinery and direction is taking place (Tilley 1993:11). These distinctive features of the museum as a theatrical place allow us to deconstruct the museum first as an institutional operation by examining its potentiality as a creator of authorized values, its status as a mediator of meaning and its role in strengthening local and national identities. Furthermore, it should be stressed that a museum as a social institution could and should have a dynamic role, leading in challenging new directions and advancing new agendas to provide new strategies in order to serve its community and fulfil its mission more effectively. To what extent the above pursuits might come to the fore in the context of new museums' management planning and how a traditional object-driven museum might become a more inclusive, extroverted and public-oriented museum, is not a matter easily assessed by 'museum' people, the archaeologists and museologists who work and run these places. In the case of Greece, it was only recently that a limited number of central museums managed to acquire a 'semi-autonomous' status (as discussed in chapter II) in which museum policy could be designed and implemented in accordance with the museum's exhibition and communication needs. This authority is, however, only partial because they still depend administratively and economically on the central service of the Ministry of Culture and Tourism (MoCT) which exercises control and supervision over the functioning of museums.

As we will see in the following case studies, strong leadership and a high standard of museum planning were critical for leading the museums through fundamental changes and shaping new visions in order to embrace the institutions' potential. To do that, it is essential to adopt new management initiatives and strategies which create new legal, ethical and professional standards and priorities, focusing on gaining public support through attendance, financial contributions and participation. The growing interest of the public in museum issues has had a great impact on museum activities. Therefore, inviting and engaging the public in discussions about the role of the museum in the community, about the preservation and registration of past objects, and about the shaping of exhibitions and educational programs might be one of the primary priorities in museum management strategies. The museum as an institution is perceived by the wider public as the place where their heritage is kept safely. It has the authority given by the law to create messages and influence the public's perceptions about the past. It thus acquires a powerful symbolic and ideological role at the local, national and international level, a role which is encouraged and fostered also by other features of museums, such as the architectural forms and styles of museum buildings.

Any analysis of museums' narratives would have to include a discussion on projecting the museum as an architectural entity. By seeking to reveal the evocative impact that the museum has on the public, such an analysis explores the dynamic of the architectural museum as a place (externally and internally) and the interrelationships which that place has with the messages and multiple readings that a museum produces. The architectural histories of the museum can be used to present the museum as a 'temple' or as a 'ritual' place or process (Duncan 2005), where the construction of a building in the style of, for example, a Greek Doric or Ionic temple or a Roman *palazzo* would ascribe to it value and ideological power through its grandiose, imposing and richly decorated architectural façade. The perception of the museum as represented by these façades has been completely in tune with their perceived roles as the keepers of the material evidence of a glorious past, whose descendants the modern countries were, thus legitimizing state power and national ideology. Thus, the museum buildings used to be located and indeed still are in a central position within the urban built environment, so that they could be explicitly marked and considered as significant social and cultural meeting points or loci of a city. In the case of Greece, the architectural concepts of the first museums[80] followed earlier European directions in the construction of temple-like

[80] See chapter II section I. It is of great interest to mention the views of the Committee of the Academy of Munich related to the architectural competition of the National Archeological Museum (NAM),

buildings, such as the National Archaeological Museum[81] in Athens, primarily in order to house the objects of classical antiquities and art. The neoclassical style of the museums was considered to be the most appropriate one to support the aspiration that the architectural form of the 'container' should be derived from the content which is to be housed in it (Ritchie 1994: 7-30). The example of the National Archaeological Museum has been followed by other museums in other geographical locations in the country[82], where the temple-like style of the external façade has been selected in order to empower the museum's image in local societies. For the museums built in the years following World War II a change in architectural style emerges as the architects' choices were to use simpler architectural forms, which were integrated into the architectural tendencies of modernism[83]. In recent times, a variety of architectural norms and forms in the construction of museum buildings can be traced, which in many cases have been influenced by the available financial resources. There are also many museums, frequently in the provinces, which find shelter by making use of listed buildings from older periods (renovated buildings) or Byzantine and early modern monuments[84], whose spatial and structural attributes and their related content allow the production of exhibitions (as will be discussed later in one case study). The adaptation and the integration of museum practices into buildings and monuments is one of the most interesting and prevailing practices in Greek museum construction. It should be stressed that many issues are raised by the representation and display of objects in these places and questions such as how the space might affect the exhibition's development and might impose a building-oriented exhibition policy are of great interest for museum studies and research. In my own experience, these reflections have been applicable during a project for which I have been responsible for many years, funded by the EU, the Ouranopolis Byzantine Tower exhibition

according to which '...the external façade of the museum buildings should be defined by the museum's aim...and the content...In Greek territory there are many ancient Greek antiquities, and so, the Greek type (rythmos) is the only that is acceptable...it is inappropriate for someone to distract anyone's sight from the remains of antiquity through useless decorative features' see Φιλιποπούλου-Μιχαΐλίδου, Έ. 1999:52.

[81] The architectural plans were made by the architect Ludvig Lange, but they were updated to some extent by P. Kalko and later by Ar. Vlacho and Ernest Ziller, the latter of whom created the final architectural image of the building and changed the arrangement of the Eastern Wing and the central room. For more details, see Κόκκου 1977.

[82] Such as the Museum of Sparta (Southern Greece), the Museum of Volos and the Museum Almyrou (Central Greece).

[83] See the Archaeological Museum of Thessaloniki (as will be discussed later in the chapter), the Museum of Herakleion (Crete) and the Archaeological Museum of Olympia, and the renovation of the Epigraphic Museum in Athens, all planned by one of the most famous architects of the era (1960-70), Professor P. Karandinos, who was a representative of modernism and the individual who introduced the 'poetics' of Le Corbusier into Greece.

[84] Such buildings consisted of a considerable number of preserved mansions of 17th and 18th century buildings dating from the period of Venetian domination (on Crete, Rhodes, Naxos...), mosques, (Thessaloniki, Edessa...), Neoclassical buildings of the 19th century and some instances of conserved and rehabilitated buildings of antiquity, such as in the Ancient Agora (Forum) in Athens (rehabilitated by the American School of Classical Studies).

project, and I should say that the building itself had defined the whole museological and museographical study of the permanent exhibitions held in it[85].

It should be noted that such re-use of older buildings was particularly characteristic of the early museums constructed in the early 19th century[86]. Some of the more notable museums in the country have within the last few years adopted more innovative architectural forms, aiming at raising the public awareness and evoking, in architectural terms, the historical place itself. That was the case in the Museum of the Acropolis, one of the larger projects, if not the largest, in museum construction, where the image of the building's greatness is analogous to (if not competitive with) the significance and greatness of the antiquities which are housed within it. It has been built to house national treasures by expressing political and symbolic values through its distinctive architectural elements and forms.

Based on the above, one could argue that the museum building itself can create multiple meanings or become a mediator carrying the symbolic and socio-political role of the museum within the society. As MacLeod states, in the discussion of the changing character of the museum, the museum space can be transformative, offering new possibilities of approaching and representing the past (MacLeod 2005:1). It is worth underlining also the impact of the museum's internal spatial structure on the creation of narratives and museum readings. The spatial structure consists of structured, divided spaces and arrangements and architectural articulations based on the themes and sub–themes of the scenarios and stories, the 'pauses' and 'starting points' that unfold through a sequence of spaces. As the Greek architect K. Krokos, who constructed the Museum of Byzantine Culture, revealed:

> 'I wanted a space where the movement within it would be provided with freedom, raising the senses, and also, where the exhibits would be a surprise along with the movements. I wanted to avoid the forced museum imperative which orders you to see objects in a row, because we remember the turbulence of the soul caused by the internal space of a little country church, but we usually forget the objects that we have seen in a museum' (Krokos 1989)[87]

The organization of the museum spaces constitutes the spatial 'syntax'[88] which provides the stage-set where the contextualized objects can communicate with the public. Thus, a considerable number of exhibition technologies are used, such as reconstructions, lighting, 3D representations and modeling, aiming at effectively engaging the public in the process of grasping some facets of the preserved past. In the Greek museums, reconstructions of objects in groups and small-scale

---

[85] For more details, see Polyzoudi 2004, the museological study and final evaluation reports, archival files on the Ouranopolis Byzantine Tower exhibition project 2000-2003 MofCT, 10th EBA;(Polyzoudi 2007; Κωνστάντιος 2003)

[86] See chapter II, section I.

[87] Available at http://www.mbp.gr/html/gr/mu_ktirio.htm accessed 25/2/2011

[88] A term borrowed from the linguistic field, referring to the way in which words (subject, verb, object) are put together in order to produce a sentence with meaning.

constructions, appropriately lit, have been extensively used as a means of focusing to offer the visitor not only the sense of place the context of the objects but also the atmosphere and the possibility of forming an emotional attachment to the exhibit[89].

In that context, we argue that an experience of the museum is a structured one, articulated out of many layers of values and constructions and re-constructions of meanings, which are exclusively dependent on what messages are to be mediated and to what extent these are interlinked with the 'spatial stories' (Tilley 1994) of the museum, thus contributing to an effective communication process. It should be stressed that all the above factors form a sort of vocabulary which operates within the museum walls and which is used by the authoritative voice of the institution, the curator, to create intended or unintended communicative acts (Bal 1996; Baxandall 1991). These acts seemingly find their expression through the 'writing' and the perception of the past as texts which recognize simultaneously the semiotic character of the objects on display and their use as vehicles of a story (didactic, emotive, and aesthetically celebratory, to name but a few) of the past, as signs in the present carrying information to the visitor (Shanks and Tilley 1992; Pearce 1990; Kavanagh 1991).

In the light of the above statements, this analysis was based on a position that views the museum also as a narrative, an authorized story-making and story-telling institution which 'speaks on behalf of objects' to an audience. So, it is the task of the experts, of archaeologists, anthropologists, sociologists and curators, to produce knowledge and to use the relevant strategies, as mentioned above, to put their messages or ideas across. Their role is that of the narrator who is responsible for creating, on the one hand, poetic museum tales which are grounded on aesthetic strategies of display and are intended to bring pleasure, and, on the other, to pursue rhetorical strategies based on those mechanisms of persuasion which are intended to instruct. It is easy to recognise the powerful role of the curator-archaeologist in the production and dissemination of meanings through museum practice. Especially in the case of Greek archaeologists working within the Greek territory that role is also becoming 'a national burden'[90] that involves dealing with issues connected to the socio-political nature of the discipline (as we discussed in chapter II). Grounded on that aspect, it is widely recognized that the museum archaeologist's task of selecting fragmented parts of past social productions and presenting them for consumption is a subjective social praxis which is endowed with the ideological and emotional background of the story-teller and, as Tilley put it, the story of the past is incorporated into the present life of the teller in order to re-interpret it or to regenerate it according to the 'linguistic' principles of past 'writing' (Tilley 1992:18).

The recognition that the museum is a product of the archaeologists is important; it is a characteristic that is especially true in cases such as the Greek museums,

---

[89] That was the case in the Museum of Byzantine Culture when it was exhibiting early Christian graves, as we will see in a later section.

[90] As one of the most eminent Greek archaeologists B. Petrakos reveals in discussing the issue of the exportation of antiquities for the purpose of an exhibition in the U.S. For more details on the issue, see Περιοδικό της Εν Αθήναις Αρχαιολογικής Εταιρείας Ο Μέντωρ, τεύχος 20 (1992).

where the fieldwork archaeologists simultaneously are working on the development of museum exhibitions and educational programs. That practice is easily explained by the fact that the majority of the displayed objects in state museums come from excavations and research and the full responsibility for the interpretation and identification of the context of the discovered remains falls on the excavator-archaeologists. On the other hand, even if this aspect seemingly assigns the dominant role to the interpreter-archaeologists, the involvement of the excavator in the exhibition process can be productive and effectively communicative, as he/she will bring not only the research accounts of the contextualized identification of the remains, but also the emotional attachment and the experience of the excavating process, thus providing the public with multiple readings for the presented objects[91]. So, an attempt to connect the archaeological aspect (i.e. the discovery of the past) with the museum activity is apparent in some Greek museum activities[92] (as we will discuss later in the chapter) but the focus generally is placed on the aesthetics and the socio-historical identification of details of the objects.

In our attempt to deconstruct the museum narrative, it was important for this analysis to take into consideration the above discussion and to pursue an investigation into these mechanisms and architectonics which make the museum socially powerful as an institution, which give it emotive and symbolic meaning as architecture and produce ideologically and culturally active and changing narratives.

III. The Archaeological Museum of Thessaloniki

The Archaeological Museum of Thessaloniki has been closely connected with a growing number of excavations and with archaeological activities in general in Macedonia, Northern Greece, since its Liberation from Turkish rule (1912). Professor M. Andronikos used to describe it as the 'National Archaeological Museum of Northern Greece' (Ανδρόνικος 1986:7) because it was the place where all the antiquities derived from excavations and surveys from all the regions of Northern Greece were gathered and kept in order to be conserved and presented to the public. With the administrative organization of the Greek Archaeological Service of Macedonia and the activity of the Aristotle University of Thessaloniki, numerous archaeological projects were initiated focusing on the big cultural centres of antiquity, the archaeological sites of Vergina, Pella and Dion and other sites of Prehistoric and Byzantine interest.

---

91 See Marthari 2002, discussing the exhibitions of Cycladic culture.

92 The Museum of Volos was the first which adopted that practice (1975) with the presentation of a stratigraphy in the exhibition of Neolithics. The case of the Museum of Byzantine Culture in Thessaloniki is the only case where a whole room is dedicated to the excavation process and where some of the theoretical issues of archaeology as a discipline are discussed. Also, a recent temporary exhibition held in the Archaeological Museum of Thessaloniki by the Department of Monuments Archive, on "...Ανέφερα εγγράφως..." Θησαυροί του Ιστορικού Αρχείου της Αρχαιολογικής Υπηρεσίας. "...Stated in writing..." Treasures of the Historical Archive of the Archaeological Service and accompanied by an educational program entitled 'Searching for lost archaeological information' which was held in September 2010, was an attempt also to present the hidden side of museums where the messages are produced and re-produced.

Founding History of the Museum and Its Significance

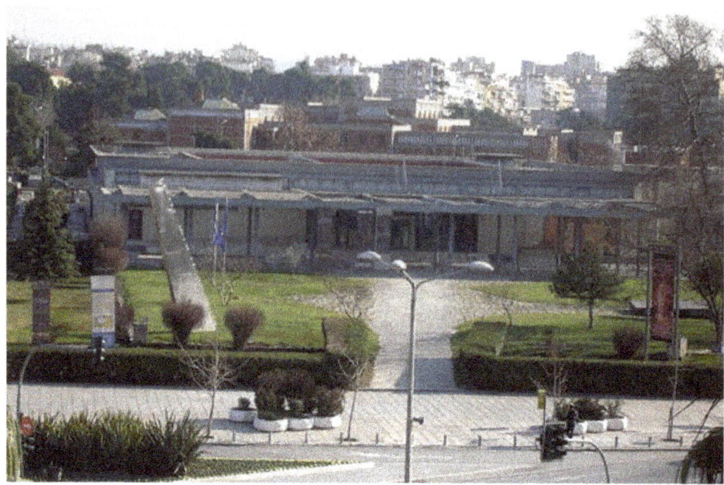

Figure 1: The Archaeological Museum of Thessaloniki

Before the official founding of the Archaeological Museum of Thessaloniki, various buildings were used for museum-like activities. The Idadie School or 'the Old Building' of the University Philosophical School was used for the exhibition of antiquities from 1912, the Dioikitirio[93] was used for storage, and the Church of Acheiropoiitos was also used as a museum storehouse from 1916 until 1922 when it was established as an Orthodox Church. In 1925, the related Ephorate of Antiquities decided to use the Yeni Tzami as a museum and the first exhibition took place there in 1931 with a second in 1953. It is worth mentioning that the antiquities were kept and hidden in trenches during World War II to avoid destruction and looting[94]. In 1959 a new place was found for the construction of a brand-new museum, which officially opened in 1961[95] based on the architectural plans of the architect

[93] The former Ministry of Macedonia and Thrace in which the office of the first Director of Antiquities in Macedonia was also located.

[94] In 1940, when World War II was still ongoing, the then Director of Antiquities, N. Kotzias, and the Curator of Antiquities, C. Makaronas, along with Professors E. Pelekidi and A. Xygopoulos, took the initiative to take measures to protect the antiquities, which were kept in different storage rooms and in the former Museum of Yeni Tzami, from any harm or deterioration. Some of the sculptures had been buried in trenches and covered with huge gravestones and a documented catalogue was sent to the Ministry of Education. Other antiquities were packaged in boxes and had been sent to Athens in order for them to be safely kept. It is worth mentioning the commitment as well as the emotional attachment of those archaeologists to these antiquities, so that, even in the most difficult moments of the war, they put themselves at risk in order to protect the 'national' treasures of the area. See I. Βοκοτοπούλου Τα πρώτα 50 χρόνια της Εφορείας Κλασσικών Αρχαιοτήτων Θεσσαλονίκης (The first fifty years of the Thessaloniki Ephorate of Classical Antiquities), Η Θεσσαλονίκη μετά το 1912, (Thessaloniki after 1912) Συμπόσιο, Conference proceedings 1-3 November 1986. Θεσσαλονίκη 1986; Χ. Μακαρόνας, *Μακεδονικά* 2, 1941-1952, 560-677

[95] The issue of the construction of the Museum was first raised in early 1931. See Βοκοτοπούλου 1986

Patroklos Karandinos[96]. Its opening, which was held in 1962, coincided with the celebration of the fifty years that had passed since the Independence of Thessaloniki from the Ottomans. The first exhibition was dedicated to the works of sculpture in the Sculpture Gallery which was researched and designed by archaeologist and then-curator of Antiquities, G. Despines, and to an exhibition of Prehistoric objects curated and researched by archaeologist A. Sakellariou. When, in 1979, new discoveries came to light with the large-scale excavation of Vergina, under Professor M. Andronikos, the museum was extended in order to house the exhibition on metal-working in Macedonia and the objects from the Royal Tombs at Aigae[97]. That was when the museum raised the public's interest in antiquities and their past, as the discoveries and the findings from the excavation of Vergina were not only of great scientific, national and international interest, but also made a considerable impact on the public's perception of their glorious past[98]. On the other hand, the importance of the museum's role as a gate-keeper and guardian of these precious relics of the past was increased in the public's eyes and minds and the museum experience was seen more as a ritual and pilgrimage to admire their ancestors' works of art as displayed by the curators, focusing on their aesthetic and historical values as dictated by the prevailing form of Classical archaeology scholarship. Later on, in 1985, Thessaloniki celebrated the 2300th anniversary of its founding with an exhibition dealing with the city which was curated by the then Director I. Vokotopoulou, archaeologist. A number of thematic exhibitions on antiquity followed in the next few years[99] until 1996, when the first extended exhibition on Prehistoric Macedonia took place under archaeologist and then-director D. Grammenos. It should be mentioned that at the stage of the initial architectural plans, a Gallery dedicated to the Byzantine antiquities of the area was designed and curated by N. Nikonanos[100], thus aiming to include all the periods of the Greek past in Macedonia and creating a diachronia in the public's perception.

The importance of the existence and the role of the Archaeological Museum of Thessaloniki reveals some interesting perspectives. On the one hand, it managed to bring together scholars at a scientific level who had been working for years in the Macedonia area[101] to create and interpret the Macedonian past based on the principles of aesthetics and on approaching the remains of the past as works of art. The museum for many years used to be an academic place, where experts and researchers on sculpture, ceramic vases, or metal works could pursue further study of these fields by the observation of authentic displayed objects of the relevant era.

---

[96] Patroklos Karandinos (1903-1976) was one of the distinguished architects of the era.

[97] This exhibition was awarded first prize by the Council of Europe, which was the first time this had happened for a Greek archaeological museum.

[98] See the newspapers *Το Βήμα [To Vima]* 25/11/1977; *Θεσσαλονίκη [Thessaloniki]* 24 and 25/11/1977.

[99] Exhibition on the Classical and Archaic period in 1989

[100] Then Director of the 10th Ephorate of Byzantine Antiquities and later Professor of Byzantine Archaeology in the Aristotle University of Thessaloniki.

[101] Apart from the projects of the Aristotle University of Thessaloniki and those carried out by the Archaeological Service, there were a considerable number of reports and findings from expeditions and missions by foreigners, such as L. Heuzey (see *Mission Archeologique de Macedoine*, 1876), M Cousinery (see *Voyages dans la Macedoine*, 1831) and M. Leak (see *Travels in Northern Greece*, 1835).

It was a purely educational place based on strict formalities and subjected to the academic directions of the current scholarship[102]. On the other hand, in the public's eyes and after the city's liberation, the museum became their landmark and a guide, which helped them to define their socio-political existence as rooted in their glorious past. It played a significant role in the formation of their local identity by emphasizing the multiple facets of the city's heritage, and it surely also played an educational role in that, through the exhibitions, people (and especially children) were visiting the museum in order to go more deeply into the history of their area. Moreover, from its beginnings the museum tried to acquire a more open and multidisciplinary character by organizing temporary exhibitions of modern art, such as that by the painter Tsarouchis held in 1981, which aimed to constitute a meeting place not only for scholars and experts but also for the wider public.

Architecture of the Museum

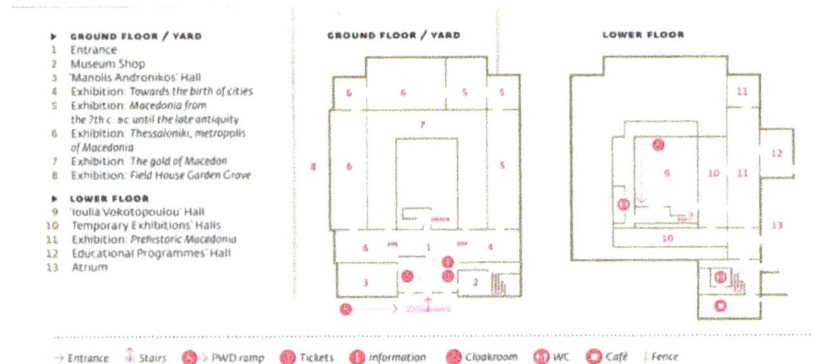

Figure 2: The Architectural Plan of the AMT

The museum building constitutes one of the most significant buildings in the city as an example of modernism[103]. It exemplifies the socio-political and cultural conditions of that period of time, which defined the framework within which the Greek architects were trying to intervene in order to provide the best architectural solutions in an attempt to regenerate of the city[104]. According to the architect, the museum and the region around it were intended to constitute a central cultural core of the city of Thessaloniki that would include an Art Gallery on the site of the

[102] The museum of Thessaloniki with its collections used to constitute (and still does) one of the main educational places for archaeology students in which courses on sculpture and aesthetics and typologies and taxonomies were held aiming to provide essential scientific knowledge of objects which were seen and studied as masterpieces of art. So, the museum was seen by the students (as I experienced this as an archaeology student at the University) as the place where the study of ancient pieces could facilitate the process of learning and the acquisition of professional skills.

[103] The most representative example of the modernism of Le Corbusier who influenced the Greek architects of the era.

[104] For more details on the movement of modernism see Φιλιππίδης, Δ. 1984. Νεοελληνική Αρχιτεκτονική Αθήνα: Μέλισσα

former military Theatre. He also suggested that the Museum should include a Byzantine section, which was built separately during the 1980s and 1990s on an adjoining lot. Furthermore, Karandinos proposed four preliminary designs: one rectangular, one cruciform in the centre, one circular and another which, when amended, became the final, i.e. the present building. The Byzantine section was incorporated into the centre and was surrounded by the section on antiquity.

The basic principles of the design were the separation of the two sections, the partitioning of the section for the offices, labs, storage rooms and library: 'a T-shaped structure with a lower horizontal arm that accommodates storage areas and workshops, while in the section perpendicular to it (due to the height difference) are the offices and the library' (Γραμμένος 2004:13). He also took into consideration the height difference in the terrain of the two exhibition areas (large and small P's) and laid them hierarchically around a natural atrium, with horizontal strips of lighting under the flat roof (the suggestion for the lighting was ultimately not implemented), visible stone masonry and the widespread use of glass bricks (ibid.).

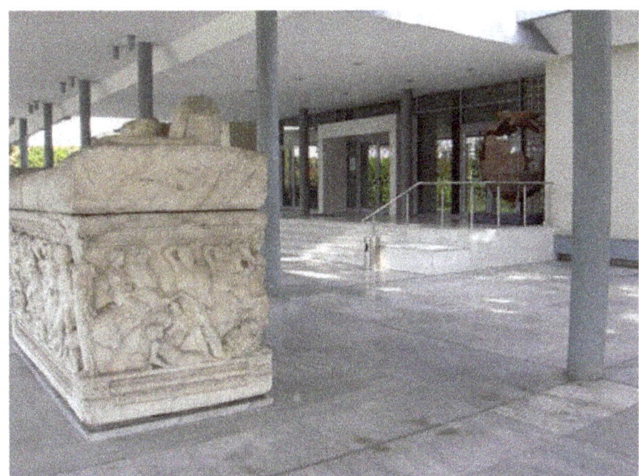

Figure 3: The main entrance of the AMT

The building met all the requirements of the era by providing bright, light, open-air, and anti-monumental forms situated in a central point of the city, which was accessible and architecturally friendly for the people of the city. It marked the city's architectural history as well as the museum history of Greece, and it has since been declared a listed building. In the following years, the new extensions for different exhibitions (as we mentioned previously) partly changed Karandinos' initial plan and, in recent years, after the CAC's approval[105] the building renovation[106] and re-

[105] No. 40/2-9-2003 CAC Committee and the related Department decision ΥΠΠΟ/ΓΔΑΠΚ/ΔΜΕΕΠ/Γ1/Φ21/54590/340/16.10.2003 'On the approval of museological and museographical re-exhibition study of the Archaeological Museum of Thessaloniki' Department of Museums, Exhibition and Educational Programs (Sub-department of state archaeological museums and collections) MofC (archival material)

[106] The preliminary study for the building renovation was made and submitted by the architect N. Fyntikakis [Ν. Φυντικάκης]

exhibition have been carried out, funded by the 3rd European Framework Support. According to the museographical plan-study[107], the main design principles were a) the restitution in its main function and form elements of Karandinos' architectural plan, b) the restitution of the atrium as the perene of the central building, acquiring a significant role both externally and internally, c) division of the basic operational units of the Museum (exhibition galleries, offices, storage rooms, labs, library, facilities), d) introduction of environmentally-friendly principles of the lighting and air-conditioning, e) construction of a basement in order to provide a new space for use, and finally f) promotion of the museological units through the renovation and through the integration of the courtyards of the museum. Internally, the great advantage of the renovation has been the covering of the atrium and its provision for multiple uses (temporary exhibitions, meetings, educational programs); 'it is the main combining idea of the proposal for giving a "moral boost" to the museum' as the architect reveals in the museographical plan-study (Φυντικάκης 1998: sect. 3 par. b). That new addition unifies the spaces, stressing Karandinos' initial plan and introducing new dynamics, providing a better and more visitor-oriented movement within the museum rooms. The architect's concerns were also with the space in the museum entrance, which used to lack some of the main facilities and the appropriate sense of unity, and with the renovation of the administrative rooms and labs. These concerns proved that the museum was attempting to become a place which could house multiple activities and provide multiple services to the visitors, including architectural interventions aimed at visitors with disabilities according to modern museum building requirements. In order to enhance the spatially-related relationships among the exhibits, and the relationship between the visitor and the space of the museum, an approach has been adopted which involves the integration of the courtyard into the museological project. Thus, a so-called 'archaeological promenade' was designed to provide ways of viewing the remains of the past, providing a variety of different routes designed and structured in accordance with a scenario built around themes and topics.

The internal organization of the space in the rooms and galleries uses a number of architectonics and technologies, consisting of bases, showcases of different sizes, free-standing constructions, panels and banners, models, and multiple types of high-tech devices, whose primary use is, according to the museological scenario-study[108], to provide an adequate, safe 'micro-space' for the most vulnerable objects and which secondarily contribute to the communication of the messages intended by the curator. The arrangements of the exhibits and the positioning of labels and panels follow some spatial and thematic taxonomies which make use of; for example, the day light or artificial lighting or the choice of colour in the topic's division. The transition from the 'micro-space' to the 'macro-space', which is the rooms'

---

[107] Preliminary architectural study for the building renovation, written and submitted by N. Fyntikakis, 1998. Archive of the Department of Museum Building Construction, MoCT

[108] Museological and Museographical Re-exhibition Study of the Archaeological Museum of Thessaloniki, written and submitted by D. Grammenos in 2003. Archive of Department of Museums, Exhibition and Educational Programs (Sub-department of state archaeological museums and collections), MofCT.

organization, and vice versa, and the relations produced in the communication process, creates rhetorical elements which are embedded in a new structured environment for the objects and their biographies (Kopytoff 1986). Then, the space is transformed into a place, a museum landscape, or 'an intensely meaningful location which excites a whole series of proprietorial feelings and close identifications' (Silverstone 1994:172) with articulated routes and 'paths' (Tilley 1994) leading to the discovery of the imagined Greek past.

That sense of place is fostered and encouraged by the way that the interpretations and identification texts are produced and the drawings and pictures are displayed in order to create the contextualized environment of the objects, which are derived from archaeological sites that were discovered and researched as a source of historical and topographical evidence.

Themes, 'Writings' and the Aim of the Museum Exhibitions

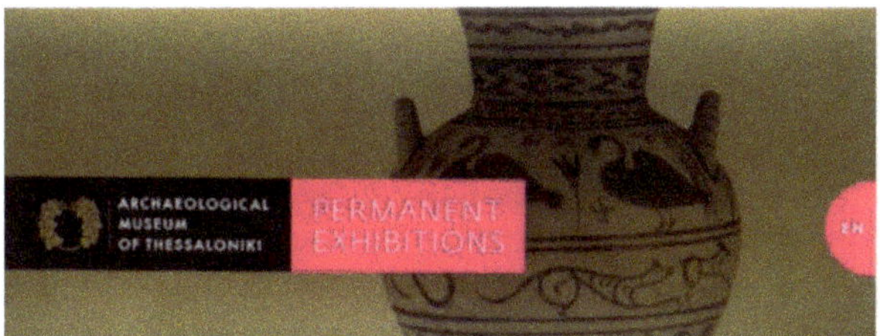

Figure 4: The Leaflet of AMT

The implementation of the museological project during the creation of the permanent exhibitions of the Museum was mainly characterized by the wide variety of artefacts from different periods. Their provenance was mostly from major excavations in cities and cemeteries, large-scale projects in prehistoric settlements and also circumstantial finds from surveys, private collections etc. The former provenance condition encouraged the curator to choose to present the objects within a comprehensive context, including a textual and visual one.

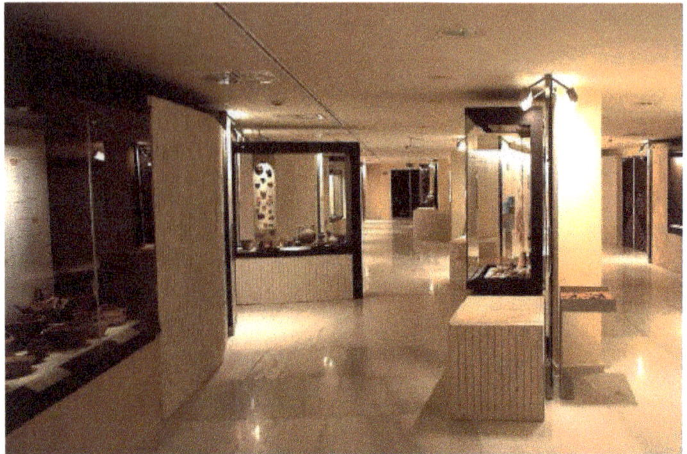

Figure 5: AMT. The *Prehistoric Macedonia* Exhibition

According to the museological and museographical plan, the museum exhibitions' aim, following modern museological principles, is to acquaint the visitor with the Macedonian past through the interpreted historical evidence. The exhibitions are structured and sub-structured in terms of thematic units, which are the following: 1) *Prehistoric Macedonia* 2) *Towards the Birth of the Cities* 3) *Macedonia from the 7th century BC until late Antiquity* 4) *Thessaloniki, Metropolis of Macedonia* 5) *The Gold of Macedon* 6) *Field, House, Garden, Grave.*

In the first thematic unit, *Prehistoric Macedonia*, bearing the introductory title *5000, 15.000, 200.000 years ago an exhibition of life in Prehistoric Macedonia*, the focus was placed mainly on the presentation of practices and activities of humans and the process connecting these social practices with the cultural history of modern society. An attempt was made to approach the visitor in a way that encouraged him/her to be critical and not only to be a recipient of structured messages, but also to develop multiple readings. The latter is accomplished by using a number of different means and structures of presentation so that the visitors avoid becoming bored and remain willing to engage more with the experience of the information provided. To that end, the use of an audiovisual application helps make visitors aware of the production of different writings or the fact that knowledge is derived from a process of discovering and interpreting the remains of the past through excavation practices; it is more like the 'words made of soil' as the Professor of Prehistory, G. Chourmouziadis, used to say of archaeological discourses. The exhibition moves on two axes: one consists of the practices and techniques developed in prehistoric societies, and issues of communication and ideology[109] (Στεφανή 2006), and the other of issues relating to the practice of Prehistoric

[109] Such as ceramics, technology, commercial exchanges, farming, hunting, cooking and storage, weaving and metal works.

Archaeology as a discipline[110] (ibid.) and its relation to other sociological and anthropological fields. This practice is apparent in many of the texts of the exhibition, as it uses aspects borrowed from the field of anthropology to support interpretative approaches (see figure 6). It should be noted that the texts are presented in a hierarchical order but they do not follow a strict chronological sequence; instead, they have a narrative style, which is interrupted by statements or questions for the purpose of facilitating the visitor's engagement in the communication process (see figures 6 and 7).

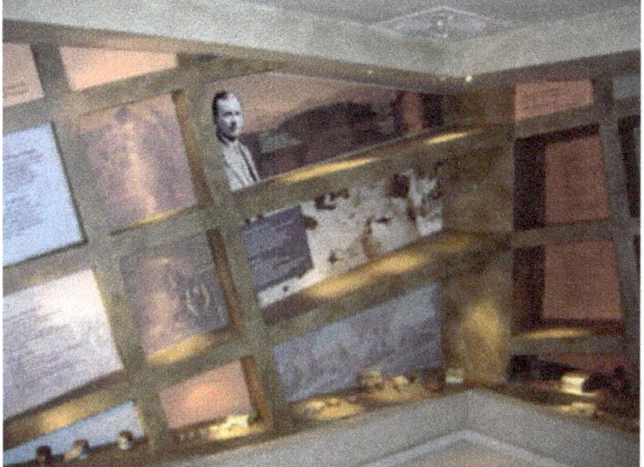

Figure 6: AMT. Exhibition panel displaying the history of research.
Prehistoric Macedonia Exhibition

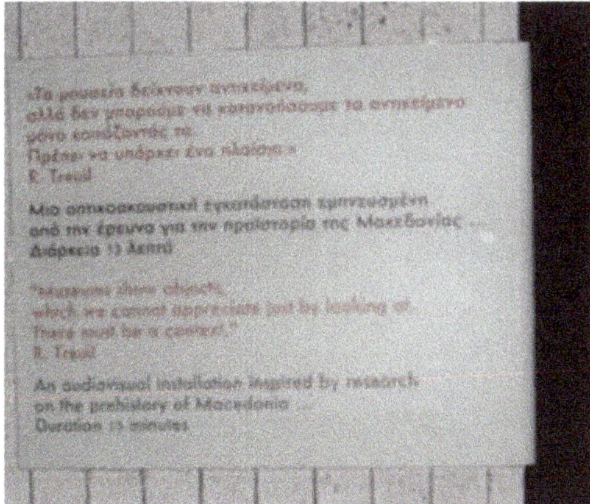

Figure 7: AMT. Text of Panel from the
Prehistoric Macedonia Exhibition

[110] Such as excavation (methodology, significance), physical anthropology, conservation, prehistoric archaeology and social archaeology.

Although the current exhibition introduced new communicative methods that depart from the traditional ones and provide new ways of experiencing the prehistoric past, its location in the basement of the museum created problems of movement and message perception. Given the fact that the displays of the museum follow a chronological order, one would expect the visitor to start his/her tour from Prehistoric times on the ground floor[111] and then move through time while receiving the exhibition's messages.

Moving to the next second thematic group of divisions or units within the museum, which are *Towards the Birth of the Cities*, *Macedonia from the 7th Century BC until late Antiquity*, and *Thessaloniki: Metropolis of Macedonia*, one easily recognizes that historic times require the most extended museum displays in terms of the space they cover and the multiple means they use. In the first thematic division, the emphasis of the narrative is placed mainly upon topographical and geographical details, as a way of providing the sense of place and the transitional time from the Iron Age to the Birth of the City. The construction of a round panel display may have a positive impact on the visitor's ability to enjoy the experience of reading, but the mixed display of drawings, pictures, cases, and objects produce a confusing impression, creating perception problems (see figure 8).

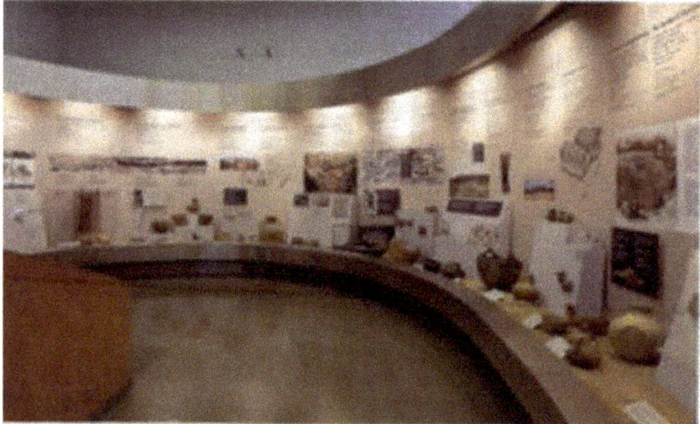

Figure 8: AMT: *The Exhibition Towards the Birth of the Cities*

[111] It should be noted that the initial plans were based on the above suggestion, but due to restricted rooms and inappropriate organization of galleries, the current solution was ultimately agreed upon. See D. Grammenos 2003 Museological and Museographical Re-exhibition Study of the Archaeological Museum of Thessaloniki. Archive of Department of Museums, Exhibition and Educational Programmes (Sub-department of state archaeological museums and collections) MoCT correspondence.

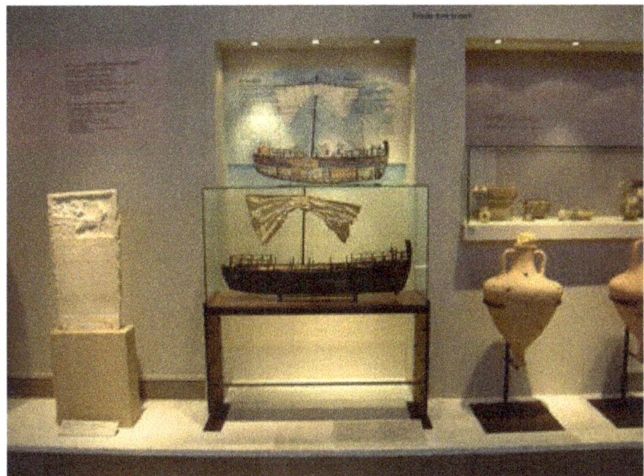

Figure 9: AMT: The Exhibition *Towards the Kingdom of Macedonia*

It is noteworthy that in the next division, an attempt was made to use objects to support thematic units as aspects of political and social life, religion, daily life etc. This created meanings in a manner that was more interesting and enjoyable for the visitor, as they could make connections with the present. The sense of place changes when the visitor reaches the thematic unit on Thessaloniki, to which a spacious room was dedicated, in stressing its dominant role as the metropolis of Macedonia. The socio-political associations are apparent in the way that a number of impressive statues are displayed, and a very interesting fresco is reconstructed in order to foster the sense of the city's prevailing position in that era. The objects displayed here are seen mostly as unique works of art of the time they represent, following the principles of Classical archaeology (see figure 10). However, that object-focused sense has been balanced by the choices of the texts and sub-themes which frame the exhibition, in trying to transform it into a more visitor-oriented experience. So, with smart questions like '*Do you know what lies in the basement of the museum of modern art?*' it provides opportunities for the visitor to engage with and wonder about the discovery and the making of knowledge (see figure 11). Also, with the audiovisual applications, a variety of information is displayed to the specialized or non-specialized visitor, elaborating on issues and themes with titles such as '*What was a city in Ancient Macedonia like?*' '*Macedonian Tombs as symbols of reference for the Macedonian Culture*' and '*The city of Thessaloniki as a city of the past and present*'.

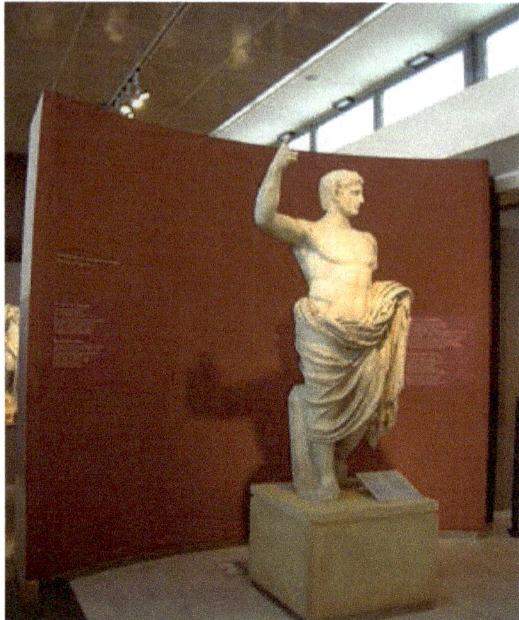

Figure 10: AMT. The Exhibition of Sculpture

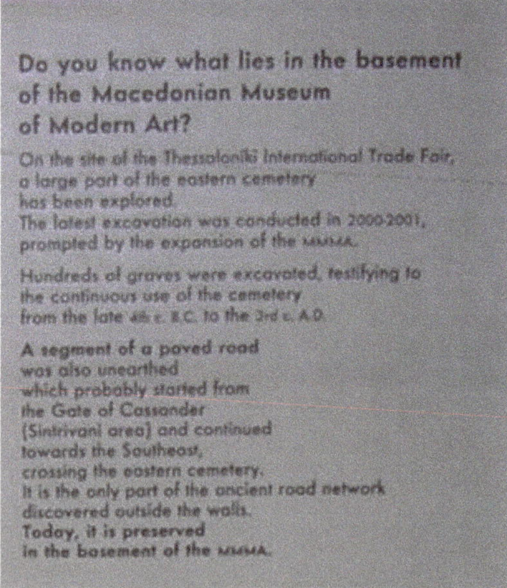

Figure 11: AMT. Text of a panel in the Exhibition
Thessaloniki: Metropolis of Macedonia

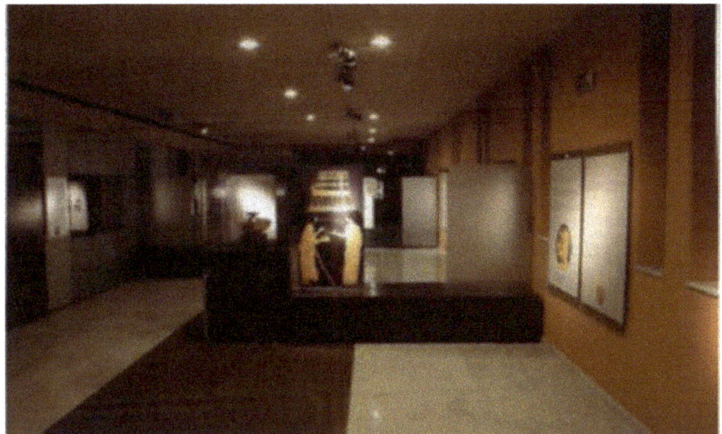

Figure 12: AMT. The exhibition *The Gold of Macedon*

The permanent exhibition *The Gold of Macedon*, although belonging chronologically to historic times, functions as an autonomous exhibition in terms of the display style and the separate space given to it. It is an exhibition based on older models (1998 and 2004), and it was created with a strong focus on object-driven display methods. The exhibition's central theme is that of its title, and the sub-themes were developed according to its usual practices, covering chronologically a period from 6th century-2nd century BC and geographically the area of Macedonia. Themes such as *'The Archaeology of Death'*; *'Gold as an expression of ideology in the mortuary ritual of the Macedonians'*; and *'Gold in the graveyards of Macedonia'* were indicative of the nature of the displayed objects. In this category of exhibits there were objects that are related to the impact that archaeology has on the public's view of the objects. For example, this is the case for the Derveni Crater (4th c. BC) found in the Derveni Tomb in 1962 (Thessaloniki), which when discovered provoked intense public interest in the antiquities from different places in the area (see figure 13). During this period, groups of tombs were coming to light, providing an increasingly number of gold finds of unique artistic significance. For many years, the crater was depicted on many of the catalogues and leaflets of the Museum, as it became the object-symbol (along with the gold finds of the Vergina Tombs) of the archaeology of Northern Greece. In these exhibitions, the 'aura' of objects as entities was fostered and this prevailed in the suggested interpretations within the texts, and the poetic possibilities of the objects were raised through the values they were given by these interpretations. The methodology of the lighting system contributes to this recognition of the main role of objects as 'actors' in the museum scene since it concentrates on the objects themselves, upgrading their decorative golden details and stressing their role as the main mediators of knowledge.

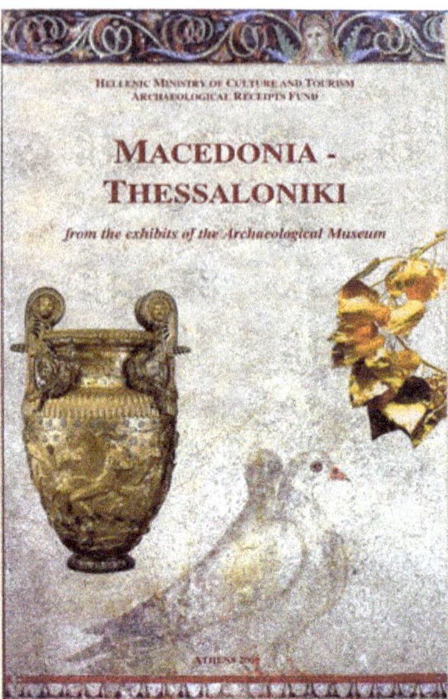

Figure 13: The Catalogue of the AMT

Another exhibition unit is found in the museum courtyard (see figure 14), which is of great importance and interest in terms of its use of texts and has proven to engage the public and be enjoyable due to the way that it elaborates its themes. The exhibits consist of funerary monuments, such as sarcophagi, altars, and stelae of the Roman period, items which usually attract the interest of specialists and not the wider public. In this case the curator, taking into consideration new trends in museum design, adopted a more sociologically- and anthropologically-oriented narrative, without reducing the scientific authenticity of the objects. He did this by engaging with the inscriptions carved on the monuments through a poetic approach and through this he created units and themes based on the information provided by each monument (see figure 15). Complementary to this exhibition there is an extended reconstruction of a Roman house, where, in a very visual and didactic way, the visitor is acquainted with architectural features and practices such as *'The art of fresco'* or *'The triclinium: dinner in bed'*. It is worth noticing the role of open space in the way that it facilitates the visitor's engagement in the meaning-making process and the 'different gazes' of the suggested museum narratives.

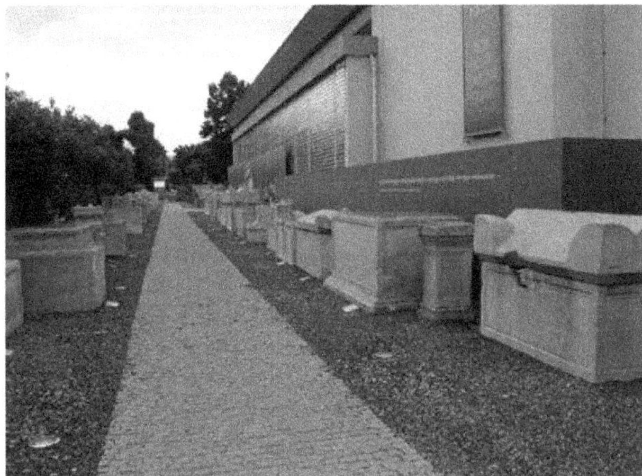

Figure 14: AMT. The Courtyard Exhibition

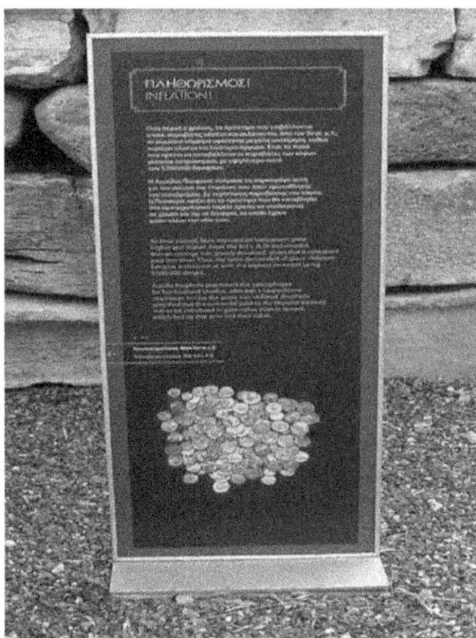

Figure 15: AMT. Panel of the Exhibition of Courtyard

In the light of the above, it should be stressed that the visitor in the museum is moving through a specifically structured spatio-temporal context in which he/she is situated and through which he/she is made to interact with the mediated stories. The role of the sequenced space is crucial as it intervenes between the visitor and the objects either by upgrading or by reducing their meanings. In the cases under study and in museums in general in Greece, as we have already noticed, the objects have close relationships with the place from which they were derived[112] (excavations)

---

[112] According to the current Director of the Museum Dr. Adam-Veleni. Personal interview Thessaloniki 20/9/2010

and that relationship is expressed in the display milieus through charts, texts and maps. Thus, the visitor is 'transferred' into the past and experiences it spatially and temporally. This effect is augmented by an artificial and newly constructed museum exterior, which provided the possibility of an exhibition taking place in the outer space of the museum and might contribute to the relationship with the space.

The Archaeological Museum of Thessaloniki, through its recent re-exhibition project has managed to bypass the traditional aspect of the temple museum and to adopt changing strategies and attitudes by making it a publically-oriented social institution. The new conditions have created a completely new role and new ground for the 'makers' behind the scene, the archaeologists of the archaeological service, who were called upon to see the potential of studying and interpreting the past and realizing the interdisciplinary nature of archaeology as a discipline. By recognizing the social, cultural and ideological role of the past and its representation and projection through the mirror of museums in modern societies, they moved towards interpretation practices which encourage multiple readings and writings of the past by the public and which view the museum as a heart of culture[113], where the visitor develops interrelationships with the museum space.

IV. The Museum of Byzantine Culture of Thessaloniki: Recreating the Byzantine Past

Thessaloniki historically reached its highest development during the Byzantine period as the second city of the Byzantine Empire, after Constantinople. Its strategic place as a crossroads of cultures[114] was of great significance, as it was the link between the old capital of the Empire (Rome) and the new one (Constantinople, modern day Istanbul). At the present day the wealth of the Byzantine monuments and the discovered sites within the city, and in Northern Greece in general, are witnesses of that Byzantine civilization. The Museum of Byzantine Culture in Thessaloniki, along with the European Centre of Byzantine and post-Byzantine Monuments (housed in the same building) were the first social, educational and academic institutions to have been dedicated to the study, research and representation of Byzantine culture.

Establishing the Museum of Byzantine Culture

The establishment of the Central Byzantine Museum in Thessaloniki has a long history. It was first mentioned in a Decree issued by a Governor General of Macedonia, Stefanos Dragoumis, in 1913[115] and a letter written by Archbishop Gennadios of Thessaloniki[116], in which it was decided that the museum was to be

[113] According to the then Director of the museum Dr Kourkoutidou-Nikolaidou.

[114] For more details on the history of Thessaloniki as a strategic place at a European level see Αρβελέρ [Arweiller] 2009.

[115] No 746/26.8.1913

[116] No 661/22.8.1913. The significance of the need for the creation of the museum is clearly evident in the sainted Archbishop's words: 'the church is most spacious, quite capable, not only at present but also

installed in the early Christian church called Acheiropoietos. In September 1913 A. Adamantiou, Professor of Byzantine Art and Archaeology, wrote a 'Memorandum on the Establishment and Organization of a Central Byzantine Museum in Macedonia' in which the eminent Byzantine scholar stressed the location of the city of Thessaloniki as the most appropriate one for the foundation of the museum[117] (Κουρκουτίδου-Νικολαΐδου 1994:11, 12). In 1914, based on the law 'On the Antiquities', the Christian and Byzantine Museum was founded in Athens and in 1916 many antiquities were transferred to it from Thessaloniki (Law no 401/1914). That museum, according to Article 1 of the law, which refers to the establishment of the museum, could contain 'works of Byzantine, medieval, and Christian art...from different locations, with the exception of those in Macedonia'; and article 9 further explains that 'a second Decree may establish another museum in Thessaloniki for the Byzantine antiquities in Macedonia'. In 1917 it was decided to move the museum from the Acheiropoietos church to the Rotonda, a Roman building at the centre of Thessaloniki. The Rotonda was designated as the place to house the new Museum of Macedonia, and a large number of sculptures were gathered there until the earthquake of 1978.

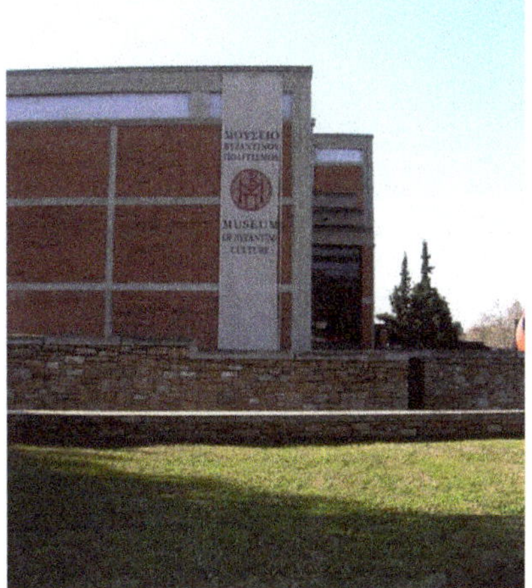
Figure 16: The Museum of Byzantine Culture (MBC)

In 1977, the CAC[118] (Central Archaeological Council) declared an architectural competition for the construction of the new museum and Kyriakos Krokos, one of the most eminent architects, undertook the construction of the museum building, but

---

in the future, of serving as the auspiciously founded Central Byzantine Museum of Greece' (Κουρκουτίδου-Νικολαΐδου 1994:11).

[117] '...where else, owing to both its geographical position between West and East and its exalted historical stature, in the fullest sense, in the Byzantine Empire, is more favorably predestined to be the finest centre of research into Christian and Byzantine art than the great and glorious Byzantine city of Thessaloniki'(ibid.:11).

[118] By an act of 18/25.5.1975

still it was not until 1984[119] that the Ministerial Council agreed that the land should be handed over and the museum built. The foundation stone was laid in 1989 by then-Minister of Culture, Melina Mercouri, and the building was finished in October 1993. In the same year, the then Minister for Culture, in consultation with the CAC, issued a decision approving the museographical-architectural plan-studies, as submitted by the Ephorate of Byzantine Antiquities responsible for the Museum, and also approving the name put forward by the Ephorate: 'the Museum of Byzantine Culture' (Κουρκουτίδου-Νικολαΐδου 1994)[120]. An issue which was of great importance for the archaeologists working in the field was always the return (from Athens) of the antiquities to their original place. As we discussed in Chapter II, the sustainability and completion of the museum would be based on those antiquities, which were finally returned in June 1994, some of which were displayed in the museum's inaugural exhibition: *Byzantine Treasures of Thessaloniki: The Return Journey*. It is quite indicative that a special exhibition was organised dedicated to the returned objects and showing the impact that the issue had on the public's and archaeologists' views on the remains of the past.

The foundation of the museum is closely related to the role of the city as a centre of cultural and spiritual life in the area, as it used to be, and it still is. The study of and research into the Byzantine past, as an archaeological field, has found fertile ground in the city of Thessaloniki which was full of sites and monuments of that period. Large-scale projects of renovation of Byzantine churches and rescue excavations have been initiated in Thessaloniki and in other cities of Northern Greece[121], especially after the earthquake of 1978, in order to reveal and study the evolution of Byzantine art. The archaeological services, along with the University of Thessaloniki, have carried out many excavation and conservation projects and many of these finds supplied the museum, which covered the gap between academic scholarship and the public. Thessaloniki is intended to be a centre for the preservation, investigation and study of those remnants of Byzantine culture which still survive in Macedonia in general and in Thessaloniki in particular. In the fields of education and art, Byzantine culture was a link in the chain of Greek cultures, an amalgam of a wide variety of cultural elements. Despite being profoundly rooted in the multifaceted tradition of late antiquity, Byzantine art nonetheless displayed an expressive coherence and developed specific artistic elements, conveyed spiritual messages and expressed the most profound religious conceptions, such as the vision of God. The transition from the ancient to the medieval world bore the defining stamp of Orthodox Christianity (Κουρκουτίδου-Νικολαΐδου 1994).

[119]Problems had arisen in relation to the location, next to the Archaeological Museum, and the studies were held up. The land (part of the former Tsiroyanni Army Camp) was owned by the National Defence Fund, which was asking far too high a price from the purchaser (the Ministry of Culture and Sciences). The personal intervention of the then Prime Minister and Minister for National Defence, Mr Andreas Papandreou, was decisive in enabling the work to proceed.

[120] See the museological scenario-study written and submitted by the then director of Ephorate and the Museum, Dr Kourkoutidou-Nikolaidou.

[121] Such as Veroia or Kozani and Kastoria (Northern Greece)

The museum's role as an institution[122] is twofold: first, to be an establishment and centre of the research and promotion of Byzantine culture, engaged in a constant dialogue with the monuments left standing or found in Thessaloniki, and to enhance and disseminate its research accounts both nationally and internationally. Due to its changing institutional status as a special administrative institution (according to the Law 2557/1997 art. 4 'On the Museum'), it constitutes a foundation which is open to the public, focusing on communicative practices, which bolsters its educational and entertainment role through different permanent and temporary exhibitions and collaborations with foreign institutions.

> '...it is a scientific institution, open to the public, with a broad cultural and educational character and aiming at the gathering, safeguarding, protection, conservation, presentation, promotion and study of works and objects of Early Christian, Byzantine, and in general the medieval and the post-Byzantine period, derived mainly from the geographical area of Macedonia...'
>
> '...it is addressed to the wider public, and it encourages through its activities increasing visitor attendance, fosters the entertainment and educational contact of the collections with the public and guarantees the scientifically documented and internationally known forms of museological presentation' (Law 2557/1997 art. 4).

Secondly, its role is also socio-political as it aims to help form and foster the city's identity at the present time. The museum symbolizes the character of the city and points out the multicultural elements of its history; it makes the city itself function as a Byzantine landscape and an open-air museum where its people seek to identify their past with specific monuments, forms and rituals in the modern city. It is interesting to stress the above point and to recognize the power of the museum to give expression in multiple meanings of and approaches to the past and to accommodate different views about the goals of a museum and the role that it is called upon to play in modern societies.

The Museum Architecture as a 'Space for Creating Freedom and Stirring up the Senses' (Krokos 1989)[123]

The museum is housed in a building constructed according to the plans of the talented architect Kyriakos Krokos (1941-1998). It comprises the permanent

[122] The MBC has been divided administratively from the 9th Ephorate of Byzantine Antiquity (Thessaloniki) by the Law 2557/1997 art. 7 par. 15 and a ministerial decision has been issued ΥΠΠΟ/ΓΝΟΣ/50304/25.10.1999 ΦΕΚ Β' 2018 by which the organization, administration and operation of a state museum must take into consideration the current museological tendencies. It was the first application of this legal principle and the first museum to be transformed into a special administrative institution which was taken as a guide to be followed by others as well as by the Archaeological Museum of Thessaloniki and the Museum of Herakleion (Crete).

[123] Available at http://www.mbp.gr/html/gr/mu_ktirio.htm accessed 25/2/2011

exhibition rooms, spacious and well-organised conservation laboratories and storerooms, a small amphitheatre, a café-restaurant and a separate wing for temporary exhibitions. The architect's intention was to build a 'space of freedom', a space for enhancing the senses where the visitor could follow a clearly routed path through the experience of Byzantine culture. The elementary concept was of a building with elements (stones, plinths and concrete)[124] where these elements or their material should 'speak' (Γιακουμάτος 2002:6). He wanted to create a space which was 'alive' in order to participate in the visitor's communication with the past and enhance the process of that perception. He believed in a building-language produced within a social and cultural context, and he introduced new guidelines into museum architecture. The visitor's senses were, for him, the initial starting point for his museum plans, and he was concerned with how communication could be accomplished through the visitor's movements within the museum (Αρβανίτη-Κρόκου 2002). It is quite remarkable to reflect on the way that, in the construction of the museum building, the scale of the human being has been used to constitute and define the scale and the character of the building itself. This anthropocentric construction policy allows the museum to adopt a spatially more visitor-centred museological and museographical strategy based not only on the written stories and tales but also on spatial narratives which are actively engaged in the meaning-making process.

The building's image externally, which is severe and austere, made with exceptionally combined modern materials and characterized by construction of high quality, fuses elements of modernism and of the Greek architectural heritage. The museum building itself is a 'closed' and 'introverted' space creating implicit associations and articulations with simple Byzantine architectural forms. This was also the reason for the construction of few and small windows[125], at least in the exhibition rooms, where the only source of daylight comes from the atrium, in some cases facilitating the public's movement and preparing them for the transition from one thematic division to another. Internally the space acquires a unique atmosphere due to the organization of the galleries which is integrated into the museological scenario. The rooms are partly organised around the central atrium and they look autonomous in that they exhibit distinctive spatial arrangements, consisting of a variety of architectural architectonics, such as showcases, bases, panels and constructions and reconstructions.

[124] '...construction is architecture. The thing should not be detrimental, or get old or dirty, it must be clean and clear...the ancient temple, its parts, washed [by the rain] and with the water gone after the rain, isn't it nice? You don't get rid of them; you don't get rid of the parts [materials] of the ancient buildings...The materials should speak' (quoted in Γιακουμάτος 2002).

[125] The opposite of the case of the Archaeological Museum in which daylight was prevalent and defined the galleries' exhibitions.

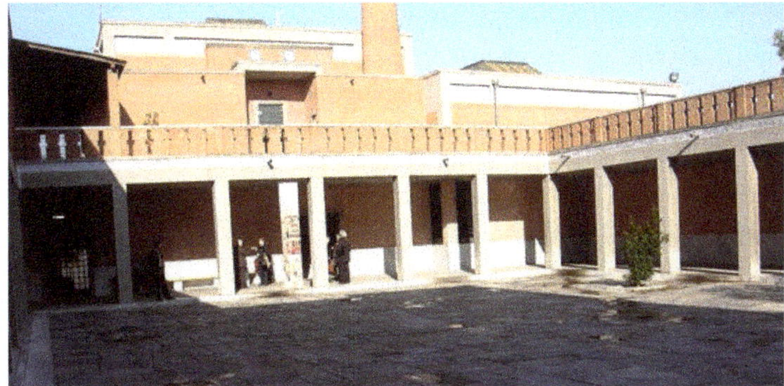

Figure 17: MBC: The Courtyard

In terms of the latter, it is interesting to note that the use of reconstructions in the museum represents the use of new interpretive methods in order to engage the visitors in new ways. However, the attempt of the curator to give the sense of a Byzantine monument-place is strengthened by the large and spacious rooms intended by the architect and elaborated as constructions in museum story-telling. It is exactly due to the curator's efforts that the place from which the objects are derived intervenes and is present in the interpretation process, creating relationships which determine the public's construction of the past.

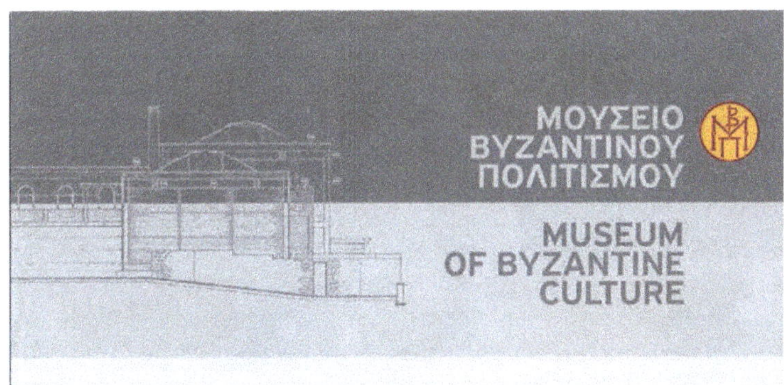

Figure 18: The Leaflet of the Museum of Byzantine Culture

The Museum of Byzantine Culture was the first museum which met all modern requirements in its construction and its functioning as a museum institution, showcasing new thinking in exhibition practices. It has received special commendation from the International Committee of the 2000 Competition of the Hellenic Institute for Architecture and in 2000 the Ministry of Culture declared it a historically listed monument and a work of art[126]. In the latter we may recognise the

[126] ΦΕΚ 1458/τβ/22-10-2001 Ministerial Decision ΥΠΠΟ/ΔΙΛΑΠ/Γ/3142/55420/19.10.2001 Department of Folklore Culture, Sub-Department of Modern Monuments.

extent to which the museum space can play a decisive communicative role by strengthening the social and cultural role of the museum as an institution.

Thematic Units and Display Philosophy

The organization of the museum's permanent exhibitions is based on chronological criteria, starting with the Early Christian period (4th -7th c.) and extending to the Post–Byzantine period (15th -19th c.), and it is divided into thematic units elaborating the daily life, art and culture of Byzantium. Two galleries are devoted to the display of the private collections of Dimitrios Economopoulos and Dori Papastratos[127], which were donated to the Museum, and the last gallery elaborates on the concepts of archaeology as a discipline and the museum as a practice.

Initially, when the museological plan[128] was approved by the CAC, the main aim was[129] to present the Byzantine culture in all its expressions: its daily life, the organization of its social and religious life and its spiritual and artistic development. Also, it aimed to explore the impact of historical developments and the political situation on the evolution of art and thought, and to examine how Byzantine culture is related to the end of late antiquity, its development, and its contribution to the shaping of modern Greek culture after the fall of Byzantium.

In the light of the concerns of the museological scenario-plan, the ancient objects were supposed to function rather as witnesses of a civilization than as objects of art, and on this basis the selection of thematic sections and the organization of the exhibition was performed as follows: *1. The Early Christian Church, 2. The Early Christian House, 3. From the Elysian Fields to the Christian Paradise, 4. From Iconoclasm to the Splendour of the Macedonian and Komnenian Dynasties, 5. The Dynasties of the Byzantine Emperors, 6. Byzantine Castles, 7. The Twilight of Byzantium, 8. The Dori Papastratou Collection, 9. The Dimitrios Ekonomopoulos Collection, 10. Byzantium after Byzantium: The Byzantine Legacy after the Fall of Constantinople*, and *11. Discovering the Past*. The scenario of the proposed exhibition program was grounded on enabling visitors to interact with the exhibits, and to acquire, through them, some idea of the human speculation, the ideological trends, the artistic sensitivity, the religious faith, and the world view which brought this culture into being (Κουρκουτίδου-Νικολαίδου 1993)[130]. Thus, the ancient objects were not meant to serve as self-contained works of art, but rather as witnesses to a whole civilization. '…It is an approach which tries to restore to an ancient object, cut off as it is from its own time and natural environment, its semantic identity within a specific thematic group, which outlines, but does not reproduce its original function' (Κουρκουτίδου-Νικολαίδου 1993:2)[131], in the words

---

[127] Dimitrios Economopoulos and Dori Papastratos are private collectors.

[128] Museological scenario-study and exhibition program of the Museum of Byzantine Culture. Archive of Department of Museums.

[129] Ministerial Decision ΥΠΠΟ/ΑΡΧ/Β2/Φ21/18240/340/13.4.1993 Department of Byzantine and Post-Byzantine Monuments.

[130] Archival material. Museological scenario-study and exhibition program of the Museum of Byzantine Culture. Archive of Department of Museums and Educational Programs MofCT.

[131] Archival material.

of the first Director who was then responsible for the display planning and philosophy[132]. The creation of the exhibition was done in stages following the funding possibilities and research on the proposed material, the majority of which came from older collections and from rescue excavations.

Drawing on aspects of the interpretations and the methods used, the displays can be analyzed in terms of groups of units. The first exhibition group in terms of chronology (galleries 1, 2 and 3) is about Early Christianity and consists of reconstructions of the Basilica of St Demetrius in Thessaloniki, of a Christian house with extended frescos, and of a Christian tomb (see figure 19).

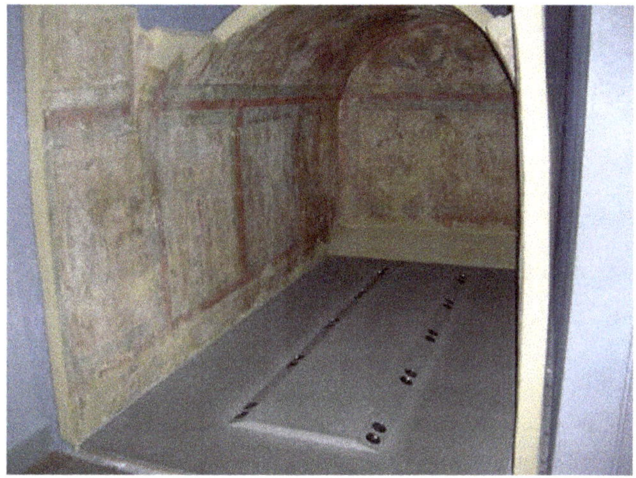

Figure 19: MBC: Christian Tomb

Aiming to illustrate the way that the new religion was created at the end of late antiquity and to examine the transition from the Ancient World to Christian ideology as well as devotional practices in the early years of the Christian era, this unit uses texts in a way that is quite descriptive and informative, giving historical and typological details in order to communicate issues that are difficult for the public, such as of Early Christian architecture. Also, a number of large-scale graphics and pictures of the monuments facilitate the visitor's attempt to re-construct and experience the locations of the displayed buildings, such as the church Basilica of St. Demetrius, which is still in use.

132 The first director of the Museum was the archaeologist Dr. Kourkoutidou-Nicolaidou, who was responsible for the initial exhibition project. In the working team for the same project were: K. Eleutheriadou. A. Loberdou-Tsigarida, D. Makropoulou, Eu. Marki, D Nalmpantis, D. Papanikola-Bakirtzi, E. Pelekanidou, A. Tourta, G. Marconi-Papadelli, E. Malli, A. Lyberi.

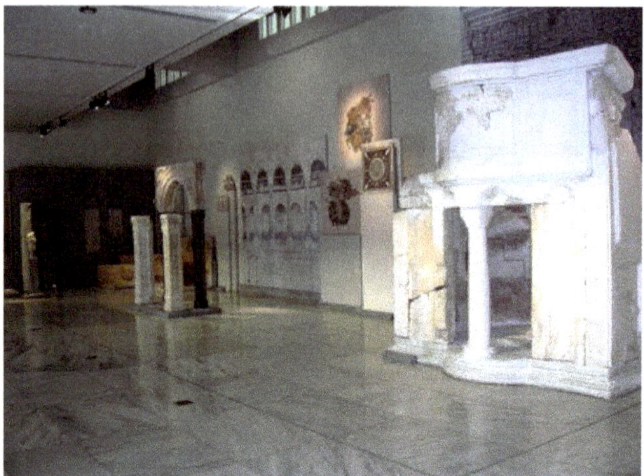

Figure 20: MBC. The Basilica of St. Demetrius

Directly linked to the new cult and the changes that it brought in religious and social life is the group of Christian cemeteries, which clearly expressed Christian ideology and world view long before these were apparent in monumental art. The specific subject of burial is included in the exhibition of the early Byzantine period, which looks at economic life, domestic handicrafts, home life, amenities, diet, and clothing, and provides information about family and social life. Of great significance, and worth emphasizing, is the way that a theme such as early Christian tomb painting, involving material too vulnerable and delicate to be treated as an exhibit, is represented through an ongoing conservation of fragile pieces carried out by the conservators of the museum in order for it to be readable by the visitor. Moreover, the limited lighting defines the routes of the perceptions and the messages by creating the atmosphere and the ambience which evoked these monuments.

Within these units, the curator's deliberate messages are conveyed through the method of displaying monuments re-structured in the museum in order to revive their 'aura'. The monuments are seen and interpreted here in relation to their context in the place where they were found or, in the case of the Basilica, are standing. But, in the museum space, they acquire a new context; their function is re-articulated and re-arranged, including their relationships with other objects.

Moving to the next chronological group, constituted by the units covering the time until the post-Byzantine era, the visitor is informed about the transition from early Byzantine times to the Iconoclastic Controversy and the middle Byzantine era, when the Empire was consolidating its power and its historical role between East and West. The art of the Macedonian and Comnenian dynasties was reflected in new forms of material culture and new iconographical programmes, and the appearance of fortification monuments and urban infrastructures in the middle of the Byzantine period provides evidence for the organization of the city in that era.

Historical elements are conveyed by illustrations of coins and lead seals, inscriptions in churches and fortresses, and miniatures in manuscripts.

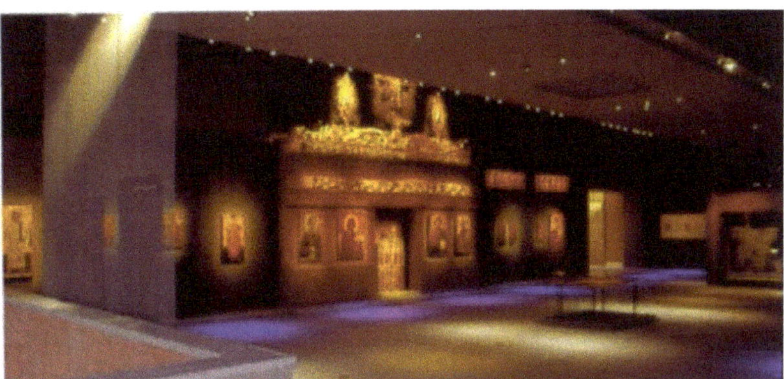

Figure 21: MBC. The Exhibition *Byzantium after Byzantium*

Another unit within this group is dedicated to the Paleologean era (1204-1453), a period of special importance for Thessaloniki and Macedonia in general. The city reached a high level of independent spiritual life and artistic output, which radiated all over the Balkans and directly influenced the Slavonic peoples. Exceptional examples of painting, sculpture and manuscripts are on display and the information provided is organized by subjects such as the Thessaloniki mint, glass-working, pottery workshops and cemeteries. The entire unit is structured around a unique exhibit of an ecclesiastical textile known as the 'Epitaphios' of Thessaloniki, dated to 1300, which is a masterpiece of gold embroidery; the perfectionism of this art object being related to that of the monumental paintings (Κουρκουτίδου-Νικολαΐδου 1994).

In these exhibition units (along with the next one, the Post-Byzantine era) the portable icons and depictions of ecclesiastical Christian circles are dominant, creating an atmosphere of mysticism and contemplation. The non-specialized visitor is captured by the deep sentiment which these images of Christianity evoke and experiences the museum story as ritual (Duncan 2005), as a place where objects are ascribed with symbolic and religious values recalling narratives and meanings related to the religious history of the area. That was the case of the exhibition on *Byzantium after Byzantium: The Byzantine legacy in the years after the Fall of Constantinople (1453-19th Century)*, which the museum curator decided to include in the permanent exhibition program in recognition of the important role which the continuity of the Byzantine tradition played in the formation of Hellenic identity in the early modern years, after Independence[133]. The prevalent features and the function of the displayed objects are aesthetic ones and the presentational means contribute to this aim by translating the exhibition text into a text on aesthetics,

[133] This issue has been discussed in chapter II. See archival material: Museological scenario-plan and exhibition program of the Museum of Byzantine Culture, 'On the exhibition in Gallery 10 and 11' Archive of Department of Museums and Educational Programs. MoCT.

aiming not only at providing an informational framework for the exhibition but also at involving the visitor's senses[134].

A third group was constituted by the exhibitions based on the two private collections (Ekonomopoulou and Papastratou); it is noticeable that they followed the above museological strategies and planning by focusing on typological features of the objects (schools of painting, chronological limits and artistic provenance). Of great scientific importance is the collection of Papastratou engravings of the 18th and 19th centuries, unique for this kind of artwork, which depict views of Byzantine monasteries with many topographical details and which constitute a valuable resource for scientific observation. The aim of these donated collections is to enrich and expand the museum's activities as an institution and reinforce the public's view of the role of private collecting when it is embedded in the museum safeguarding, interpretation and management decision-making process[135].

In the last unit (gallery 11), which consists of the gallery *'Discovering the Past'*, a different method of approach was applied with a focus on interpreting and presenting the story[136], effectively succeeding in communicating different messages and providing a rest for the visitor from the museum journey. The gallery tries to connect archaeological activity as a primary source of material culture (excavation and study of the past) with museum practice as an institution for the secondary production of meaning. It is divided into two thematic parts: the first part is about archaeological research, the practice of archaeology as a discipline and theoretical trends of interpretation of material culture, and the second part is about the museum as a place of keeping, presenting, conserving and contextualizing the material evidence of the past. According to the museological plan for the gallery, the exhibition attempts to reveal the whole process that is hidden behind the museum 'scene', the meaning-making process, the role of the curator, and the transitional stage of objects moving from their functional and ideological status in past societies to providing material evidence as precious relics kept in museums[137]. The visitor is seen as an active message recipient, engaging in the production of writings by tracing the history of an object, starting with its discovery, and proceeding through the documentation and conservation process to the museum display in which it is contextualized and interpreted in a new context and new interrelationships are formed. A number of digital applications are made available to the visitor who is encouraged to intervene in the museum display and to define his/her own method of perception. It is worth pointing out that it is the first time that a state museum has

---

[134] According to the museological scenario-plan 'On the means of presentation' '...The suggested way to present and communicate the messages is mainly aesthetic in the way elements of objects' form are articulated in a communicative order creating stimuli for causing: emotional attachment, surprise, joy of discovery...' G. Marconi-Papadeli and E. Stephanou-Katsanika. Archive of Department of Museums and Educational Programmes.

[135] It should be stressed that the state museums are not allowed by the law to accept donations. In the case of the related museum the donation process has been done through an '...approved...institution aiming exclusively at serving museums goals' the institution of Friends of MBC.

[136] The museological scenario-plan of that gallery has been carried out at a different stage (final) in relation to other exhibitions.

[137] Museological scenario-plan of Gallery 11 Department of Museums and Educational Programmes, MoCT.

introduced such a thematic unit as a museological project, thus showing the shifting in the thinking about museum policy in recent times in Greece.

The Museum of Byzantine Culture, which was awarded the Council of Europe's Museum prize for the year 2005, constitutes one of the first steps forward in establishing new ways of presenting and thinking about the museum as an institution in Greece. Although the nature and the character of the exhibitions' content are based on objects carrying historical, religious and symbolic associations, the museum in practice has managed to serve both its role as an educator and mediator and as an important meeting-place for the city, being recognized nationally and internationally in the field of Byzantine studies, according to its initial goals which were set in 1993.

V. The Folk Life and Ethnological Museum of Thessaloniki: Approaching the Recent Past

In our attempt to approach and draw upon the poetics and rhetoric of the Folk life[138] and Ethnological Museum and its exhibitions, a brief historical overview of the establishment of the Greek museums of this type and the related theoretical scholarship of the research field needs to be provided in order to sketch the necessary framework for our analysis.

Historical Framework for the Folk Life and Ethnological Museums in Greece

The foundation of the first Museum of Historical and Folklore Material coincided with the foundation of the Historical and Ethnological Etaireias (institution) in 1882 under the supervision of one of the most eminent literary scholars, Nikolaos Politis. According to its founding constitution, the aim of the museum was the gathering of historical and ethnological material, and every object should contribute to the enlightenment of Greek history and philology; the life and language of the Greek nation; and also to the establishment of a museum in which these objects could be kept as evidence of national life[139]. The above aims and goals led to the activities leading to the creation of the first ethnographic state museum in 1918, 'The Museum of Greek Crafts', which in 1959 was renamed the 'Museum of Greek Folklore Art', and whose main responsibility was the documentation and registration of material evidence of the recent tangible Greek folklore tradition (Βουδούρη 2003:77-80). It is evident that the promotion of the idea of the unbroken continuity of the Greek past defined all the attempts of the construction of the first museum, and this is related to the formation of the identity of the Greek nation, as we have discussed in previous chapters. A large number of private collections and small local museums were created within the next few years, based mainly on the

---

[138] Laographic, Λαογραφικό in Greek.

[139] Foundation Constitution of 15.2.1889 approved by ΒΔ of 27.3.1889 ΦΕΚ Α' 85 art. 2. See Βουδούρη 2003:77.

efforts of people and collectors who used to collect, in a scattered way, different objects inherited from generation to generation. Also, a number of scholars attempted to organize the field in academic terms in order to form a research framework for the study of numerous materials and objects gathered mainly in regional areas. For that purpose, the university departments all created over the country in recent years have, in collaboration with local communities, conducted research in order to map out the tangible and, more recently, also the intangible heritage of the Greek territory, pursuing sociological and ethnological observations and taxonomies.

Moreover, in an attempt to form a legal protection framework for that aspect of the Greek past, the state, through the Ministry of the Environment in 1979, moved towards the setting of legal principles by declaring a measure concerning traditional villages and settlements, thus contributing to the regeneration and re-planning of local development. Also, further legal measures were taken by the then Ministry of Culture and Sciences by appointing the National Centre of Social Research to conduct for the first-time research on the folklore museums of the country, which proved to be very significant for the future. The new Department of Folk Life Culture[140], created by the Ministry of Culture and Science in 1977, initiated a number of measures in order to protect overall early Greek cultural heritage (neoclassical and traditional architecture, early modern cultural resources, folk life museums and collections, ecclesiastical and traditional-demotic music and dancing etc.). The formation of the Greek ICOM has been decisive for these sorts of museums as well (as discussed in chapter II) because new trends and new museological tendencies and forms of collaboration were pursued and disseminated to the directors of the museums, whose appeal was, and still is, remarkable[141]. It should be noted that the status of the majority of these ethnological museums (i.e. private) facilitated their abilities to take initiatives and advanced measures in terms of museological strategies especially in the sector of the planning of educational programs[142]. Thus, museums such as the Benaki Museum collection (founded in 1930), the Pelloponesian Institution in Nafplion, awarded the European Museum of the Year Award in 1981 (Papantoniou 1983), and various other cultural institutions and foundations[143] gave new directions to the interpretation and representation of the rural Greek past by adopting new techniques and exhibition methods.

However, despite the above efforts to create an advanced museum policy and exhibition practice, the interdisciplinary nature (Παπαδόπουλος 2003) of the study and research of this facet of the material past has not been fully recognized and in many cases exhibitions and displays of daily life looked like store rooms and still served national and deeply ideological purposes. Additionally, in many local collections-museums, the exhibition units and the objects were recognized and

[140] ΠΔ 941/77 'Περί Οργανισμού του Υπουργείου Πολιτισμού και Επιστημών' [On organization of the Ministry of Culture and Sciences] (ΦΕΚ 320 Α', 17.10.1977).

[141] According to the President of the ICOM and the Director of the Directorate of Early Modern Cultural Heritage MofCT, T. Chadjinicolaou (personal interview. Athens, Ministry of Culture and Tourism 4-6-2009).

[142] Chatjinicolaou (personal interview, Athens, Ministry of Culture and Tourism 4-6-2009).

[143] Such as ETBA, Pireus Bank Group Cultural Foundation.

interpreted in terms of typological taxonomies without any specific spatio-temporal context, leaving them unable to communicate with the public[144]. Recently, the new archaeological law introduced a new framework for the ethnological museums concerned with, on the one hand, administrative matters, and, on the other hand, scholarly-based operations (see discussion in the previous chapter).

The Folklife and Ethnological Museum of Macedonia and Thrace, Thessaloniki: History and Architecture

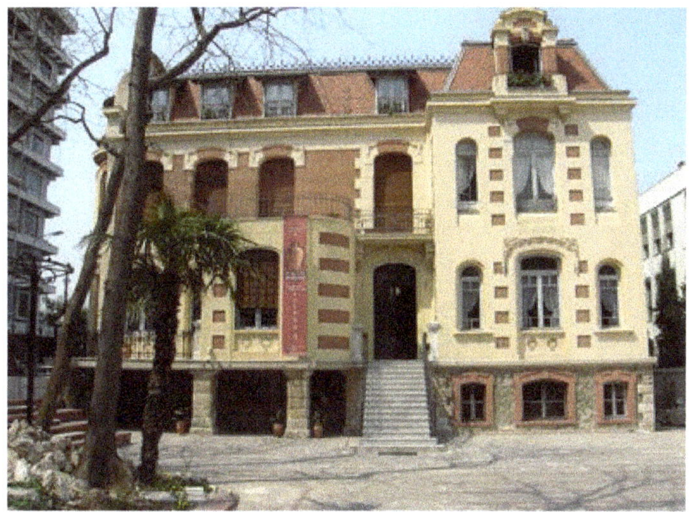

Figure 22: The Folk life and Ethnological Museum of Macedonia and Thrace, Thessaloniki

The foundation of the Folklife and Ethnological Museum of Thessaloniki in 1957 was based on the activity of the Μακεδονική Φιλεκπαιδευτική Αδελφότητα (Letters Amateurs, Educational Macedonian Fraternity-Community), which was established in Constantinople in 1821 and extended its activities to Thessaloniki in 1931. Its aim, under its then-president, I. Taris, was to collect folklore material consisting of objects illustrating rural life, found mainly in Northern Greece. At the beginning of its existence, the Museum was established as a legal entity in private law and in 1971 it came under the supervision of the newly established Ministry of Culture as a legal entity in public law, based in Thessaloniki and with a research spectrum covering all the areas of Northern Greece. In 1986, for a short period, the administrative supervision was placed under the supervision of the Ministry of Macedonia and Thrace, concerning the geographical spectrum of its research activity, and it was then transferred again to the MoC in 1993, where it remains. In the following few years, the museum underwent many renovations and reconstructions related to the building in which it was housed, known as 'the Old Governor's Residence', and the re-organization and documentation of its material.

[144]Chadjinicolaou (personal Interview, Athens, Ministry of Culture and Tourism 4-6-2009).

In 2005 the museum opening took place and today it pursues scientific research (ethnological and ethnographic) and projects in collaboration with universities and institutions (Greek and foreign) with the aim of collecting and gathering traditional material evidence of the recent Greek past. Also, among its aims is the preservation and the establishment of a digital directory of the objects which are open to the public as well as researchers. Of great importance for the goals of the museum is that it has arranged for the creation of educational programs on a wide range of subjects, addressed mainly to children, who used to be, and still are, the highest percentage of its visitors[145].

It should be noted that the educational program planning has found very fertile ground in these kinds of museums (folk life and ethnological) due to their administrative status, as they were private or were organized by foundations and so they had the flexibility (financially and administratively) to conduct many activities that enhanced their openness to the public. Also, because of the nature of the objects, derived from collections, which dated from the early modern period, they were easy to manage and to form into groups illustrating a recent and more familiar past to the wider public. The architectural elements of the museum building also contributed to this familiarity with past stories, since it used to be a villa-residence known as 'The Modiano Villa' at the beginning of the 20th century, when it was the main house of the banker Y. Modiano and his family, and it later housed (in turn) the Commander of Macedonia and the Minister of Northern Greece.

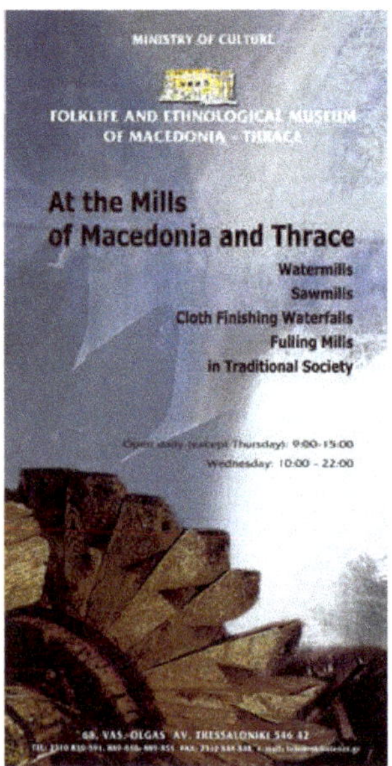

Figure 23: The FEMMT Leaflet

[145]According to the current Museum Director F. Oikonomidou, 85% of the public visitors are children (personal interview, Thessaloniki 24/9/2009).

The building is one of the best architectural examples of the Eclectic style and was constructed in 1905-1906 by the architect Eli Modiano in the eastern district of Thessaloniki known as the Tower district. It is developed on four levels with an octagonal central area and asymmetrically organized designs around the rooms of the house pointing out the main architectural features of the eclectic style of this villa. The decoration of the façades follows the typical division of 'base-stem-head', with the use of irregular stone in the basement, a finer elaboration with plastered surfaces, layers of bricks and big windows at the top of the roof. Internally, there have been roof-decorations and fine constructions of details according to the style of the era. The building has been used to house different activities and services through the years, and it has experienced many damages and detrimental activities, motivating the initiative of restoring it back to its initial appearance. In 1971, under the supervision of Professor N. Moutsopoulos, work started on its transformation into a museum, which was completed with the conservation works by the 4th Ephorate of early modern buildings during the period 1995-2000[146].

The museum building belongs to the type of museum architecture which re-uses older period buildings (as discussed in section II of the present chapter) to house the collections, engaging in that way in museum dialogue and exhibition stories, in the poetics of building narratives. In terms of the image of the villa-house, it gives the museum a distinctive position in the city's-built environment, due to its delicate and fine architectural characteristics. Also, the fact that it used to be a residential house influences and enhances the character of the related exhibitions, consisting mainly of objects associated with daily and rural life (such as costumes, furniture and house tools) of the recent past. On the other hand, the arrangement of the rooms of the house imposes its own 'philosophy' and leaves limited room to the curator to plan the movement of visitors through the museum. In order to reflect on the above considerations, it should be noted that in this case the aesthetics of the building itself might function as a stimulus and might attract more visitors who would seek to explore that distinctive atmosphere of the place, provoking their senses and leading them to have an emotional experience and an engagement with the museum-space. And, as Uzzell and Ballandyne have put it insightfully, 'the space is endowed with "atmosphere" because of the activities and memories of what has occurred there' (Uzzell and Ballandyne 1988:158). In our case the museum space is interpreted and re-interpreted by the visitors looking for information about the initial use of the building, the persons occupying it and the activities that have taken place there. So, a panel comprising all the information about the building (and a model, in this case) is usually provided in order to help visitors in grasping the meaning of the place that they experience.

In the light of the above, it may be argued that it is quite unavoidable for the curator who works with museums in used buildings to adopt a building-centered museological program in which the exhibition planning follows the building narratives associated with the poetics and the rhetoric of the already structured

[146]This work has been funded by the EU, the Organization 'Thessaloniki, Cultural Capital of Europe, 1997', the Ministry of Culture and the Ministry of Macedonia and Thrace. The building was declared as a 'listed building' in 1980.

space as it was constructed in the past. However, the layout of the exhibition and the choices of the themes and stories to be told through it could still be directed towards a more visitor-oriented engagement.

Exhibition Units and Themes

> '...What I want to do in order to understand traditional culture is to rebuild it, to set it up before my eyes in its entirety, as a system "in operation"...We need to resort to the tangible factors of culture, like technology, institutions, behaviours, and to study them, not in isolation, but in relation to one another, as phenomena that are not static, but dynamic, and continually changing' (Kyriakidou-Nestoros 1985, quoted in exhibition panel).

One of the main introductory texts at the opening of the permanent museum exhibitions is the one quoted above, written by one of the most eminent anthropologists of the era whose theoretical accounts have had a profound impact on study and research on the traditional culture of Greece. The use of this statement by the curator at the beginning of the exhibition is intended to set the goal of the museum itself: based on research and a thorough study of the evidence of the recent past, to re-build it, to re-generate it by giving it life again through use. That statement thus turns into a message to the visitor who is called to read and interpret the witnesses of the past through the process of their re-constructed functions and to produce a new knowledge by approaching them actively and engaging in their operational features. It is very important also that the visitor is encouraged to see the exhibits developing their dynamic relationships with other exhibits and producing a constant flux and constantly changing museum stories.

The exhibition units in the museum were organized following a thematic order focusing on the presentation of the traditional culture of rural Greek life of the 18th, 19th, and early 20th centuries. The themes made use of a central topic and moved in different directions depending on the meaning to be pursued through the objects.

The first theme that was developed in the layout of the exhibition is '*At the Mills of Macedonia and Thrace: Watermills, Sawmills, Cloth-finishing in Traditional Society*' The core theme of this exhibition is the water-powered constructions that were used in the traditional pre-industrial society of Northern Greece. A number of reconstructions of these machines (see figure 24) were used to familiarize the visitor with their function and to illustrate their contribution to the transition from the hand-tools period to one of new technological developments and their possibilities, which marked the social and the economic life of the area. Also, based on these reconstructions, the visitor is encouraged to explore the impact that these evolutions had on human life in creating social hierarchies and classes. So, new professions and social divisions are demonstrated, such as the miller, the sawyer and the fuller, providing information on the practices and the products of these new 'technologies'. A map and a historical framework are provided in order to locate the public historically and geographically and panels with texts and sub-texts inform them about the techniques and methods of the new production tools. It is worth noting that in many cases the texts are informed by anthropological and sociological writings and many quotations are used in order to create socio-cultural linkages of the traditional past seen and studied as part of the many Greek pasts. This , for example, was the case with the sub-theme called Bread with statements like "*So I sent men to find out who the eaters of bread in that land were...*" (by Homer, Odyssey, I, 88), "*We are still savouring the discoveries of Neolithic man...*" (by Levi-Strauss, 1952), "*...with agriculture the land became, from a habitat, a homeland*" (by D. Theocharis, 1973) and "*I am the Living Bread*", illustrating the intention of the curator to create multiple articulations of the exhibits by giving an opportunity for the visitor to develop new associations of the produced meanings. The inclusion also of quotations from research fieldwork (in the form of interviews) and the use of parts of texts derived from Greek traditional literature, such as proverbs, enigmas or songs, embedded in the informational texts, is an attempt to make those texts enjoyable and entertaining as well as informational (see figure 25).

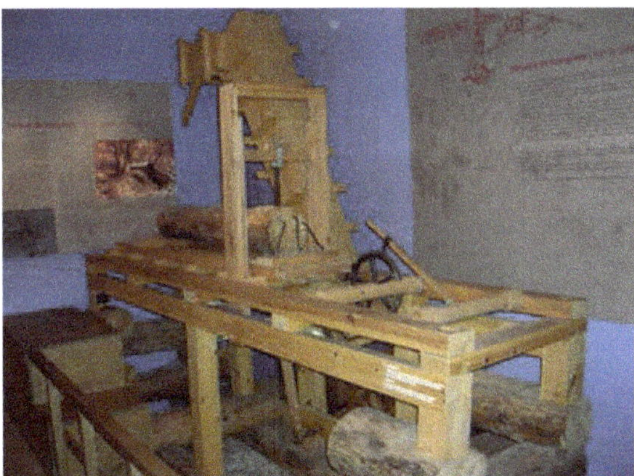

Figure 24: FEMMT. The Exhibition of *Sawmills*

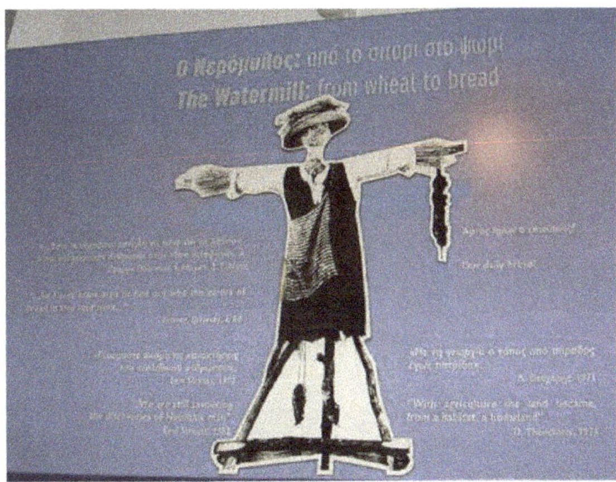

Figure 25: FEMMT. Panel of the Exhibition on the theme of *Bread*

Additionally, moving in that direction, the educational program-exhibit *The water mill at school*, where environmental issues and the promotion of traditional methods of producing energy are displayed, raises public awareness of the concerns of modern life (see figure 26).

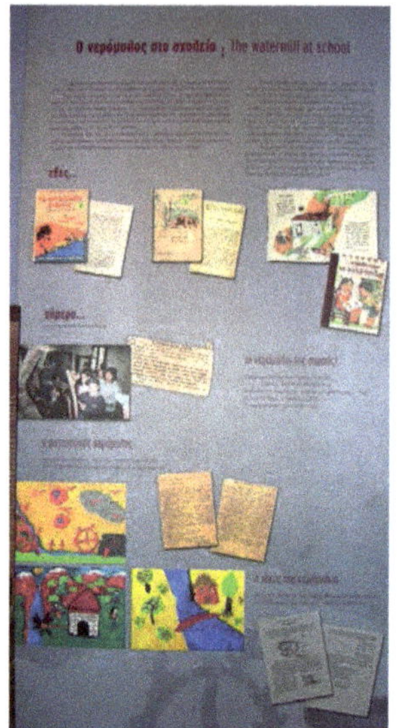

Figure 26: FEMMT. The Exhibition
The water mill at school

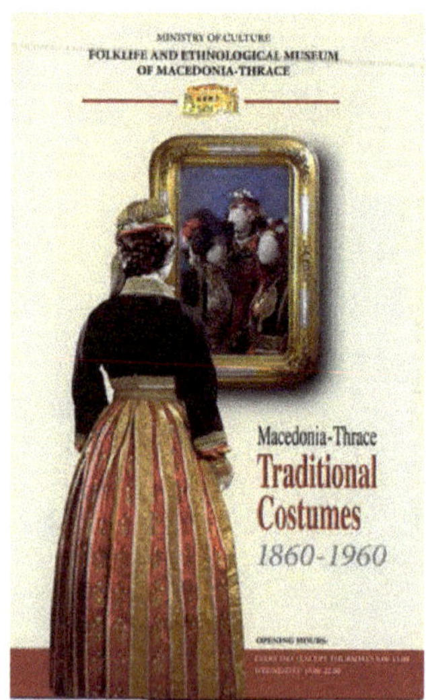

Figure 27: The FEMMT Leaflet of the Exhibition *Traditional Costumes*

The second permanent exhibition's unit develops the theme of Traditional costumes in *Macedonia and Thrace 1860-1960* and displays a large number of costumes from Macedonia, Thrace and the neighbouring areas (Northern Macedonia, Eastern Thrace, Eastern Roumelia, the Black Sea and Asia Minor) in a way that inform the viewer about the evolution of these costumes, their symbolism, their associations with rituals and ceremonies and the process of their making. Again, in this unit, the reconstruction of the main clothing machines is extensive, and their educational role is prominent along with the informational panel. The evolution of traditional clothing and the influences it received from various different geographical locations is traced within an historical framework in which historical approaches and interpretations are demonstrated to support the variety of styles and decorative features of the costumes. Added to this, engravings, maps and showcases function as aids to support the attitudes and stories relating to costumes and clothing as expressions of multicultural societies by making the exhibited costumes themselves into symbols and objects of power, which are representative of the social, cultural and economic status of the specific historical era.

In the light of the above, one could argue that the predominant aim of the museum is that of the educator and instructor, through the multiple exhibition settings and devices (with an emphasis on reconstructions) as powerful communicative means addressed to the public, mainly children, who come to obtain information and to acquire an insight of recent years of Greek history. According to the current director of the museum, it has been among the goals of the museum to design exhibitions in such a way as to make them places where the visitor should have the opportunity to become engaged in the process of experience and to interact with the exhibits with all his/her senses[147]. The idea of traditional thought and of a return to environmentally-friendly solutions was fostered by the curator (especially in the exhibition of water-powered machines), making the museum in that way a mediator not only of 'past' messages but also one suggesting future alternatives and perspectives on modern life.

VI. Conclusions: Visualising the Greek Past

This section summarizes the main points of the analysis of the three museums and discusses the museum as a dynamic place for creating and visualizing pasts.

In the above discussion of the case studies, an attempt has been made to investigate the representation of the Greek past through three major museums in Thessaloniki, which essentially are geographically and historically representatives of the history of archaeology as a discipline and the museum as a practice operating in Northern Greece. Building on the recognition that archaeology as a practice and the museum as an institution are functioning as 'translator agencies' which translate, creating, or to put it more correctly re-creating, new rules, 'syntax', and 'linguistic' patterns to form persuasive stories, one can readily realize that the room that is left for many versions of that translation is potentially broad, subject to socio-political

[147] F. Oikonimidou, Director of the Museum (personal interview Thessaloniki 24/9/2009).

conditions, intentions and approaches which affect the decision-making process of the storytelling. To bring about the creation of that translation, which is visually perceived by the public, the curator relies on the poetic nature of the museum narratives in which, following Aristotle's work in the *Poetics*, the museum exhibition is perceived as a theatrical stage and a performance place for a tragedy with a plot, characters and performers (the artefacts themselves) which can evoke emotional effects. The different themes of an exhibition function as *episodes* which narrate the actions and practices of past societies, posing dilemmas and establishing interrelationships between the audience and the objects as carriers of the story's messages.

In the cases we analyzed in this chapter, the museum is a place where the Greek past is visualized through the tradition of visual representation which is inherent to the discipline of archaeology. It is where human visual experience and visual intelligence are formed and grounded on practices of spectatorship, like the glance, the look, the observation, and surveillance (Bennett 1998). The legibility of the objects within the three museums is based on this visualization of the past culture, where the objects create visions of glorious, emotive, symbolic, ideological, instructive—to name but a few—Greek pasts. That visualization or 'visual expressionism' of the archaeological discipline, operating in different parts of the Greek historical territory, has found fertile ground in the museum's representational arena and its meaning-producing exhibition space. The aesthetic values of the objects, rooted in the historical traditional approach of Greek archaeology, are balanced now, in some exhibition attempts, with the introduction of new interpretive methods influenced by anthropological and sociological writings which encourage a multidimensional experience of the museum. The exhibition planning has been based on a more holistic perception of the museum, creating in that way a place where the voices of the three 'makers' of meanings, or 'namers', as Taborsky called them (Taborsky 1990:66), the object maker, the curator, and the visitor, encounter one another in a dialectical process in which meanings and messages are communicated.

Recognizing that the museum is 'probably the main institutional connection between archaeology as a profession and a discipline and the wider public (Shanks and Tilley 1992:68), it is important to reflect upon the museum as an institution in Greece which is essentially related (if not identical) to archaeological practice. The initiative of giving both museums, i.e, AMT and MBC, a semi-autonomous status[148] has been a very significant step forward and a direction for new thinking on museums as places of interaction and places in which alternative meanings can be mediated and the visitor can actively engage in creating his/her own understanding of the past. It can be easily argued that museums, which in administrative terms are subject to strict official directions, have few possibilities of building an effective management decision-making project aimed at their primary goals as social institutions. And, in the case of Greece, that statement is evidenced by these museums where, in all three cases, their autonomy has allowed them to pursue more

[148] As issued by the Law 2557/1997 (as discussed in chapter II).

effective museological and museographical scenario and architectural plan-studies in which the museum's role as a social and cultural institution in modern society could be fulfilled. On the other hand, it should be noted that traditional trends and tendencies still exist in interpreting and representing the traces of the past in exhibition settings, which reflecting the well-grounded tradition of classical scholarship where archaeology is perceived as part of the history of art. So, tensions and conflicts between traditional and modern archaeologists—museologists are easily traced in the museum space where new powerful interrelationships are developed, and these create the stimuli for a re-theorizing of the Greek museum. Moreover, the archaeological museums in Greece are museums containing mainly exhibitions of groups of excavation finds on which they rely for their authenticity, their uniqueness and the richness of their exhibits, according to the current Director of AMT[149], a practice which creates a sort of implicit reliance in terms of the continuous supply to the museum from the recently separated 'mother Ephorate' and the publishing rights relating to the excavated exhibits[150].

In the overview of the historical museum's foundation, it is worth pointing out that the museums still serve their primary role as symbolic places, where national treasures are held, and as witnesses of the historical continuity of the Greek past. In all cases, that time sequence of the various pasts is stressed throughout the exhibitions (which are either chronologically or thematically organized) and many of the exhibits are fetishized and acquire a symbolic power as witnesses of past societies, reaching a higher level of art and craftsmanship.

Finally, in the attempt to discuss the museum space relationships, what is remarkable and needs to be noted is that the spatio-temporal context within which the past is interpreted and told, in the three cases, participates in the visitors' perceptions of meanings and messages, building in this way spatial narratives which compete for the dominance of the exhibition's textuality or inter-textuality. Thus, for example, in the case of the MBC, the building-voice has been stated at the beginning of its construction and defines profoundly and emotionally the exhibition's development, while in the AMT case, a close relationship of the exhibits with their provenance and their places of origin is essentially implied and fostered by the architectural syntax of space, and organizational choices such as that of the outdoor permanent exhibition. Taking the discussion further, the museum is seen as a multi-spaced place with definitely structured layers of time and space that consists of 'micro-spaces' (showcases and constructions for the objects) and 'macro-spaces', arrangements of rooms according to themes and topics. The visitor is in the middle of the process of the interrelationships that are produced by this transition between micro and macro-spaces, as he/she attempts to form a context of meaning, relying and also making claims upon his/her spatio-temporal experiences.

It is important to realize that the objects, the archaeological place and the museum space are interlinked, producing a dialogue that is encountered by the

[149] Dr. G. Adam-Veleni, archaeologist director of AMT (personal interview Thessaloniki 20/9/2010).

[150] These observations are of the main concern for the museum, as the director of AMT stated, in discussing the principles of the new law and the new regulations which will provide a framework in which this major issue will be under study by the MoCT (personal interview Thessaloniki 20/9/2010).

visitor to the Greek museums, transforming them into active, dynamic, and living places. The exploration of other forms of museums, such as site museums, can contribute to the development of new approaches to the museum, perceived as a multi-vocal and multi-interpreted place.

CHAPTER 4

Archaeological Site Museums as Symbols and Places of Reference: Case Studies of the Archaeological Sites of Vergina and Mount Athos

The face of Greece is a palimpsest.

(Kazantzakis 1965:7)

I. INTRODUCTION

This chapter examines the second group of case studies to explore the alternative practices of reconstructions of the past, and to discuss the ways in which site museums can be treated as places of reference. The discussion developed in the previous chapter provided us with stimuli to pursue further research and to reflect on the concepts of museum space and the archaeological landscape (archaeological, historical, and heritage sites) and how these could be interrelated and communicated in the production of meanings.

The museum is seen and examined here as a living space which is fully interactive with the exhibited remains of the past. The historical and archaeological landscape fully imposes its ideological and social character and is thereby involved decisively in the interpretation process. In our attempt to pursue alternative approaches and readings of past remains, the chapter explores two cases, the Museum of the Royal Tombs in Aigae and the archaeological-historical site of Mount Athos, as landscapes in which social 'paths' (Tilley 1994:29-31) of experiencing the place generate spatial narratives (archaeological site features, values and social articulations) intermingle with the museum story-telling practice (objects and artefacts as message carriers). The goal is to challenge the traditional image of museum practices and to foster the interpretation perspectives of 'new museology' by proposing a framework in which methods and practices operate to form a new, more holistic approach that aims to encompass more possibilities for interpreting and presenting the past. These practices might include approaches that generate new forms of relationships between the archaeological remains of the past and their spatial context (archaeological, historical landscape) and stress the impact of these relationships on the public understanding of the past.

Dealing with the above issues, a new term is introduced in order to elucidate our critical thought on representation practices and to question the conventional aspect of the museum. The 'museumscape' as a term is a synthesis of words that associates the museum and landscape discourses, reflecting the reciprocal relationships created between the museum and the landscape as containers, not only of material remains and values of the past, but also as places of social actions and articulations reproduced and structured through organized processes. Through the analysis I suggest an alternative way of viewing the past and a new, more holistic way of thinking, reflecting the need for a broadening of theoretical approaches to the past.

II. MUSEUMS *IN SITU* IN GREECE AND A SENSE OF PLACE AS PALIMPSEST

It has been argued that the site museums are the most effective communicative museums in the way they make direct links between the site, the findings and their context (Swain 2007:246). It has been stated by the director of UNESCO's division of Cultural Heritage, in a discussion on theoretical and practical implications of site museums, that '…the site and the museum each designate a space of heritage whose limits adapt and transform themselves, occasionally overlapping when a heritage space takes on the characteristics of a museum' (Mgomezulu 2004: 4). It is widely recognised that the interest in the development of these types of museums, built and located at an archaeological site, is significantly being pursued. In this way, excavated material from the site itself and from other related structures of the archaeological landscape are displayed and interpreted within their own context in order to develop communication 'channels' between the interpreted past and the public. And it is exactly this latter point that makes site museums so popular and effective in producing and mediating meaning. 'The museum is an integral part of the site. It is not a substitute for the site but part of it' (Kirshenblatt-Gilbert 1998:169). Reflecting on this point, we need to remember that archaeology is inextricably connected to landscapes, sites, monuments and context, and museums are considered as the places where new contexts are supposed to be constructed to receive the material evidence of the past. In the case of site museums, all the archaeological interpretation-making process and museum activities are taking place *in situ* and in that way giving the visitor the opportunity to gain an experience and to be encouraged towards a more comprehensive engagement with the place-context[151]. So, the term '*in situ* museums' is archaeologically understood to possess all those articulations of contexts, time, landscape and natural environment and to produce stories and narratives of the past using the rhetorical tangible and intangible remnants of past societies. What is interesting, considering the role and the character of the *in situ* museum, is the fact that it brings together the experience of an archaeological landscape focusing on the acquisition of the sense of place, and the experience of museum space based on the interpretive methods and strategies of the material of the past projecting into the present. So, the concept of place and how

[151] The term *in situ* has a very 'strong' notion in archaeological terminology and defines overarching methods and practices of the discipline. An interesting discussion is provided by Sutton and Stroulia (eds.) 2010.

it is experienced is profoundly crucial for the aims and goals of these museums, namely, to pursue effective approaches for the production of meanings.

In the case of Greece, *in situ* preservation and the creation of archaeological site museums is one of the primary strategies within archaeological heritage management and museum policy. Over the past twenty years, extensive excavation projects and the great number of finds that have come to light have created the need for the Greek Archaeological Service to initiate the changing use of these places. They were initially intended as storage rooms to house all the finds from the diggings, and only at a later stage have they been transformed into a museum place comprising all the relevant display technologies. Thus, almost all the large- and small-scale organized archaeological sites in Greece, such as Delphi, Knossos, Olympia or Dion and Vergina, to name but a few[152], are accompanied by their own museums, in an attempt to provide to the visitor a complete experience of the site and its history. It should be noted, as already argued, that archaeology as a discipline in Greece has mainly been based on pursuing the excavation of cities, sanctuaries and sites of antiquity based on detailed descriptions of written sources as directed by the scholarship of classical archaeology. At the same time, the still standing, or, to put it differently, the 'living' ruins of many of the big sites of antiquity have from the very beginning enabled the public to acquire a sense of place of the past and to develop an emotional attachment to these traces, valuing them differently subjected to socio-cultural conditions of the present (as discussed in chapter II). That sense of living ruins is apparent not only among the big modern cities with multilayered pasts such as Athens, but even more so in rural and isolated areas, where the archaeological landscape, formed of different chronological layers of human past and present activities, uncovered, excavated and researched by experts, interferes in the life of modern locals, establishing new forms and layers of relationships and new codes of communication, and contributing to the perception of the landscape as palimpsest. These relationships, underscored by the impact that the past has on public perception, create a network of associations with past traces, monuments, sites, and objects evoking aesthetic, symbolic, historical, and economic values and establish new parameters of management for experts to take into consideration.

So, in many cases the *in situ* museum, demonstrating these sorts of relationships, functions as the intermediary between the site and the public, and as a 'facilitator' (Walsh 1992) by which it contributes to an organized and effective accessing of the past remains of an archaeological place and reinforces the interrelationships between people (and especially locals) and the sites. At the same time, the museum activities can establish significant tourist mobilization fostering economic development and regeneration of rural and isolated areas. It could arguably be said that these twofold, or manifold—if we consider the multiple implications of the museum relations as a practice—qualities of the nature of museum sites is challenging for museum personnel who are called upon to perceive the museum not as a distinct institution separated from the archaeological context

[152] For a detailed catalogue of archaeological sites and their museums see the website of the Ministry of Culture www.culture.gr.

and the everyday life, but instead to see it as a dynamic living and integral part of an ongoing social practice. In this respect, the environment of the archaeological place, consisting of the past traces, buildings and constructions along with the natural features of the landscaping, forms the staging scene on which the networking of interpretation processes and presentation strategies will be developed through conservation and museum practices.

Focusing on Greece, it should be noted that the construction of museums *in situ* constitutes, in recent years and under the funding of the EU, an essential practice which had, and still has, a major impact not only on the country's museum policy thinking but also on the overall management of the archaeological sites, challenging the traditional methods and mechanisms of approaching and interacting with the past adopted by Greek archaeology. Thus, recently designed projects in Greece focusing on the construction of museum sites, which open or demonstrate their activities to the public, attempt to pursue a different approach to the past by which the visitor is involved in museum practices and experiences different ways of seeing as discussed in the following section.

Museums as a Practice *In Situ*

One of the main pursuits of the so-called 'new museology' is the involvement of the community in developing an appreciation of its own place and the fostering of the active museum, open to receive new voices in interpretative and representative museum practices (Vergo 1989; Walsh 1992). In order for that attempt to succeed, a public-driven museum policy should be developed in which many activities that used to take place behind the scenes of the museum should come to the forefront of the exhibition practice. So, the conservation process, which is considered one of the primary methods leading to interpretive approaches of the past material, could be part of the exhibits of a museum calling for the visitor to interact with the caring and reading of the excavated evidence. These initiatives can lead the museum to be perceived as an extroverted and communicative mechanism promoting the social and cultural upgrading of a society.

The conservation practice *in situ*, as part of museum activities, has been implemented recently by many museums in Greece, especially in open-air archaeological sites and in local cases, where the museological policy attempts to adopt more holistic initiatives of presentation and interpretation of the past. It is, for instance, worth noting the case of the open conservation labs[153] created by the 10th Ephorate of Byzantine Antiquities (EBA), Chalkidiki[154] (Northern Greece), funded by the EU. Located in a rural, isolated area and being part of a heritage landscape consisting of buildings restored and transformed into a museum (exhibition, storage, administrative rooms, and conservation labs), these labs are expressions of an extroverted attempt made by the overall museum project and have had a

[153] Three conservation labs have been created: for paper, manuscripts and books, for painting on portable icons and for ceramics.

[154] Archive of 10th Ephorate of Byzantine Antiquities, Ministry of Culture. 'Restoration and rehabilitation of buildings in N. Flogeta, Chalkidiki' Funded by 3rd EFFP.

considerable impact on the locals of the area. Among the aims of the director of the Ephorate[155] was to establish the conservation process as part of the museological scenario in which the visitor would have the opportunity not only to observe the conservation stages being performed on the finds but also to interact with the specialists and to get more insight of the specific conservation techniques applied to the excavated material[156]. Educational programs have also been designed, based precisely on the interactivity promoted by the museum people, and have proved to be very effective and communicative[157]. Reflecting on the above example, it should additionally be noted that setting the conservation practice as an exhibit is quite challenging and provoking in the way that it encourages and stresses the multivocal role of the museum as an institution. The conservation as an object to be displayed and contemplated is now considered not only as an educational and instructive vehicle but also as a practice subject to being negotiated, interpreted, and re-interpreted by the public.

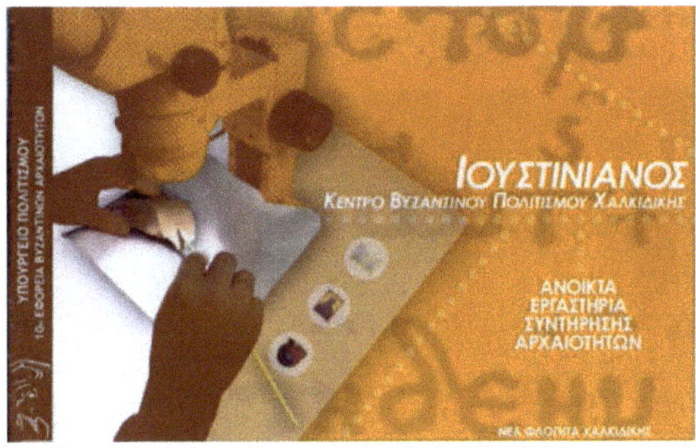

Figure 1: The Leaflet of the 'Open Conservation Labs' in N. Flogeta, Justinian-Centre of Byzantine Culture, Chalkidiki

In the same sphere of new alternative ways of engaging the public with the interpretation and experience of the past lies the attempt made by archaeologists and curators to display the archaeological process of monument or site excavation and to constitute it as part of a museum's articulations. In many cases the excavation itself is the main 'exhibit,' or supplementary to what is displayed in the related museum site. So, the visitor is encouraged to obtain information and to experience in situ how the archaeological narratives are constructed and produced and how they are transmitted. This experience is effectively acquired due to the immediate contact of the visitor with the place or landscape defined and researched and their spatio-temporal articulations. This practice is very popular and promoted by the practitioners in many countries in order to accomplish a raising of public awareness about the past remains of their area and to pursue more effective management

[155] Dr. I. Tavlakis is the director of the 10th EBA and responsible for this project.
[156] Personal interview with the director.
[157] Polyzoudi 2004, 2005 Archive of 10th EBA.

protection methods. Generally, in the case of Greece, archaeological promenade projects, consisting of a combination of experiences within a museum and outside it on the excavated archaeological site, have become a prevailing practice for how to approach and present the past. The so-called 'museums without walls', referring to open-air archaeological sites such as the Prehistoric settlement of Dispilio in Kastoria[158] (Northern Greece) or to museums which have a direct view to the excavated site or monument, such as the newly built Acropolis museum in Athens, can be considered as indicative evidence for the current tendency of museum practice to conceive of inclusive interactive spaces and to encompass the sense of place more conceptually in their operation.

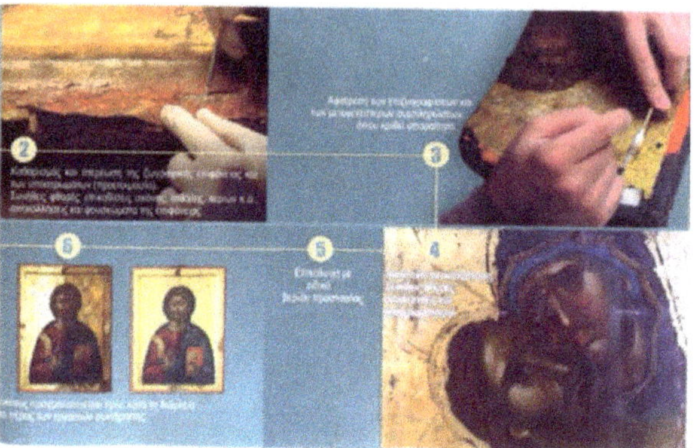

Figure 2: Various stages of the conservation lab of icons, as described in the related leaflet

'Museumscape': Promoting a Dialectic Relationship

Recognising the complexities and implications of a theoretical discussion of the interpretive attitudes and presentation of the past within the realm of archaeological landscape and museums, this study introduces the term 'museumscape' in order to add a critical reflection to the above discussion. The development of the investigation of the museum roles and the archaeological and historical landscape has been quite lively in the past twenty years with the growing interest in the new museology, a new geography, which provide the means to pursue new readings and writings of the past (Vergo 1989; Merriman 2000 Daniels and Cosgrove 1988; Bender 1993, 1998; Barret et al.1991; Knapp1999; Tilley 1994).

The 'museumscape' is a synthesis of two terms—museum and landscape—which essentially define the spectrum of archaeology as a discipline. It brings together all the features and theoretical discourses developed recently in these two fields and attempts to investigate new alternatives and critical considerations for approaching and interpreting the past. It is mainly a concept which allows us, on the one hand, to understand the inclusive role of the museum as a space and the form it could take as a mediator of the meanings produced, and on the other, the powerful

[158] On the open-air museum of Dispilio see Χουρμουζιάδης 2001; Χουρμουζιάδη 2002.

and meaningful impact of landscape constructed of physical compounds and spatio-temporal layers of human activity. Through this term the museum is considered to be in a constant dialogue with the archaeological place producing effective communicative museum narratives and encouraging public involvement. On the other side, the archaeological-historical place itself is conceived of as a museum developing its own space and temporal narratives endowed by historic, symbolic and political values, embedded in specific constructions in the past but projecting them and experiencing them under the socio-political conditions of the present, as we are going to see in the following sections. The visitor moving between these two entities is called to use the channels created by this interrelationship and to form his/her own approach to the remains of the past, evaluating them differently and ascribing them significance, power and sacredness (as will be discussed in the case studies). And given that 'landscape is never inert, people engage with it, re-work it, appropriate and contest it' (Bender 1993:3), it should be stressed that the landscapes (archaeological, historical) acquire a multivocal and polysemic character (Bender ibid.) which demand a pluralistic means of perception and interpretation. Building on that and recognizing that 'places, like persons, have biographies inasmuch as they are formed, used and transformed in relation to practice' (Tilley 1994:33) we can argue that places, consisting of buildings, constructions and other remains, form their own patterns of creating stories and disseminating them to the public through different channels of communication. This ability of the archaeological places constitutes the key issue for the archaeologists and the museum people in terms of realizing the multifaceted character of the decision-making management practice and the need to develop multidisciplinary methods and strategies.

Taking as a starting point the idea that the space is a medium rather than a container for action (Tilley 1994), which enables us to perceive ourselves as *being in*, following the Aristotelian concepts of space, it is important to understand to what extend we can experience that being in, the belonging, the sense of place within the boundaries of 'termed sites' (Knapp 1999) and what the rhetorical strategies are for investigating different ways of seeing and reading the past. The pursuit of both lies within the dialectical interrelationship of the archaeological landscape and the museum. The former relies on the perception of the place as a 'reference system which passes on and encodes information about the ancestral past and is integral to the message' (Tilley 1994:40), the latter rests on the activities and interpretive technologies of the museum practice.

The 'museumscape' in this study is conceived at two levels, as a concept and as a method. As a concept it attempts to describe and investigate the museums in situ, site museums and their activities, and what kind of articulations and associations are developed through the inter-connections of museums as institutions and sites, and landscapes as 'referent systems'. As a method it accommodates different practices and expressions of experiencing the past, within a museum and on the site, but using a common vocabulary and codes of translation to formulate an inclusive framework in which to establish a dialogue about different readings of past remains by the public and how these readings and perceptions are subjected to change and challenge, as discussed in the following sections.

III. The Archaeological Site Museum of the Royal Graves of Aigae, Vergina: How the Traditional Museum is Being Challenged

> 'An endless dialogue with those distanced persons in the night, as I was staring at them again and again, and they were supposed (forced) to look at me; I expected them to answer me who they are' (Ανδρόνικος 2006:157)

The archaeological site of Vergina has been one of the first large-scale projects carried out in Northern Greece and has marked a new age in Greek archaeology. The wealth of its discoveries with findings, objects and constructions, revealed an extended archaeological landscape which contributed to the broadening of existing evidence of the life of inhabitants in Northern Greece during antiquity and gave new directions for archaeology as a discipline. Excavated for years by the eminent archaeologist M. Andronikos, Professor of Archaeology at the University of Thessaloniki, and the archaeological service of MoCT, 17th (IZ') Ephorate of Prehistoric and Classical Antiquities, the site became a World Heritage Site in 1996 on the basis of cultural criteria (i) and (iii): '...considering that the site is of outstanding universal value representing an exceptional testimony to a significant development in European civilization, at the transition from classical city-state to the imperial structure of the Hellenistic and Roman periods' (UNESCO 1996)[159].

[159] See UNESCO, World Heritage Sites directory, available at http://whc.unesco.org/en/list/780.

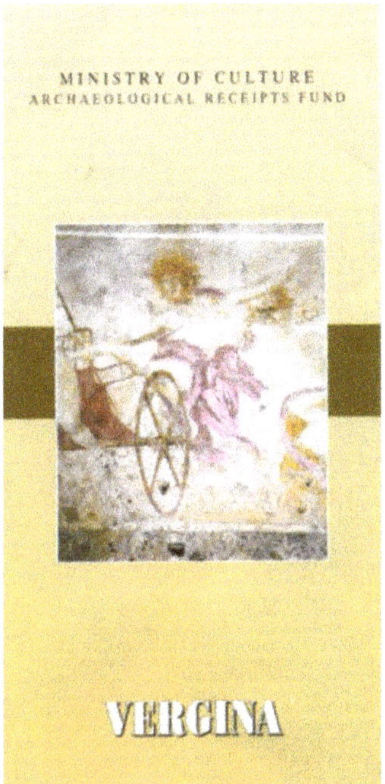

Figure 3: The Leaflet of the Archaeological Site of Vergina

History of the Site

Based on archaeological evidence, the site was continuously inhabited from the Early Bronze Age (3rd millennium BC); in the Early Iron Age (11th-8th centuries BC), it became an important cultural and economic centre, densely inhabited. The wealth and density of over 300 grave-mounds in the Cemetery of the Tumuli testifies to the importance of Aigae in the early Iron Age. Elegantly decorated vases and other significant finds revealed communication and cultural exchange between Aigae and other geographical parts of the ancient world. Also, the richness of decorated copper jewelry of fine quality produced in local workshops illustrates the central role and significance of the place even in the early years of its existence. The ancient city (historical period) in the northern foothills of the Pierian mountain identified Aigae as the capital of the kingdom of Macedonia and the first Macedonian city-centre. The city was located at a crossroads which connected Macedonia with the South of Greece. As the capital of the Macedonian kingdom and site of the royal court, Aigai was the most important urban centre in the region throughout the archaic period (800-500 BC) and the following century. The grave-goods in a series of tombs dating from the 6th and 5th centuries BC demonstrate commercial and cultural links with Greek centres of eastern Ionia and the south. At the end of the 5th century, the Aigae courtyard becomes a cultural centre in which artists, poets and philosophers from all over the Greek world are gathered. In the 4th century BC the administrative centre was transferred to Pella, but Aigai retained importance, and the royal tombs. It was here in 336 BC that Philip II was assassinated in the theatre and Alexander the Great was proclaimed king. The fierce struggles between the heirs of Alexander, the *Diadochoi*, in the 3rd century adversely affected the city, and it was further slighted after the overthrow of the Macedonian kingdom by the Romans in 168 BC. Nevertheless, it was rebuilt and survived into early imperial times. However, between the 2nd and 5th centuries AD the population progressively moved down from the foothills of the Pierian mountains to the plain, so that all that remained was a small settlement whose name, *Palatitsia* (or palace), alone indicated its former importance.

The first excavations on the archaeological site were carried out in the 19th century by the French archaeologist L. Heuzey. Thereafter, K. Rhomaios, Professor of archaeology at the Aristotle University, excavated in the 1930s, after the liberation of Macedonia. After the Second World War, in the 1950s and 1960s, Professor M. Andronikos, through the University of Thessaloniki, undertook the direction of the excavations, and he investigated the cemetery of the tumuli. At the same time, the palace was excavated by the above institution and part of the necropolis by the archaeological service of the MoCT. In 1977, Professor M. Andronikos started bringing to light the royal tombs in the Great Tumulus of Vergina (Megali Toumba). The most remarkable of these was the tomb of Philip II (359-336 BC) and its discovery is considered to be one of the most important archaeological events of the century. Since then, the excavations on the site have been carrying on and they have so far revealed a considerable number of significant monuments and findings. The most significant monuments on the site are: a) The royal tombs in the Great Tumulus consisting of three Macedonian tombs and one cist-grave. One of them was the tomb of King Philip II and another probably belonged to King Alexander IV. These two graves were found unplundered and are lavishly decorated with splendid wall paintings, made by great and famous artists. b) The royal tombs to the NW of the city. Two Macedonian tombs are included in this group, the so-called 'Rhomaios Tomb', an Ionic, temple-shaped structure dated to the beginning of the 3rd century BC and the 'Tomb of Eurydice', which probably belongs to the mother of Philip II and is dated to ca. 340 BC To the same group belong another three cist-graves dating from the 5th and 4th centuries BC, as well as four pit-graves of the late Archaic period. c) The cemetery of the tumuli. This is the imposing necropolis of the Iron Age (11th-8th centuries BC), which includes more than 300 small earthen tumuli, constructed over clusters of burials, which contained rich offerings. d) The Palace and the Theatre dated to the 4th century B.C. The palace is organized around a large, central peristyle court and comprises a circular shrine (Tholos) dedicated to Herakles Patroos and luxurious banquet halls for the king and his officers. One of these rooms has a fine mosaic floor. e) The temple of Eukleia lies at the northern end of the theatre and includes two temples of the 4th and 3rd centuries BC). The acropolis and the city walls are located on a steep hill to the south of the settlement. The fortification wall extends to the east of the city. The fortification of Aigai dates to the early Hellenistic period (end of 4th-beginning of 3rd century BC).

The Meaning of the Place and Conflicting Interests

As already noted, the archaeological site of Vergina has been recognised locally, nationally, and internationally as a place of great archaeological and historical value which adds to our understanding of the past. Large-scale preservation of the buildings, reconstructions and conservation works have been carried out by the archaeologists and specialists in order to prevent them from destruction and decay. The management planning has been based on official policy dictated by principles of making the place accessible and open for the public to experience the site through designed and organized pathways. But as Tilley argued '...places are always far more than points and locations because they have distinctive meanings and values' (Tilley 1994:15). Based on this statement it could be argued that Vergina expresses this multi-sited aspect which directs us to recognise the place as a site-symbol and as a place of reference. From the very beginning of the impressive discoveries by Professor M. Andronikos, the place attracted the interest not only of the archaeological community but of the wider public as well, by ascribing to these finds socio-political and ideological values. It is quite remarkable to note that the meetings organized[160] for the presentation of the excavation have resulted in the gathering of numerous people of different class coming to listen to the new archaeological evidence. 'I was surprised...within some time there was no place to sit, the corridors [of the conference room] were full of people...nobody was leaving, and the people started gathering outside the building, in the main road causing problems to the cars' circulation' states Professor Andronikos in his book, touched and moved by what he experienced in those moments (Ανδρόνικος, 2006:198)[161]. The Vergina artifacts had a great impact on the Greeks and their perception of the past. They have been perceived as proofs of the Greek identity and they were emblems of a glorious past. '...for once again the legend of Alexander the Great had touched the hearts of Macedonians' (Andronikos, 2006:176).

As in other cases such as the Acropolis, Knossos, or Delphi, the archaeological landscape has been perceived by the public '...as sacred, symbolic and mythic spaces replete with social meanings wrapped around buildings, objects...providing reference points and planes of emotional orientation for human attachment and involvement' (Tilley 1994:17). Building on the above, it should be stressed that the public, in the case of Greece, conceives and uses the archaeological places in two

[160] In Thessaloniki at the University, Department of Archaeology 24 November 1977; in Athens at the Archaeological Society January 1978 and at the ΕΣΗΕΑ room January 1978. At the conference of Classical Archaeology held in London 4-9 September 1978, foreign newspapers reported 'We have never seen scientists react as children, as they did on the sight of Vergina's finds' (Ανδρόνικος, 2006:223)

[161] The same incident was experienced by a witness, Dr. Kokkou, archaeologist, when she was attending Professor Andronikos' talk '...it was something that I cannot describe. All people were coming to hear and to see the beautiful findings...not archaeologists but people from different social layers it was really touching to see it...it was something unforeseeable...' (personal interview, Athens 10/6/2009).

'...we were crying hearing Professor Andronikos saying about the Philip tomb and showing us the photos of the gold larnax and other finds...' remembers one of the citizens of the city of Veroia where Andronikos gave one of the first talks after the discovery (personal discussion with Mrs Kazantzidou, Thessaloniki 20/12/2010).

realms, on one hand as vehicles to foster their local or national identity rooted in the ancestral past (as discussed in chapter II) and on the other, to define themselves as *being in* and *acting* within a historical place creating meaning and significance through the inter-relationships produced within it. On the latter relation is based the aspect of the perception of the past as an economic resource inviting possible development through the tourist consumption of the monumental material of the archaeological place of Vergina. So, the site has been museuficated and its material has been fetishized by the locals who now fervently clamour for the return of the finds to the place they were found (as they have been removed and kept for exhibition in the Museum of Thessaloniki) and raise conflicts with the archaeologists-excavators. Reflecting on this tension, one could argue that the above approaches point up the issue of inclusiveness that the 'new museology' attempts to bring to the fore in the museum's future goals. But this inclusiveness can take many forms and shapes depending on the socio-political and cultural conditions of the present, and in the case of Vergina the factor of public approach was decisive for the understanding and interpretation of the site.

The importance of the preservation and the archaeological research of the site has been high among the priorities for archaeologists, especially for the vulnerable paintings in the royal tombs. For that reason, Andronikos initiated the conduct of measures and principles for effective protection and management of the site. Additionally, the historical significance of the site dictated the pursuits of large-scale excavation projects and the well-researched evaluation and identification of the past material in order to lead to archaeological results. So, in this case any form of management plan of the archaeological site should take into consideration all the parameters, giving priority to the safeguarding and conservation of the site, in order to be accessible to the public.

On the other hand, the archaeological approach to the material evidence of the past has been translated by many locals as an obstacle and a delay to their way of experiencing and conceiving the monuments, which are seen mainly as a great opportunity for the economic regeneration of the area and a tourist attraction. The symbolic and historical values ascribed to the site, nationally and internationally recognised, transformed an isolated area and landscape into a place of significance and interest. Based on that, locals were claiming their share of the task of understanding and interpreting the site by projecting the ruins and the site into the modern societal framework and interpreting them under present socio-cultural conditions. So, local claims have been fiercely[162] expressed on the right of a site-local museum to be created in order to house the popular Vergina findings, thus establishing the future sustainability not only of the ancient place but mainly of the villages nearby. It is interesting to stress that once again (as discussed in the MBC of Thessaloniki in chapter III) a museum comes to give expression to local claims and different approaches and evaluations of past traces and it becomes a vehicle of 'power' for locals and the wider public who see a different future through the lens of the museum.

---

[162] The claims at the modern Vergina have been so intense that many locals have hindered the progress of the excavation works (Ανδρεάδης 2010: 123,124).

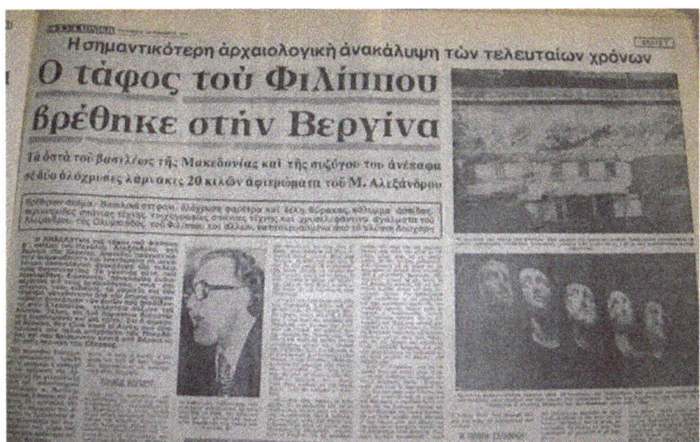

Η σημαντικότερη ἀρχαιολογική ἀνακάλυψη τῶν τελευταίων χρόνων

Ο τάφος τοῦ Φιλίππου βρέθηκε στὴν Βεργίνα

Figure 4: Extract from the daily newspaper of *Thessaloniki* bearing the tile: 'The most significant archaeological discovery of the last years; the Philip Tomb was found in Vergina' referring to Androniko's discoveries and the public reactions (25/11/1977)

In the light of the above it should be noted that these sorts of conflicting interests can provoke many forms of reactions and always prove the political nature of archaeology as a discipline and as a regulator of the production and the dissemination of meaning. In the case of Vergina, the power and the significance of the place and the values ascribed by archaeologists and locals have defined the 'channels' of communication with the public. These 'channels', consisting of a new approach and rhetorical strategy of presentation, were put into force by the creation of the Museum of the Royal Tombs.

The Museum of the Royal Tombs as a Place of Creating Meaning

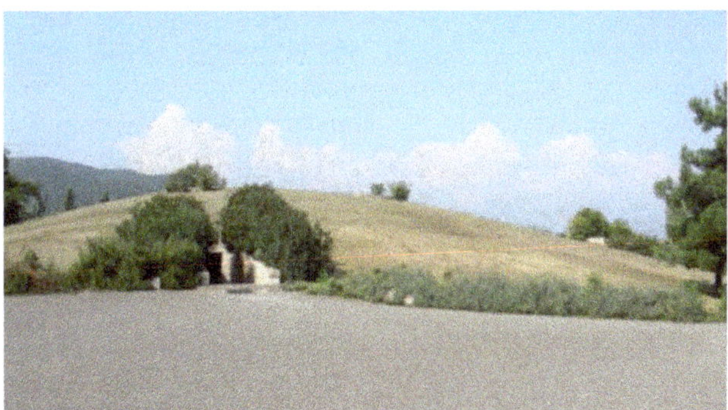

Figure 5: External View of the Museum of Royal Tombs (The Great Tumulus)

The creation of the Museum of the Royal Tombs was dictated by the need firstly to protect findings and then to promote public awareness according to the current Greek archaeological Law (3028/2002) and the international conventions on the protection of archaeological heritage (Valetta 1992). The monuments uncovered by

Professor Andronikos and his colleagues (today Professors Stella Drougou and Chrysoula Paliadeli) during the course of the excavation seasons 1977, 1978 and 1980 in the great Tumulus were: the royal Tomb, the Tomb of the Prince, the Tomb of the free-standing columns, the Tomb of Persephone and the Heroon (a building connected with the cult of the dead). All created at different dates, the five monuments were buried at different depths beneath the earth deposits of the Great Tumulus, a pine-clad hill some 12m high.

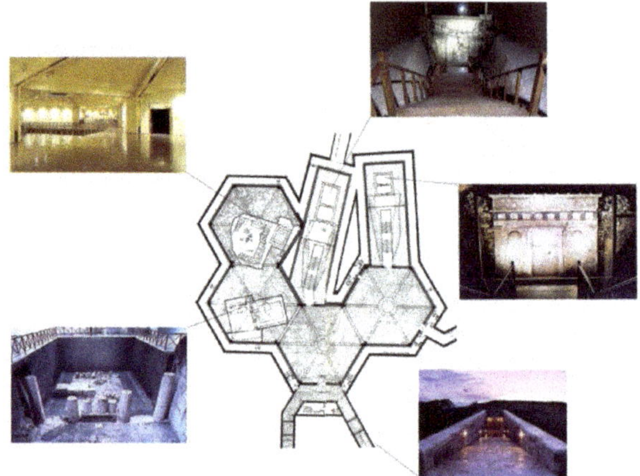

Figure 6: Plan of the Museum of Royal Tombs (The Great Tumulus)

Immediately after each monument was uncovered, Professor M. Andronikos' primary concern was to protect it from the rain and the sunlight especially in the case of those which had painted decoration. In 1977, an immediate programme was launched to preserve the magnificent murals which adorned the monuments. At the same time, a conservation laboratory was set up on the spot to save and restore the extremely important portable objects they contained. For the preservation of the Royal Tombs themselves, a subterranean structure was built in 1993 to protect the ancient monuments by maintaining a constant temperature and humidity, both indispensable for the preservation of the wall paintings. It has been suggested to build a structure which externally would have the form of an earth mound and internally would house, as a museum exhibition, the treasures found in the Royal Tombs.

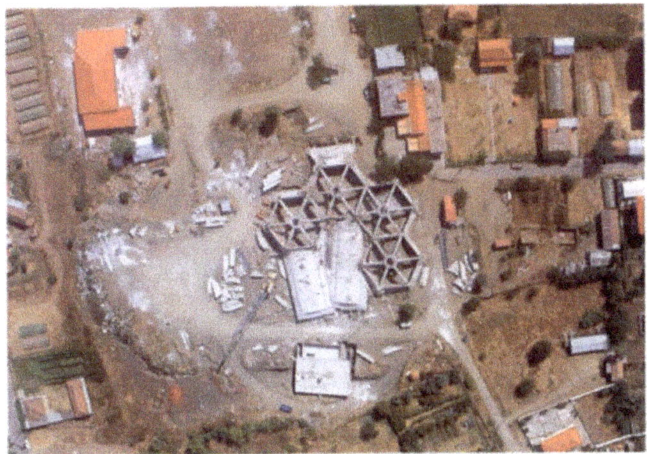

Figure 7: Aerial view of the ongoing construction of the Museum of Royal Tombs (1992)

The work carried out by the Directorate of Restoration Works, Ministry of Culture, on the five monuments in the Great Tumulus took the form of *preventive conservation*, a well-known practice in architectural conservation (Demacopoulos 1995). Also, extra care was taken with the immediate environment of the Tumulus in order to acquire a similar image of the past landscape. In that way, it would be possible after all these years for visitors to approach and experience the monuments '...in some comfort, in a manner that does not imitate, but hints at a much earlier situation, at least as far as the external (surrounding) space is concerned' (ibid.:27).

Considering the above constructive and architectural framework of spatial narratives, the museum exhibition units and the 'paths' of experience as they look today follow a structure which has been organized on the basis of and around these in situ monuments and their associations. The character of the museum, in terms of its thematic focus on graves, tombs and the celebration of death and memory, approaches the definition of a 'museum-mausoleum' according to the current director of the 17th Ephorate of Prehistoric and Classical Antiquities (EPCA) Dr Kottaridi, who stresses the unique nature of the museum's theme and how it is expressed in the rooms of the crypt-museum (Kottaridi 2003)[163]. The buildings themselves—the graves—are accessible and experienced by the visitor, who enjoys the approach to a tangible heritage that was originally (in past times) built to be hidden from human sight. Also, the visitor is encouraged to experience the 'atmosphere' and the awe that these monuments evoke, producing emotional attachment and deep sentiments. That emotional side of these constructions of the past has been pursued by the exhibition creators who attempted to guide the public's interest towards '...the things, not usable any more nevertheless useful, raised on their pedestals, become monuments, fragments of memory, ideas rather than objects...' (Kottaridi 2003:48). The main museological scenario has been based on

[163] And personal interview with Dr Kottaridi, Vergina, 15/9/2010.

the idea that '...death, the past, earth and oblivion are shadow and absence of light, whereas life and memory are light and colour' (ibid: 49). This aspect directed the main parameters of the organizational structure of the exhibition and defined the operational museum networking. So, light played a decisive role in the production of the appropriate ambience of the space, and the limited use of showcases and other display constructions indicates the 'minimalistic' morphological character of the exhibition mechanism.

The exhibition path, as designed for the visitor, is intended to be followed gradually in order to reach the highest meeting point with the most significant exhibit-building, the royal tomb. Thus, the visitor entering the exhibition, walking down the road paved with stones, *dromos* (as it was called in ancient times), has a reconstructed image of the space and the monuments that he/she is approaching. A model of the landscape monument of the mound (Megali Toumba), under which the graves were situated, introduces the visitor to the museum environment and orientates him/her spatially within the landscape narratives (see figure 8). In the next step, grave stelae and finds from the tombs of ordinary Macedonian citizens, inscribed on the marble, are displayed with identification texts providing historical information (see figure 9). The next in situ monument that the visitor encounters is a ruined 3rd c. BC tomb, called a free-standing tomb, with the four restored Doric columns, forming a portico at the façade, an architectural element that indicates the monumentality of the building. Unfortunately, this tomb was plundered, and the displayed finds are merely indicative of the splendid content it used to have. The other exhibit-building is the collapsed Heroon, cult place of the kings, which was initially above ground. Along with the cult place the visitor has also the opportunity to experience the first of the royal tombs, the tomb of Persephone, which takes its name from the mural painting depicting the abduction of Persephone by Hades.

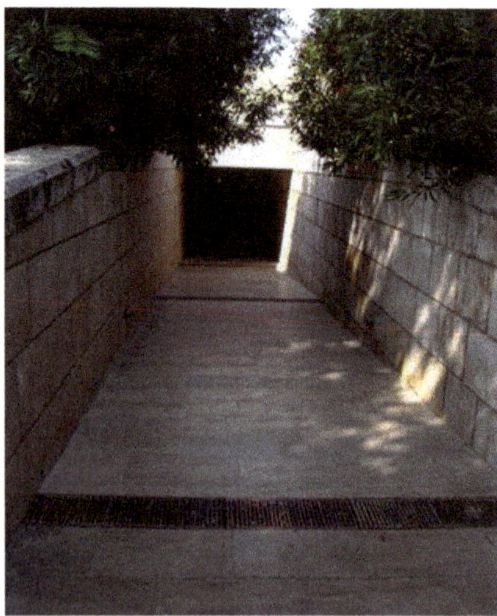

Figure 8: The so-called dromos leading to the entrance of the Museum of Royal Tombs

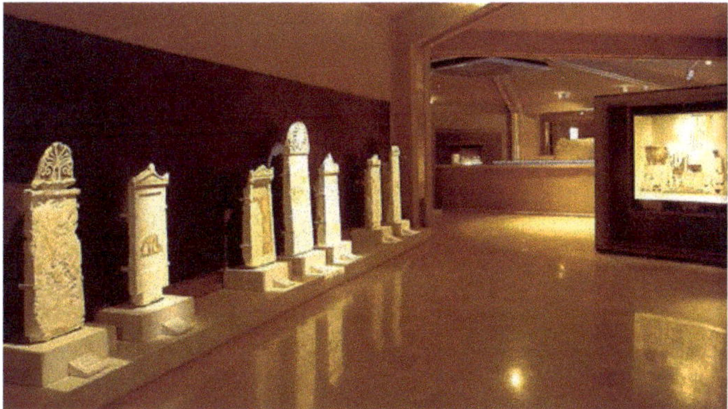

Figure 9: Internal view of the Museum of Royal Tombs.

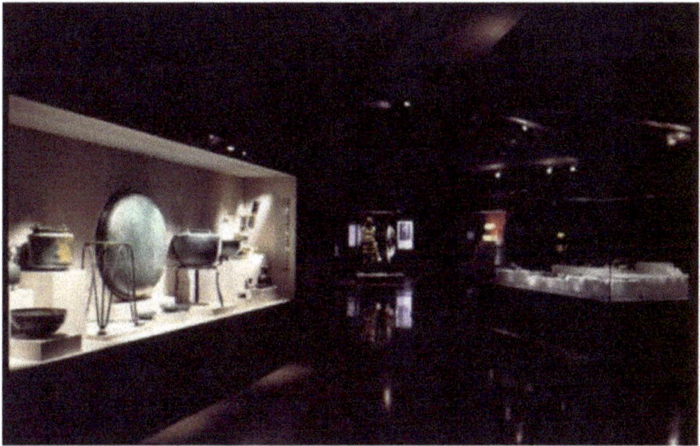

Figure 10: Internal view of the Museum of Royal Tombs. The light in present display is limited.

In a number of showcases along the visitors' exhibition pathway, impressive finds, weapons, suits of armour and other objects of metallurgy are displayed as symbols of power. Some of those are the hieratic diadem and the torch bearer, the wine jug and the *patera* of the ritual libations which are all associated with the sacred nature of the grave of King Philip II, father of Alexander the Great and consolidator of Macedonian power. The pile remains of the funerary pyre, found scattered all over the tomb, are reminders of his tragic death and at the same time an allusion to his passing into another dimension. The famous gold coffin (*larnax*) that contained the bones of the heroized King Philip II and the oak crown worn by the dead man are displayed as powerful symbol objects attracting the visitor's gaze and contemplation. The lid of the larnax is decorated with a 16-ray star symbol and two rosettes, the inner being filled with blue enamel[164].

[164] For more details see the website of the MoCT www.culture.gr

Having admired and contemplated the impressive 'world of gold' the visitor reaches the grave-building, the Macedonian tomb of Philip II, and has the opportunity to encounter one of the first monumental paintings of the period, the royal hunting depicted on the façade of the tomb. The next 'exhibition' unit is the tomb of Alexander IV (the tomb of the Prince), son of Alexander the Great who was buried after 310 BC. The finds from both tombs are displayed in showcases in which the visitor is encouraged to obtain information on the objects related to the ceremonies of the dead and the art of some of the masterpieces of the period. The exhibition journey concludes with a picture of the excavator of the graves, Professor M. Andronikos, bringing us again to the present after a journey to the world of the dead and reminding us of the significant role of the archaeology as a discipline, which studies the past, and the social role of the museum as an institution, creating and mediating meaning to the public.

It is important to stress that the above recognition is fostered by the style of the museum construction and exhibition settings which manage, on the one hand, to challenge traditional forms and exhibition practices, and on the other, to encourage a more holistic method and strategy of management, focusing more on the space-experience rather than on object-experience. Thus, despite the richness and magnificence of the object-findings displayed in the museum, what captures the visitor's feelings is the space itself, consisting of buildings and constructions of the past, carrying not only the information about the past framework itself, but also bearing the meanings and the messages of present practices of discovering, studying and representing the past. Here, the museum as a place operates to 'humanize and enculture landscape linking together topographical features…with patterns of human intentionality' (Tilley 1994:24). Through simple exhibition settings and mechanisms, the creation of meanings within the museum rely mainly on those rhetorical strategies which are based on the potentialities of the space aiming at the emotional engagement and involvement of the visitor. And if the rhetoric was concerned with persuasion and closely related to dialectic, following Aristotle's definitions and terms, it could be argued that the museum narratives in our case, as created and experienced through the designed exhibitions, strengthen an immediate dialogue between the visitor, as message recipient and maker, and the remains of the past presented in an intentional space. This space of the past (partly original (the constructions) and partly recreated (the museum)) is powerful and fully imposed in the present, participating fully in the museological process by its character, and defining the rules by its atmosphere acquired through centuries. Thus, a framework is established for a 'hot interpretation', a term introduced by Uzzell, defining the entertainment and the emotive and ideological involvement of the visitor (Uzzell 1988).

Recognizing the above it should also be noted that the nature of the presented buildings (graves, tombs) raises new considerations on the representation of these kinds of past remains which in our case initially defined the goals of the museum. Presenting graves as exhibits and seeing them as monuments of the past, once constructed and planned to be deliberately concealed from the world of the living, creates a dilemma for the people who are responsible for their protection and management, which demands the achievement of a balance in the museum practices. The desire of the public to experience and to have access to a glorious and symbolic heritage creates an innate contradiction in relation to the original purpose of these monuments. However, in this case the museum in the form of a tumulus manages to achieve, in my opinion, an effective balance representing essentially the many-fold character of archaeology as a discipline. On one side, within the archaeological site (underground landscape) defined by institutional boundaries, it maintains the scientific integrity of buildings and constructions and also the academically documented archaeological stratigraphy, and on the other, it serves its role as a social institution and a place of communication by providing a space where interrelationships among people and traces of the past are stressed and fostered.

It should be noted that the above museum suggestion has been adopted by other Greek archaeological-museum projects as it has proved the most effective approach appropriate to these sorts of monuments (graves, tombs) and constitutes an example to follow in the framework of an effective museum policy. This is, for instance, the case of the museum-tumulus in an isolated area in Thrace (Northern Greece) which is expected to house a wealthy family's tumulus, excavated by the 19th (ΙΘ') Ephorate of Prehistoric and Classical Antiquities, dated to 2000 years ago and containing rich finds, chariots and equine symbols[165]. According to the excavators the main aim of the suggested project is the presentation of the findings (horses, chariots and horse accessories) *in situ* in order '...to show to the public the image of finds during the excavation' (*Kathimerini* 2011)[166]. The concern of archaeologists to pursue management decision-making which will primarily ensure the protection and preservation of the archaeological site, but also access to and effective experience of the past remains, is apparent in many Greek cases. In these cases, the site-museum comes to achieve the appropriate balance between various interests and objectives.

Along with the recognised success of the Museum of Royal Graves at Aigae it is interesting to note that the archaeological landscape-site of the Vergina area, as it has been formed based on the archaeological evidence so far, has recently induced the implementation of a new museum-project, supplementing the existent one. According to the director of the related Ephorate, Dr Kottaridi, a poly-centric museum is being prepared to frame the entire archaeological site of Aigai with a variety of exhibition units and significant museum practices. The main aim of this attempt is 'to encourage and strengthen the dialectic conversation between the visitor and the material remains of the site...'[167] as Dr Kottaridi stated, stressing the ideological and social role of the museum as an institution, and the archaeological landscape 'as a backdrop against which...remains are plotted' (Knapp and Ashmore 1999:1). The plethora of groups of significant graves, and other important constructions of the site, have led those responsible for the management plan to

[165] The archaeological site came to light in 2004 and the museum-project is expected to be funded by the 4th EU Program. Responsible for the site excavation and the proposal of the museum project is the archaeologist D. Triantaphyllos, of the related Ephorate.
[166] Newspaper Καθημερινή [Kathimerini] (digital edition).
[167] Personal interview with Dr Kottaridi, archaeological site of Vergina 15/09/2010

initiate[168] a number of museum units, similar to the museum of the Royal Graves in the case of underground constructions or in the form of an 'archaeological park-promenade' for the necropolis of the site, creating in that way a multi-sited approach to interpreting and experiencing the material remains of the past. 'The scenario is given by the site itself consisting of different units (archaeological-exhibitional) with themes changing dependent on the archaeological evidence' (Kottaridi ibid.). It can be argued that the above attempts show an interesting shift of museum policy in Greece towards more holistic and inclusive approaches to interpreting and presenting the past remains to the public, focusing not only on the impact of the isolated objects displayed within a museum space but rather on the stories of the wider archaeological landscape as it has been created through centuries. The architectural assemblages of the archaeological site of the past provide the scene in which the archaeologists of the present, as 'regulators' of 'past memory', will create those narratives and relations enabling the establishment of a nexus of interconnections among the remains of past societies and the present local communities. Seen from that dialectical perspective what is interesting and necessary for Greek archaeology to pursue is the openness and the creation of communication channels among the past and present messengers or 'makers' of material culture; as Sutton and Stroulia put it, '...a new recontextualization that reconnects sites to the living, breathing contemporary world around them' (Sutton and Stroulia 2010:32). This recontextualization demands recognition of the social and political role of archaeology as a discipline practiced in the present and creating present stories which involve not only historical information about an archaeological past but mainly narratives of that past, projecting and interpreting them into a living and vibrant present whose occupants have their say and share.

In the case of Vergina, the concept of 'museumscape' is applied in order to enable us to recognize exactly what is argued above, the interrelations of the archaeological museumscape with the local communities, and additionally to establish a nexus of channels through which museum practices could contribute to an understanding of the past and the pursuit of a sustainable future. Based on that recognition it could be argued that the symbolic character of the Vergina site could rest not only on the historical and archaeological evidence but also on the way that these archaeological remnants and places are valued as sacred and symbolic capital by the contemporary societies and as vehicles for a sustainable socio-economic framework for future generations.

IV. Mount Athos: The Place as a Museum-Ritual

> 'Oh, this Athos unduly doomed to death, as if by a vow of self-destruction! And so, imbued with deep-felt poetry! Yes, to go there requires physical courage not to doze off in the slow narcosis of so-called prayer but to embark, rather, upon the immense vocation of a trappist—*the silence, the*

[168] The project has been suggested and approved for funding by 4th European Funding Framework (Kottaridi ibid.)

> *almost superhuman struggle within oneself to be able to embrace death with an ancient smile!*...I thought we had landed on some island of long ago, since every vestige evoked *a poetry shaped by an adoration of the past*. The moment was not simply bucolic. *It was also sacred, filled with silence and peace*'
> (Le Corbusier 1987:173, emphasis added).

In this study's attempt to approach the historical, archaeological and symbolic aspects of the internationally recognized place of Mount Athos, the introductory words of Le Corbusier above inspire us to investigate that polysemic and meaning-rich location and its associations. By attempting to perceive it as an uninterrupted living place, replete of cultural, socio-political, and economic values, we experience this place's many-fold character which makes it unique and challenging as an historical place. Mount Athos has enjoyed recognition as a World Heritage Site since 1988 (cultural and natural criteria)[169] and it is widely recognized as a museum due to the richness of unique works of art (architecture, painting, etc.) of great artistic value and at the same time being 'a living organism' with the monastic practice uninterrupted since the 10th century. As UNESCO's statement of significance puts it, 'Le Mont Athos est véritablement un musée unique au monde...un organisme vivant'[170]. One can easily realise the multiplicity of approaches and roles that this place could play in our present attempts to seek multi-routed management practices for this kind of heritage site. It is remarkably challenging for the contemporary expertise, archaeologist, anthropologist, and other specialists, to recognise in this case those features that the place has acquired through time and to succeed in reaching a balance between present management imperatives and the practices expressed as rituals of the past.

[169]Criteria: (i)(ii)(iv)(v)(vi)(vii) See http://whc.unesco.org/en/list/454/

[170] http://whc.unesco.org/en/list/454/ accessed 10/4/2011 '...Mount Athos is truly a museum unique in the world...a living organism' (my translation)

History of the Site

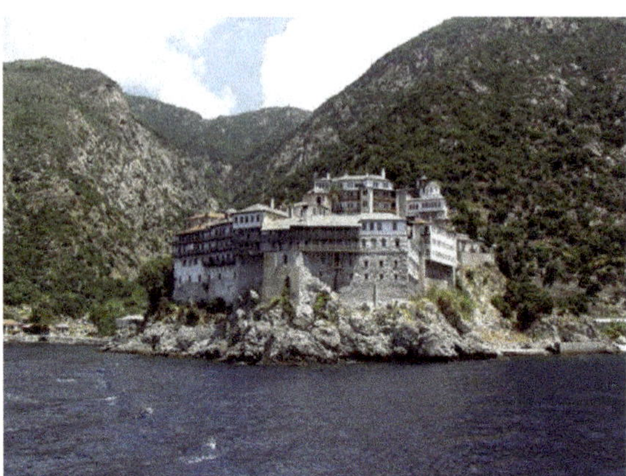

Figure 11: The Monastery of Grigoriou, Mount Athos

The peninsula of Mount Athos, located in northern Greece, has been settled from prehistoric and historic times, according to archaeological evidence found in different parts of the area in the course of rescue and systematic excavations[171]. The location was most active during the Byzantine period, when Christian monasticism developed, and which is still in force in comparison to other monastic centres of the world, such as Egypt, Syria, Asia Minor, Palestine and Constantinople where most of the centres are in ruins or inhabited by only a limited number of monks. The 'holy mountain' could claim the title of being the only monastic centre of this period with a continuous and diachronic history up to the present. Mount Athos consists of twenty monasteries which enjoy an autonomous statute since Byzantine times, and they are inhabited by some 1,400 monks. The monastic movement began to intensify in 963, when Saint Athanasius the Athonite founded Great Lavra on the tip of the peninsula. In 972, the first Typikon (agreement) was concluded at Karyes between the Emperor Ioannes Tsimiskes and the monks of Mount Athos. It was the basis for the exceptional status still enjoyed by the 'Holy Mount' today. Saint Athanasios attracted many hermits, including Georgians, Armenians and Latins, who lived isolated in separate dwellings. Along with the Great Lavra, two other large monasteries, Vatopedi and Iveron, were established during the 10th century, and the monasteries of Docheiariou, Philotheou and Xenophontos followed the presence of numerous monks and the establishment of coenobitic life on the mount in the eleventh century. At the end of this period the Mountain suffered by frequent pirate raids in which many monasteries were pillaged, and others completely destroyed. During the period of Latin Occupation (1204-1261) Mount Athos was under the jurisdiction of the Latin Kingdom of Salonika and the monks were

[171] For a detailed description of the excavations, surveys and research on the area see multiple archaeological reports of 10th Ephorate of Byzantine Antiquities, MoCT and multiple articles on the book: Άγιον Όρος και Προχριστιανική Αρχαιότητα 2006 [Holy Mountain and Pre-Christian Antiquity] Θεσσαλονίκη: ΚΕΔΑΚ ΥΜΑΘ.

subjected to pressing conditions to accept the union of the two churches East and West. After the death of the Emperor Michael his son and successor Andronicos II was opposed to the Latin rites and the union and it was he and his successors who helped the monks to restore their monasteries after the Catalan raids to the mountain, which plundered, massacred monks, burned down monasteries and took with them priceless treasures. During the fifteenth century the monks continued their resistance to the union of the churches and took an active part in the struggle for Orthodoxy. After the fall of Thessaloniki (1430) and Constantinople (1453), Mount Athos was under the rule of the Sultan of Turkey with whom the monks had good relations and enjoyed many privileges. The role of Mount Athos in the enlightenment of the enslaved Greek people during that period was recognized and remarkable. It became the educational and spiritual centre from which patriarchs, bishops and teachers tried to encourage Greeks and strengthen their faith in their rebirth and liberation. The Athonite Academy was the witness of that movement, and many distinguished teachers lived on the mountain during the period offering their services to the Greek attempt for national independence in 1821. In the last century many monks from abroad, mainly Romanians, Bulgarians, and Russians, arrived on the Mount contributing to its increasing population. Today, Mount Athos remains a sacred place and an integral part of the Greek state in which the community of monks enjoy a coenobitic and idiorhythmic way of life, which is internationally unique.

The Management of a 'Sacred Place': Conflicts and Interests.

The institutional organization of the twenty monasteries of Mount Athos is based on a network of legislative and administrative principles which form the governing framework of the peninsula. According to the constitutional charter dated 10 September 1926, 'Mount Athos is an autonomous part of the Greek state, which retains complete sovereignty over it', whereas the Greek Constitution of 1927 places the Mountain within the Greek State as 'a decentralized part of the Greek State...with its immemorial special status...[which] is subject to the jurisdiction of the Ecumenical Patriarchate'. The Holy Community (Holy Epistasia and Holy Assembly) consisting of twenty members, that is, one from each monastery, is the main administrative authority responsible for legislative and canonical enactments covering the organization, administration and government of the monastic life. The presence of the Greek State is defined by the existence of services supervised by the political administrator responsible for the law's implementation. The Greek Law is fully applied to the area of Mount Athos and the principles issued by the monasteries constitute strict codes of social behavior. Added to the national charters are also the charters issued by international committees and organizations such as ICOMOS, ICCROM, and UNESCO related not only to the cultural and artistic architectural value of the Byzantine heritage but also to its recognition as a sacred natural site. This is the Delos initiative which was established in 2004 within the framework of the Cultural and Spiritual Values of Protected Areas (CSVPA) Specialist Group of the International Union for Conservation of Nature (IUCN). In these initiatives the focus is placed on the uniqueness of natural elements of the Holy Mount landscape whose recognition defines the implementation of the appropriate protective measures and codes[172].

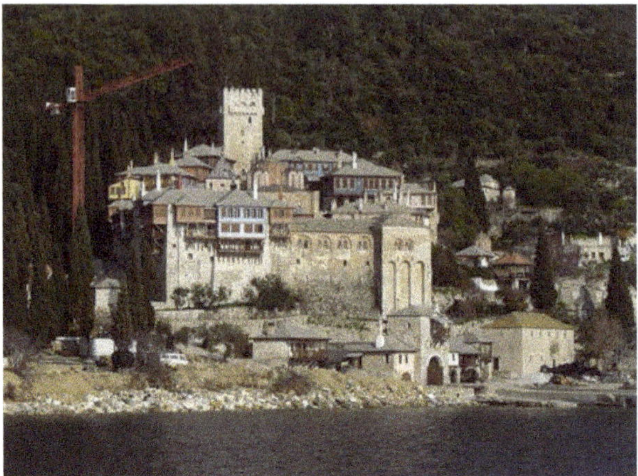

Figure 12: The Monastery of Docheiariou, Mount Athos

The central issue of the above national and international organizations is the protection and preservation of this valuable site, which is rich in structures, objects, works of art, garments and traditions, a heritage which has survived almost intact and living for over one thousand years. This living religious heritage expresses its existence and continuous presence through the meaning of tangible and intangible values ascribed to manifestations of sacred structures and objects, on one hand, and through rituals and celebrations, on the other. The implementation of methods and practices of conservation and preservation of the plethora of sacred, tangible and intangible, relics of the past found within the boundaries of the peninsula has proved to be a challenge not only for the Greek archaeologists working for years on the site but also for scholars who study and seek to approach the phenomenon of 'Mount Athos' more broadly. The multi-faceted character of the site creates many complexities and implications that the contemporary management attempts should take into consideration. In the light of these concerns it should be noted that a considerable number of large-scale projects have been initiated by the Ministry of Culture, through its responsible archaeological service, the 10th Ephorate of Byzantine Antiquities, and other organisations, such as the Centre for the Preservation of Mount Athos, within the last 20 years. These projects were funded, and still are, by the EU[173], showing the attempts that are made to 'de-isolate' the

[172] See Proceedings of the second workshop of the Delos Initiative, Ouranoupolis 2007.

[173]The 3rd European Fund Framework provided an extended network of large and small-scale conservation projects which allowed *in situ* preservation and conservation works on architectural structures and objects like icons and manuscripts to be carried out by the 10th Ephorate of Byzantine Antiquities, MoCT

place and make it accessible in the realm of the modernization and to ensure effective conservation practices and the future sustainability of the place.

Consequently, these pursuits created tensions and conflicts in the attempts of different groups and communities to find a sustainable and appropriate framework in which conservation and preservation methods and management strategies could function. Thus, the community of archaeologists, as legally responsible for the protection of the area, encountered, and still do, many difficulties in their attempts to approach and pursue research investigations in order to interpret and study the evolution of Byzantine culture that the remains of Mount Athos evoke. These difficulties mainly arose from the unclear and confusing legislative principles, which define the lines and grades of authority in the conservation decision-making management about the architectural heritage (structures, buildings), the ecclesiastical objects (icons), and the monumental wall painting in the monasteries. Under these conditions the dilemma of who is responsible for the assessment, evaluation and management of this heritage often preoccupies the director of the relevant Ephorate, who struggles to maintain the balance between various interests ensuring the archaeological research and study of these valuable remains of the Byzantine past[174] and the adoption of rescue measures for the safeguarding of the vulnerable heritage. Within this framework many issues are raised in terms of large-scale projects of restoration and renovation of architectural heritage, which is often at risk of demolition. In the attempt to reconcile the traditional methods of preservation, based on the archaeological evidence and technical building information found in the past structures, with innovative but at the same time interventionist and modern approaches which modernize the structures for contemporary use, there are many conflicts among the archaeologists (Ministry of Culture), representing the former aspect, and the architects (Centre for the Preservation of Mount Athos) representing the latter.

On the other side, the Athonite community has its share in the management planning as guardians and producers of a living religious heritage trying to establish those conditions which will ensure the historical continuity of that symbolic place and its future sustainability. Thus, making use of the guidelines as defined by their constitutional charter, the monks appeared as 'owners' of a Byzantine heritage, exercising full control over how and to what extent this heritage should be preserved, under what conditions, and how should it be interpreted by or presented to the public. That monolithic attitude had created many conflicts in the past among the services related to the protection of Greek cultural heritage, especially when exhibitions and cultural events would have been organized concerning the heritage of Mount Athos. That was the case of the exhibition titled 'Treasures of Mount Athos' at the Museum of Byzantine Culture in Thessaloniki, in connection with the celebration of the city as European Capital of Culture in 1997, where for the first time religious objects and works of art from the Mount Athos were exhibited to the public. It was really a great moment for the Greek public who came from all over

[174] According to the Law 2557/1997 and Presidential Decrees 941/1977, 191/2003 the protection and the safeguarding not only of the Byzantine and post-Byzantine heritage but also of the pre-Christian antiquities lies with the 10th Ephorate of Byzantine Antiquities with current director Dr Tavlakis.

the country to see the symbolic 'objects of Orthodoxy' and to admire the cultural and natural landscape of that geographically and spiritually isolated place. That 'spirit of place' is perceived in a different way by the Athonite community, who value the place based on the religious significance and intangible elements of Byzantine heritage, such as customs, holy living, spiritual ethics, hymns etc. and require full respect for these principles and practices. In this framework is involved a so-called *avaton*, meaning the prohibition of entrance of any female or child to the holy mountain as dictated by the constitutional charter[175]. Although that practice seems to imply monolithic and exclusive approaches to the interpretation and representation of the past, it should be conceived as part of an intangible heritage consisting of values and codes created many years ago forming the idiorhythmic and distinctive regime of Mount Athos.

Recognising the above perspective, heritage practitioners should conduct a policy which fosters the respect and protection of not only the tangible architectural assemblages and objects, movable and immovable, but also the intangible acquired values, which in cases of living religious sites often constitute the core of their distinctiveness. And to that direction, it should be noted that the last Greek archaeological law (3028/2002, as discussed in chapter II) has proved preventative of damage by extending the protection framework not only to the tangible cultural heritage, but also to the intangible, thus pursuing the safeguarding of numerous areas and cultures at risk in Greece.

Considering all of the above, what is most interesting is that the significance, evaluation, and pursuit of a management policy in a place depends on the way that the different communities and groups perceive that place. The values ascribed to the relics of the past define the extent and the quality of perception and experience of the site, which profoundly defines the place-making process. Thus, whereas for the heritage practitioners the place is conceived as a scientific ground for exercising the methods and practices of a scientific approach and interpretation, for the community of monks it is a place endowed with rituals and ceremonies of past activities and their respect ensures their historical continuity. On the other hand, the general public, the visitor, or to put it differently the consumer approaches and interprets the place according to the values ascribed to the institutionalized heritage, ideologically and symbolically marked by the historical continuity and the emblematic character of the place. Also, the economic and tourist evaluation of this place raises many conflicting issues for the preservation management and the sustainable protection of the tangible and intangible facets of that heritage, proving the need for a multi-routed and multisided interpretation and evaluation approach and method for these kinds of archaeological sites.

Beyond the Site

In the light of the above considerations and recognising that value, intrinsic or extrinsic, is formed in the nexus between ideas and things (Mason 2010:100), one

[175] Further discussion on the *avaton* of Mount Athos is provided in Hatzinikolaou 2005.

may argue that places like Mount Athos, inherently sacred and empowered, could be experienced as living 'museum-scenes', wherein the socio-cultural relations of past societies are reproduced and represented forming a fertile ground for new modes and technologies of communication with the public. The history of architectural heritage of Byzantine monasteries and a variety of other structures can be traced in situ and the visitor can encounter practices and ways of living still in use that were formed years ago. That possibility of experiencing the past provides the visitor with the opportunity to get insight of the past and to develop dialectical relations with the present. Furthermore, the landscape of the holy mountain becomes a place of interactivity where people not only admire and contemplate the works of art of a glorious past but also are engaged in the production of the symbolic and social relations that these objects evoke. They become witnesses of a living past which is re-created and re-interpreted though objects and structures that maintain their primary functional and symbolic character and continue to play their active role. They are not *synecdoches* but rather they are alive, still in use to be offered to the process of socio-cultural production.

On the other side, the sense of exclusivity that is created by the founding principle of *avaton* requires that efforts be made to initiate projects which aim to make the heritage of the holy Mount accessible to all. These projects consist, on one hand, of digitization and creation of portals, such as web-sites, to the various aspects of Mount Athos's Byzantine heritage and, on the other hand, of the planning and organization of many exhibitions (national and international) thus providing different approaches and interpretations[176].

Moreover, Mount Athos, perceived as a 'living museum', provides us with an alternative example of a place where the three agents (Baxandall 1991) of material culture of the past could be encountered. So, the monks act as 'producers' and successors of a culture within an unchanged tangible and intangible landscape, which forms the informational context of the stories. The second agent, the narrator-maker or the story-teller, the archaeologist, as a regulator and responsible for the preservation and protection of an institutionalized heritage, creates the framework of experience and develops strategies for approaching the relics of the past. Thirdly, we have the recipients and consumers of the constructed messages, the viewers or visitors, who attempt to travel into a sacred place with the purpose of getting a grasp of a living pastness in order to locate themselves in the present. We could argue that all the three are active 'makers', participants and at the same time carriers of their own preconceptions, which interact to create meaning within a place transformed into a 'museumscape'.

[176] Exhibitions were organised in Helsinki at the City Art Museum, Finland from 18th August 2006 to 21st of January 2007 and in Paris at Petit Palais from 9th of April to 7th of July 2009.

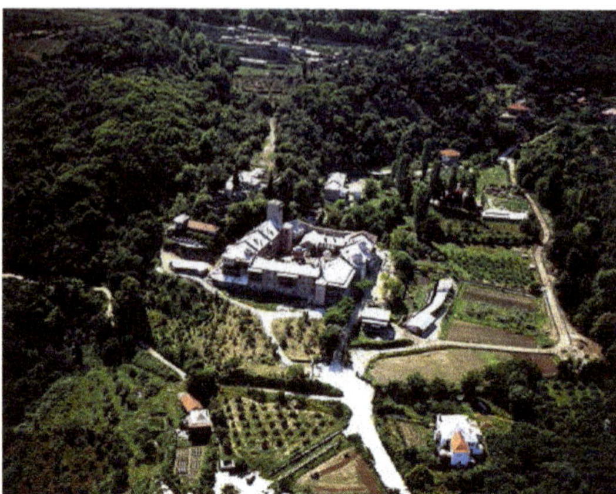

Figure 13: The Monastery of Koutloumousiou, Mount Athos (aerial view)

The recognition of the above transformation would help us to understand those complexities and implications that these heritage sites could have in the public's attempt to perceive them and interpret them. In the case of the distinctive and unique place of the holy mountain, seeing it as a museum and adequately conducting a phenomenological interpretation approach would prove eventually a more effective method for all the groups interested and involved in the heritage discourses, and on this basis further mechanisms which would encourage a language for the understanding and protection of this living culture could be developed. Based on that, the 'museumscape' approach could provide a framework in which multi-sided 'channels' could be created in order to facilitate the engagement of the public in an understanding of the past, while the encouragement of stimulating practices of decision-making management would foster the polysemic character of the place and ensure its sustainability.

V. Conclusions: Challenges and Perspectives

In this chapter, an attempt has been made to investigate methods and practices which could lead to the development of alternative methods of interpreting and new readings of the past. The two cases evoke institutionalized and 'authorized' (Smith 2006) aspects of internationally recognised tangible and intangible heritage. Both sites are approached as archaeological-historical landscapes replete with socio-cultural meanings and at the same time as museum-places where strategies of representation are taking place. This duality of approach has had as its main aim to unfold all those potentialities that the archaeological place as a defined site transformed into museum space could have on the experience of the past. The recognition of this could enable us to understand and approach the past not as a dead entity but rather as active and dynamic, always under transformation and changing. This would introduce new methods and strategies for how we may perceive and experience the past. Both sites provide us with fertile ground to investigate aspects which challenge the traditional image of the museum as 'keeper' and 'guardian' of valuable things and promote the holistic perspective and potential of experiencing the past, focusing rather on the recognition of the socio-cultural role of the museum within modern society and the perception of an archaeological and historical landscape as a place of social action (past and present) that creates layers of relations.

Within this framework, practitioners working in the field of management and representation of the past should seek alternative and inclusive ways to approach the past and make it accessible. The focus should move to *being in* a place and how one can perceive and experience the dynamic of the place. That sense of place and its meaning could be reinforced by initiatives which integrate, for example, environmental issues with representational and educational projects. That was the case in the planning of educational projects at the 10th EBA (designed and organized by the author). The main structure of the projects was based not only on the provision of historical and archaeological interpretative information, but also on the integration and further contextualization of natural and cultural settings of a specific area, broadening in that way the spectrum of investigation and analysis of past remains. The title of the projects 'Monument, Museum and Environment' called the visitor to approach the monument-tower (Byzantine Tower at Ouranoupolis, Chalkidiki) not only as evidence of the past historical and archaeological setting but also as presenting a symbolic monument transformed into a museum in the contemporary local society, as well as calling attention to its meaning and its connections with the wider natural and cultural landscape of the village (Polyzoudi 2004, 2005)[177]. Supplementary to the above educational project was one designed for Mount Athos (as the place is at the border of the Mount), putting emphasis on the presentation of Byzantine monasteries (through digital applications) and also on the natural and religious dimensions of that 'living' place (ibid. 2005). The aim of these attempts is to conduct a public-oriented policy of museums and monument management that integrates the present locals' approaches and perceptions about past remains. In that way, active involvement in the experience and safeguarding of local heritage is fostered and a raising of public awareness in the protection of past relics is encouraged. It was remarkable to note the inclusion of this in both the cases of Vergina and Mount Athos.

[177] Archive of the 10th Ephorate of Byzantine Antiquities, Ministry of Culture. Educational Programmes.

Figure 14: The Leaflet of Educational Programmes.10th EBA. MoCT

The recognition of the potentialities of site museums and the conception of the archaeological and historical place as museum space could offer an inclusive framework in which theoretical approaches of interpretation and representation of material culture, on the one hand, and museum practices and technologies, which produce stories and narratives of the past projected to the present, on the other, enter into a dialogue where the visitor is not a passive recipient but rather an active one participating in that dialectical process. That perspective challenges the traditional roles of the museum and sets new guidelines on our way to pursue multifaceted approaches to the representation of the past and the creation of a multivocal museum space. The expression of this multivocality of the museum space is going to be investigated in the next chapter through the analysis of private collecting.

CHAPTER 5

Collecting Objects and Searching for Identities: Cultural Interactions in the Private Museums of Greece

We navigate through life from one experience to the next,
framing our perceptions of the world and sending them
into the future as formalised memories from which
we hope the next generation will benefit
(Tapsell 2003:242)

I. INTRODUCTION

So far, this study has examined concepts and museum discourses developed in a framework constructed and controlled fully by the state sector. In order for this study to provide a complete and comprehensive insight into museum evolution and archaeological management in Greece, it is critical also to explore museum and collecting practices as developed in a private sphere and on a more decentralized, local basis. Thus, in the present chapter an effort is made at the beginning to articulate a structure of thought that will enable an understanding of the private collecting policies within a general intellectual, social, historical and museological context. It will examine the framework in which private collecting operates today in Greece and future perspectives on their contribution to museum policy planning. Also, the process of integrating local, private collections of traditional material with the museological scenarios of state museum exhibitions will be a significant issue in our attempt to investigate different approaches towards an authorized past. Based on the author's experience leading a museum project in Ouranoupolis, Chalkidiki, northern Greece, management practices and theoretical reflections are discussed on the way that local people could be engaged in the production of stories, which in turn could provide valuable evidence for practitioners who seek new inclusive ways of thinking and presenting the past, local or national.

Next, the chapter investigates, through the presentation of a case study of the local museum in Alexandroupolis of northern Greece, how cultural diversity and identities are expressed through private collecting policies and to explore the interpretive tools of making histories and alternative identities in museum exhibitions. Concepts such as locality, memory, and remembrance are engaged in our attempt to map and define the significant role of the decentralized local museums in the perception of one or various pasts, raising issues of the multivocality and plurality of approaches to past remains displayed in the museum space. By focusing on management practices as manifested in the decision-making process, it reveals the potential of private collections in empowering cultural diversity and intercultural dialogue.

II. Private Collecting in Greece: A New Imperative

Over the past twenty years, a broad range of critical analyses have emerged on the process of collecting, unmasking the structures by which the act of collecting takes place and their implications. Thus, scholars and theorists of museums such as Pearce (1991; 1992; 1994; 1995); Elsner and Cardinal (1994); and Pomian (1990) have studied the history and the evolution of collections in a Western framework and conducted research on the theoretical background of the formation of collecting practices, examining the socio-politics of collections. Recognizing the essential and significant role that a collection-container, as supplier, has in the process of the creation of museum exhibitions, and further informed by the related literature on collection studies, the emphasis in this study is placed mainly on the way that collections and collecting objects can motivate reflection on a new way of, on the one hand, inducing museum practitioners to seek more inclusive and open ways and methods of interpreting the past remains, and on the other, influencing non-experts such as locals and the wider public to adopt a holistic attitude to approaching and understanding their heritage. To achieve these goals, what is needed is the recognition of a broadening of the roles and aims of the museum as a social institution within a society and an admission of the 'power' of the museum to change and fundamentally impact on the social, cultural and economic development of modern societies, especially at a local level.

This study has stressed that the preservation and management of antiquities in Greece is the full responsibility of the state through a networking of central and regional services and a number of legal principles forming the framework of study, research, and protection of antiquities (as discussed in chapter II). However, it should be stated that collecting activities in a private sphere have been expressed in two forms in the Greek territory: first, collections that were mainly created by wealthy people at the beginning of the 20th century, becoming ultimately the primary sources for the creation of a considerable number of significant museums (mainly in Athens) rich in antiquities and remains of the past. These museums today are either recognized by the state as private museums (funded partly by the state), such as the Benaki Museum and the Goulandris of Cycladic Art (both in Athens), or their collections have been placed under the administrative regulation of the state (state museums), such as the museum of Asian art in Corfu. Secondly, there are collections which have given rise to numerous ethnological and folk life museums, which are supervised by the state. The above categories together constitute the image of private collecting in Greece today[178]. It should be noted that in the state's

[178] Another category of non-state museums are the Ecclesiastic museums whose study and research are allowed to be performed by the related archaeological service of the Ministry, though the ownership rests with the monastery or church to which they belong as 'sacred objects' Laws 590/1977 and 2557/1997 for a detailed discussion see Βουδούρη 2003.

attempt to control the illegal trafficking of antiquities, interest has been directed to the private collections predominantly containing objects from ancient times. This includes measures and legal principles which regulate the function and the aims of the above collections as museum collections and the framework in which the collectors are allowed to act within the museum context in order to offer to society (Law 3028/2002 articles 31 and 45).

However, the majority of private collections were created at a regional level and mostly consist of objects from traditional Greek heritage, often reflecting the ideology of historical continuity (as discussed in chapter III). Given that observation, this study considers these decentralized cases to be interesting for addressing issues related to the development of concepts of locality, memory and identity and to investigate how these concepts are articulated in a socio-cultural context. Although most of these collections are not based on specific taxonomies and typologies of material culture, but rather are created in a random and scattered way, based on the principle of gathering and accumulating everything old, they nevertheless sketch a significant public tendency to preserve and to protect something precious, memorable, or worth remembering from the past. The act of collecting objects of traditional heritage started to emerge in Greece mainly after World War II and especially during the 1970s and 1980s when rural life was being replaced by the civic life of big cities and people wished to have memories from a recent past. Also, historical events with sociological and anthropological dimensions such as these of the Greek population exchanges of Asia Minor in 1922-1923 and during the Balkan wars of 1912-1913 marked the economic and social life of the newly established Greek nation and formed new anthropological landscaping of the country. These events were exactly the stimuli for the people to 'keep their past alive', establishing their rootedness by accumulating and gathering tangible and intangible objects regarded as channels of communication. The collectors used to be either individuals or local unions and cultural communities, whose role was the gathering of objects mainly representing rural economic and social contexts for people in the regions. This activity took a more official and carefully researched form when the systematic study of traditional culture of Greece started through the development of the discipline of anthropology and ethnography in academic terms, as we discussed in the chapter III. By then, a huge quantity of objects dating from the post-Byzantine period until the beginning of 20th century had been found by researchers studying and documenting the remains of the folk life of Greeks. These objects have created the main core of the local private folk life museums which have the strongest identity associations with the recent past. The aim of these museums was related to the fostering of the sense of belonging and the concept of locality linked and legitimized by reference to a recent memorable past, rather than to a nationalistic distant glorious past. 'Their' past was a past that they could remember and in which they could recall historical events and personal histories through the 'metaphors' of the objects (Saunders 2002). But mainly it was a sedimented, emotional, and personal past, replete with experiences and memories that could be made alive again through the museums' activities and local exhibits, facilitating the interactive relations between the producers of the past and the consumers of the present. Considering the above aspects, it is important to observe the way that the museum, its functions and its methods are changed and adapted to integrate the needs and the pursuits of the local context.

III. LOCAL HISTORY EXHIBITIONS AS AN *AIDE-MÉMOIRE*

In the light of the last observation, it is interesting to reflect on the recognition of the museums as *aide-mémoires*, or as memory-spaces or places where memories are recreated. To understand the way that memory is developed and reshaped within the museum context, it is necessary to explore the creation of local history exhibitions. Based on a project I conducted while pursuing research and study for the creation of a number of museum exhibitions, I have engaged in museum discourse, which challenged me to recognize the multi-faceted character of the museum as a social institution operating in a local framework, and to seek new ways to foster inclusive and integrating strategies in the management of museological planning.

The project, called the 'museum exhibitions of Ouranoupolis', was funded by the 3rd European Funding Framework Support and carried out by the 10th Ephorate of Byzantine Antiquities. It consisted of a number of restoration and museum activities focusing on the transformation into a museum of a Byzantine tower (tower of Prosforiou) located in the eastern peninsula (Mount Athos) of Chalkidiki, Northern Greece[179]. Due to the significance of the Byzantine tower as evidence of the Byzantine past, closely related, geographically and historically, to the important archaeological place of Mount Athos, emphasis was initially placed on the creation of exhibitions focusing on the historical and informational presentation of the Byzantine culture of the Mount Athos monasteries and the pre-Mount Athos area remains of the post-Byzantine period. However, further study and research on the development of a museological scenario that potentially could cover a wider range of chronological periods, on the one hand, and would enable us to include broader approaches to the existing material evidence, on the other, came to the forefront of the exhibition planning. As the principal researcher/organizer for the museological project, I wanted to pursue the creation of exhibitions that would inform the visitor historically and diachronically about the heritage of the area, but at the same time to stress the role of the locality through the recognition of the museum not only as a place where the glorious ancient past was kept, but rather as a place of memory, where a more personal past could be reshaped and experienced. To reach that goal, among other research and documentary study of the archaeological material derived from the excavations in the area, ethnological research on a local collection was initiated in order to capture the historical profile of the region.

Historically, the area of Ouranoupolis witnessed the same periods as those in Mount Athos (discussed in the previous chapter), as it is located exactly at the boundaries of the Holy Mountain. Archaeological evidence from Prehistoric times until the post-Byzantine period showed that the region has been inhabited

[179] The museum project consisted of the creation of exhibitions dedicated to 1) the Prehistory 2) the historical times 3) Byzantine and post-Byzantine period and 4) the early modern times (end of 19th and beginning of 20th centuries).

throughout that time due to the close relations with the mountain. Besides, the excavation in recent years of one of the first Byzantine monasteries, the monastery of Moni Zygou outside the administrative boundaries of the Mount, indicates the religious importance of the area during those times. The recent historical past of the region was marked by the settlement of Greek refugees coming from Asia Minor in 1922, who produced new development and new economic and socio-cultural perspectives in the area. This facet of the local history of the area has never been researched, expressed, or presented in local terms by a representation of this recent past that the locals felt more attached to and which they felt needed to be expressed[180].

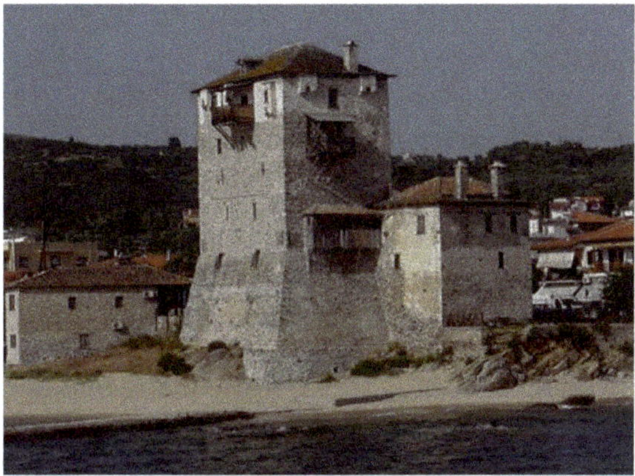

Figure 1: The Byzantine Tower of Ouranoupolis, Chalkidiki

Within the above framework, our concern was to create a mélange of means through which local memory could be recreated. Those means consisted of archival documentation, oral traditions, customs and practices, ethnographic mementoes that were found in a local collection (that of the Lochs). Having been an active archaeologist for years and being challenged by the opportunity and necessity of this project, I conducted the study of the collection, and encountered and engaged with the question of what was 'worthy of memory' (Alcock 2002) in order to integrate this material into the suggested museological scenario of a state museum. It should be noted that my research focused on those practices which were essentially associated with the life (customs, practices) of the refugees and constituted vivid affirmations of their local identity. In this investigation, a key element was my personal approach and communication with the locals in order to explore their attitudes and the values that they ascribe to a recent past. What is interesting to stress is the fact that so far locals' perceptions of the past have been closely related to and associated with an authored past, the image of the imposing Byzantine heritage of Mount Athos, which has always been and continues to be a

180 According to the research I conducted during the museum-study planning, a number of people who claimed forcefully that their recent history was not presented adequately and that they would be willing participants in any attempt to express their local traditional heritage.

source of national and international interest. In the museum's attempts to integrate a more local past into its museological scenario, the local public found a perfect opportunity to express their emotional attachment and to rebuild their own memories localizing them in objects and places.

Based on the recognition that museums have the ability to trigger individual memories and personal experiences, the exhibition, which was dedicated chronologically to early modern times in Ouranoupolis, was organised around a traditional practice which has been treated as symbolic and has functioned as an identifier for the community of refugees, and especially for women. This is the art of making traditional rugs, unique in their designs and their quality as they used natural substances for the dying of the wool (see figure 2). This is a practice that people were to use in their homes within their daily life and which, through the exhibition-making, has become an exhibit evoking nostalgia and emotional reaction. Crucially important to the presentation of these traditional household practices has been the role of the couple Loch, whose private collection constituted the primary source of the exhibition. The couple Loch lived for years in the tower (1928-1982), where they also died, and their name was connected with the village and the locals, who they helped in their first years of settlement in the new area. The idea of the re-learning of the art of rug making belongs to the persistence and creativity of Mrs Joice Loch who helped the local residents by providing the means for them to recall past ways of living and to acquire again their past practices and customs. These historical manifestations constituted the core elements for the story-telling of the exhibition, aiming to provide the stimulation which would enable the locals and the visitors to respond with an emotional engagement to the presented past.

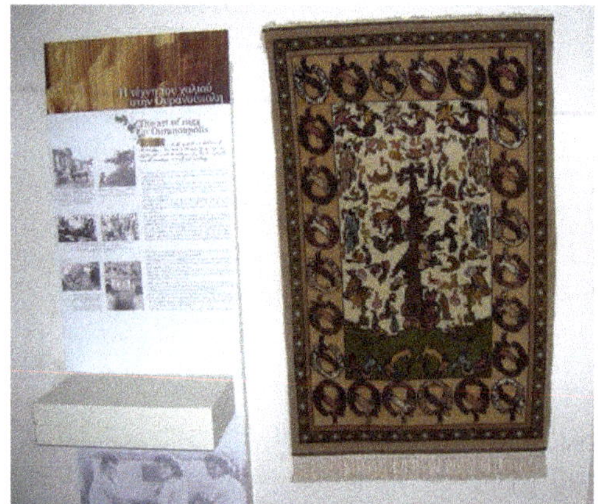

Figure 2: Ouranoupolis Tower, Lochs Exhibition
The Art of Rugs in Ouranoupolis

Recognising the assertion that the museum space is active in the making of meaning (Macleod 2005), the two rooms in the Byzantine tower dedicated to the early modern history of Ouranoupolis have attempted to re-create a recent past in which the tower itself plays its role. So, in one of these rooms a small-scale reconstruction of the room as it was when Mrs. Joice Loch was living there was carried out in order to connect the past activities that occurred in the tower with present practices and feelings (see figure 3). This sort of representation had a positive response from the public, as the room managed to capture the atmosphere of the era and trigger individual memories and personal experiences. Many locals who lived through that period have visited the exhibitions and engaged in a rebuilding of their memories from events and celebrations that occurred in the tower, relating their lives to the life of the tower-monument. For them it was not perceived only as a monument that is authorized to tell the stories of the past, but rather it is part of their daily lives which is replete of memories and is a place where community life is celebrated. Its transformation into a museum has facilitated this process and it has played the role of a *lieu de mémoire*, a place where the past is not frozen but is active in historical understanding through the re-enactments of tangible and intangible elements of local cultures. It is interesting to note at this point that during the documentary research for the project and its implementation, the interest on the part of the local residents was aroused by the representation of 'their recent, local past' rather than by the presentation of the other periods (Prehistoric, Classical, or Byzantine). They enthusiastically embraced the challenge to engage in this process of recollection and the production of stories in this way, either by providing information and objects, or by giving consultancy and confirmation of the accuracy of some texts which provided the evidence. I would say that it came as a surprise for many of the locals that an institutionalized place such as a state museum (Byzantine Tower) would take such an initiative to include facets of the local recent past and to become open and accessible not only for the consumption of historical information derived from different periods of time, but also for these methods and practices of reproduction and dissemination which might lead to a wider understanding and a greater affective engagement with the recent past (Gregory and Witcomb 2007).

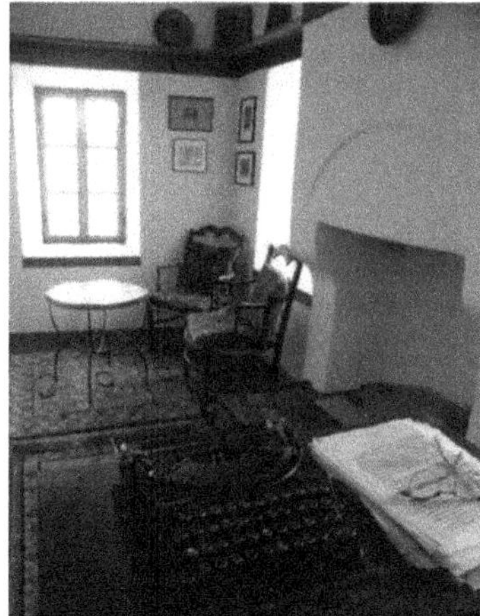

Figure 3: Ouranoupolis Tower, Lochs Exhibition. Reconstruction of the room.

On the part of the agents of the museological and museographical scenario-study team, the decision to integrate a local historical collection and exhibition into a state museum proved to be a thought-provoking initiative which challenged the traditional and well-established image of the museum, whose primary role was to present and celebrate impressive and glorious facets of the Greek past provoking admiration and contemplation. This attempt has been implemented under the shadow of many conflicts among archaeologists and archaeologist-museologists, which is indicative of the discursive nature of archaeology and the museum practice. The former were representatives of the traditional view of the museum exhibition to show the past just as a sequence of events, celebrating the artworks of different pasts, while the latter favoured the introduction of a more holistic approach focusing on the integration of multiple aspects. By attempting to incorporate into the museum narratives and manifestations, practices and experiences that belong to a more familiar and local historical past, the museum managed to express its dynamic and potential character, its capacity to be transformed into a place which is able to communicate multiple messages, to invoke multiple approaches and to foster alternative visions of history and culture. Additionally, we may argue that the creation of local history exhibitions and their integration into archaeological museum scenarios, given the widely recognised public response that they have received, reveal clearly the tendency of the audience to localize their own past and project it into the present in order to acquire a better understanding. The experience of a nostalgic and emotionally charged recent past creates a different spectrum on which the museum can be seen as a place that enables them to communicate their own histories and interpret their own cultures, thus encouraging the diversity of narrated stories and the multivocality of meanings, as we will see in the next section.

IV. The Ethnological Museum of Thrace, Alexandroupolis: Making Histories and Identities in Museum Exhibitions

The Ethnological Museum of Thrace is situated in north-eastern Greece in the city of Alexandroupolis on the borders with Turkey and Bulgaria. It was founded in 2001 and administratively is classified with the non-state as a private museum supervised by the state[181], but has its own foundational constitution. However, according to the new Law and the regulations related to the official accreditation of an institution as a museum (as was discussed in chapter II) the museum's planning exhibition programs and management are supervised and controlled by the related Directorate of the Ministry, which in this case is the Directorate of Cultural-Traditional Heritage. The Ethnological Museum of Alexandroupolis in recent years has become one of the most important private museums, with an increasing interest in collecting the tangible and intangible heritage (songs, oral tales, customs etc.) of

[181] Document of the Directorate of Cultural-Traditional Heritage, Ministry of Culture ΥΠΠΟ/ΔΙΑΛΑΠ/Γ/4403/65150/8.12.2000 concerning the supervision of Folk life museums and collections

the wider area of Thrace and in activities which create an interesting framework for discussion of the role of a local museum in the representation of cultures. Its location is significant, as in past years up to today the whole area constitutes a crossroads of cultural, social, and economic interactivities which define the contemporary identities.

The History of the Site

Greek Thrace constitutes only a small part of the geographical and historical Great Thrace whose borders, from the 1st century until the 19th century, were defined by the mountains of Aimos (North), by the Aegean Archipelagos and Propontis (South), by the Black Sea (East) and by the Nestos River (West). According to the historians of ancient times and the evidence of archaeological research, the culture of the ancient Thracians had elements deriving from different tribes and peoples. According to Herodotus, it had a numerous population of various united tribes (Γιαννακίδου 2002). In 46 AD, Thrace came under Roman conquest. In the Byzantine time, Thrace witnessed a great period, as Constantinople, the capital of the Empire, was located within its territory, resulting in the growth of the population which consisted, apart from Greeks, also of Slavs and Bulgarians (6th and 7th centuries) in its northern geographical part. During the Ottoman conquest (14th to 15th century) the southern part of Thrace was inhabited by Turkish people and the image of Great Thrace took the form of a multicultural mosaic in which Greeks, Bulgarians, and Turks cohabitated peacefully together. Due to the Balkan Wars at the end of the 19th century, Thrace, as an economic crossroads and place of political and strategic importance, was divided into three parts in three countries, resulting in great population movements and a huge number of refugees. The northern part (the so-called Eastern Roumelia) joined the country of Bulgaria in 1885; the south-western part joined Greece in 1920; and the south-eastern part joined Turkey in 1922. These historical events caused major population movements, resulting in waves of refugees and exchanges that led to the contemporary administrative situation of the area. Today in Greek Thrace, as well as in Greece, there are several different communities (numbering around 350,000 people) including Muslims such as Turkish Slav and Roma Pomaks, Armenians, and Jews, who define their identities through social and cultural interactions.

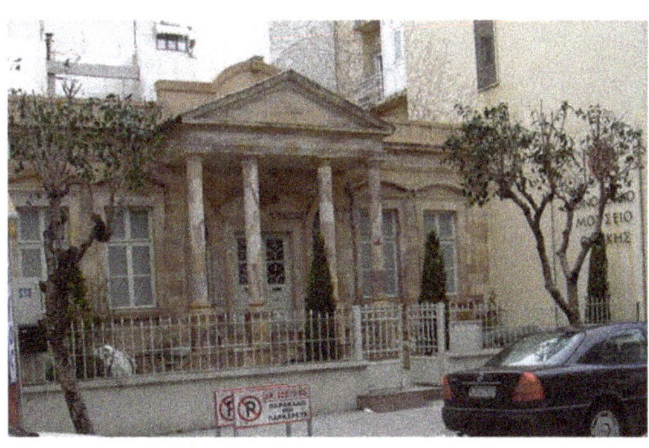

Figure 4: The Ethnological Museum of Thrace (Alexandroupolis)

These minority communities are dispersed throughout the three administrative prefectures of Thrace (nomoi)[182] and live and produce their own local histories and social relations, thus defining their identities. They constitute the source communities (Peers and Brown 2003) upon which new forms of research and the new dimensions of the role of the museum in modern society are increasingly focusing in order to turn the museum experts' interests into more inclusive practices, as this study is attempting to investigate.

The Collector and the Collections

The collector Aggeliki Giannakidou started her collecting activity in 1967 when she settled in Alexandroupolis for the first time. Her interest has been focused on the research and study of the traditional tangible and intangible heritage of the area. 'I found myself very lucky to live in Thrace in a period where the traditional way of life was a 'living' reality', Mrs. Giannakidou remarks, stressing her duty to document these witnesses of multiple 'pasts' (Γιαννακίδου 2002:7). She has focused on the collection of ethnographic material relating to rural life derived from personal archives in houses kept as relics by the owners, natives and refugees, acting as strong memories reminding them of their roots and family origins. The main stimulus for the collector was that sense of 'the place, the topos, the memory, the space, a place of coexistence and co-living' (Giannakidou 2007)[183]. The primary stage of her research lasted for five years and involved conducting a thorough study by traveling to distant villages and isolated areas in order to come into contact with those communities and identify them. It was a difficult task for her, as she confessed, but quite rewarding as 'I experienced for myself different ways of living and realized the multi-cultural face of modern Thrace' (ibid.). For her it was fascinating to work with people coming from different cultural and political backgrounds and to try to map the differences and similarities among them. Her anthropological research, from the beginning until the present, has been supported scholarly by many national and foreign institutions (universities, archaeological services) and has elicited responses from many local unions and groups studying the socio-cultural landscaping of the area. Her collaboration with source communities was more effective than she expected, which led to an establishment of a network of relationships that could offer valuable advice and consultation to the museum management.

[182] The prefectures (nomoi) of Xanthi, Rodopi, and Evros.
[183] Personal interview with Mrs Giannakidou. Alexandroupolis 27/5/2007

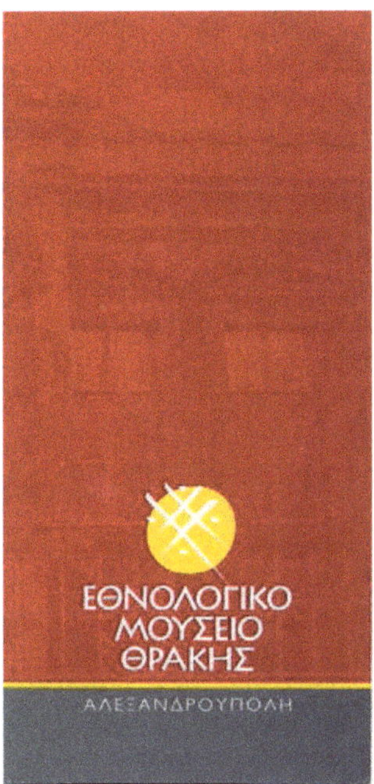

Figure 5: The Leaflet of the EMT.

The trust-building process with museum sources is considered one of the main priorities of the museum curator, as important as writing and story-telling. It is in the curator's hands to establish relationships which are based on full respect for different cultures, customs and religions, and to show the potential of the museum to include and present multiple pasts and messages. It is of great importance for the collector to approach these differences or this otherness not only in academic terms but also in a sensitive and distinctive way which allows community members to see the museum researchers as people who seek to promote cross-cultural dialogues and learning rather than creating databases of material cultures. In that way, the museum as an institution acquires the image of being a place where the curatorial praxis enables the incorporation and integration into its exhibition projects of the source community's needs and perspectives. Considering this and taking into account the socio-political context of the wider area as defined through the centuries, the above pursuit would be a challenge for any collector-curator seeking to conduct research projects in order to explore and represent the plurality of cultural histories, given the political disputes and conflicts that have existed and have been cultivated in the area, driven mostly by isolated nationalistic views. However, as this study suggests, a museum could play a very important role in balancing conflicts and lessening disputes by creating a place of expression and intercultural interaction, a place of 'contact zones' (Clifford 1997; Herle 2003; Boast et al. 2001; Boast 1997).

The collections consist of a broad range of tangible and intangible forms of evidence of cultures. So far, more than 5000 objects and photographic archives have been collected and kept in the museum; these are dated from 1681 to the beginning of the 21st century. The objects range from traditional clothing to household items and tools that are representative of a rural pre-industrial way of living. Also, bigger items, such as constructions related to the production of food or clothing are gathered in order to document practices and customs used in past times in the different communities' environments. Another category of objects is that related to the cult practiced in Thrace, such as portable icons and books. Of great importance is the archive of sound-recorded and video-recorded material documenting the contacts and interviews undertaken by the collector during the research, which is used not only as an informational source but also as a basis for the creation of a number of digital exhibits with authentic material integrating them with the museological scenario of the exhibitions.

It should be stated that the collection has been based on thorough research and a systematic study of the documented material gathering all the identification information relating to the objects and creating classifications and taxonomies in a registration system in order to facilitate the exhibition process and the structuring of story-telling. Mrs Giannakidou stated, 'My aim is to safeguard every original item that has "produced" the place of Thrace, to present and promote its *distinctive and multiply-shaped expression of communities, "in origins"*, as it is inscribed for centuries in the wider area' (Γιαννακίδου 2002:7, emphasis added). The objects of her collection bear witness and constitute an introduction to a local history formed by multiple meanings and stories which need to be told. The museum, based on her collection, undertook the goal of implementing and creating exhibitions and museum activities aiming, on the one hand, to represent many 'voices', many cultures and the many local histories of communities, and on the other, to foster the social role of the museum and a radical re-envisioning of the nature of museums.

Architectural Script and Display Philosophy

The museum found shelter in one of the many houses in a neoclassical style which used to be found in Alexandroupolis during the 19th century. According to the outdoor inscription, it was built in 1899, and it was used as a second residence by a wealthy man named Altinalmazi. It was fully restored and renovated following the architectural elements of the house by a family of collectors in 1998, and it was redesigned internally to house the exhibitions of the museum following the initial organization of the building. The rooms were organized in terms of themes according to the museological scenario. At some points, the limited use of showcases gives the sense that there are not clear lines and categories among the thematic units as developed within the place. In many cases the objects appear as though they have been left there without purpose, but they are deliberately placed in order to stimulate the visitor's imagination, not following a kind of taxonomy or classification system but rather to make him/her recall memories from a recent past and often to make comparisons and references to modern items of daily use. This practice of 'letting the objects speak' is often found in exhibitions of folk life objects where the curator, using the relatively recent production of the material ethnologically as local evidence, attempts to trigger visitors' or locals' minds to reflect upon the functional and spatial identification of the displayed items. This 'museological' technique is also observed in some exhibitions of archaeological material, often presented with the purpose of comparing archaeological and modern objects and thus aiming at the production of educational experience (as part of the design of education programs).

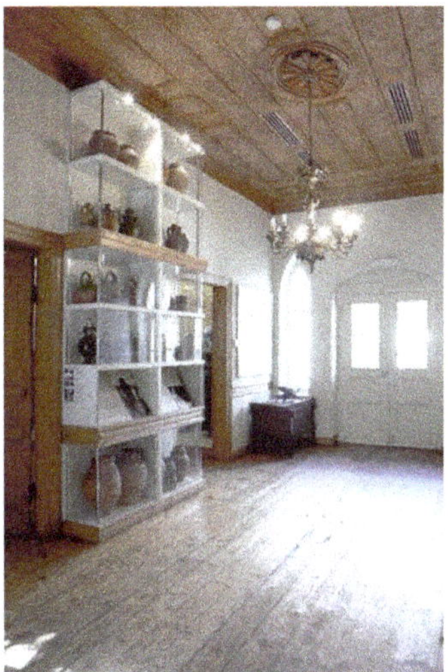
Figure 6: EMT: The internal rooms

The separation of the exhibition units is done mainly by large introductory panels and the spatial sequence of the rooms creating a thematic linear museum narrative. The use of charts and photographs is extensive, providing the visitor with the information needed to get into the story of the exhibition. The exhibitions are developed in three main spaces: the ground floor, the basement and the courtyard, where a rest area and a museum shop are at the disposal of the visitors and rooms are also provided for meetings and educational programmes. Given that the exhibitions are housed in a neoclassical house, the architectural designs of the displays have been subjected to spatial restrictions and compromises. However, the atmosphere of the house in some cases reinforces the exhibition intentions of the curator, who has attempted to create an adequate emotional framework in which the locals can experience and spatially visualize their heritage. So, in the case of the basement rooms, the original (and partly restored) construction built in a traditional way from stones and wood fosters the process of capturing the traditional and rural character of the displayed objects and facilitating the visitors' engagement with the representation of the past and its associations. This is the reason for the curator's introduction of 'sound and smell settings', technical tools and devices to stimulate all the senses of the visitor by transferring him/her to a place of memory and of the remembrance of different episodes of the past. Thus, the museum space becomes dynamic and active using multiple techniques and choices which contribute to the visitor's effort to get involved in the process of understanding and capturing the meaning of past societies.

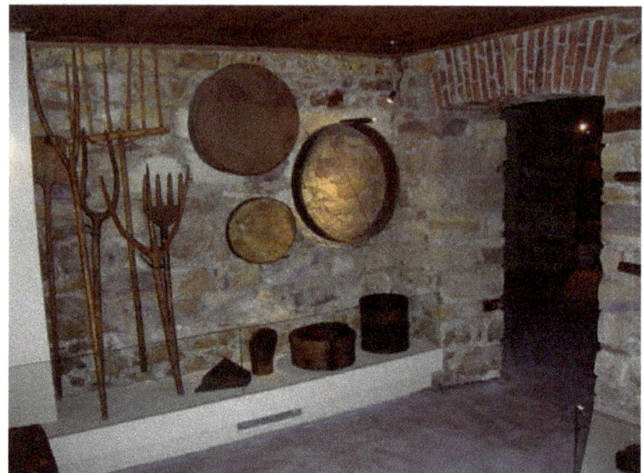

Figure 7: EMT: The exhibition rooms at the Basement

Within the above-described architectural framework and on the basis of an ethnological collection that is rich in tangible and intangible material, the aim of the exhibitions, according to the museological study as planned by the collector, has been to present the economic and social life of people of the area and to activate the visitor's memory enabling him/her to approach and interpret the remains of a recent past. As Mrs Giannakidou has stated:

> 'the primary goal of the museum and its exhibitions was not the preservation of a folklore aspect of life, nor was it only the aesthetically and museologically accepted exhibition of objects, but mainly it was to connect the tradition and the embedded information with the concerns of modern society...by establishing the museum as a reason for a re-evaluation [and re-assessment] of tradition' (Giannakidou 2007)[184].

Considering the above, what is interesting to note is that the collector's pursuit and concern is not only with the museum as a place for displaying beautiful things but mainly making the museum intervene and participate in the modern life of people through its multiple activities.

The thematic units of the exhibitions cover a chronological period from the end of the 17th until the beginning of the 20th century and the displayed material was organized on two axes: first, the linear time of historical presence in Thrace, and second, the agricultural cycle of rural life. Themes like *Clothing, Men's and Women's Costumes, Cults in Thrace,* and *Nutrition (Pre-Industrial Baking in*

---

[184] Personal interview with Mrs Giannakidou, Alexandroupolis 27/5/2007.

Thrace) make up the main exhibition groups of objects displayed on the ground floor. The texts of the panels using a number of photographs and a map adequately provide all the information about the history of the related objects. The curator's primary aim is to give complete information of the identification of the items, such as costumes, which belong to the community and embody its symbolic values within the society. The display provides comparative information of distinctive elements, e.g. stressing the wide range of designs and techniques of clothing, thus indicating the multifarious influences that the area has received through time. That intention flows into almost all of the developments of the thematic units, making apparent the goal of the museum, i.e. to present a multi-voiced approach rather than a monolithic one. The rooms in the basement are dedicated to rural activities related to *Cultivation, Honey, Cereals, Wine and Tobacco*, addressed to a number of rural occupations that local residents in the area still practice following the traditional techniques and methods of their ancestors. Thus, the local visitors who would probably be members of a 'source community' interact with the exhibition messages through the evocative role of objects and they make efforts to introduce their own approaches in the identification of the material culture of past societies. This engagement could have a twofold result: on the one hand, it can facilitate the visitor in tracing the distinct elements of his/her community and to define its identity and, on the other, it helps them to locate themselves within a modern social framework where diversities and multiple cultures might coexist and produce stories. Recognizing that point, it should be noted that the role of the curators and the museum people is becoming significantly demanding in respect of the process of displaying objects and cultures and making efforts to balance inequalities in the representation and interpretation of past remains.

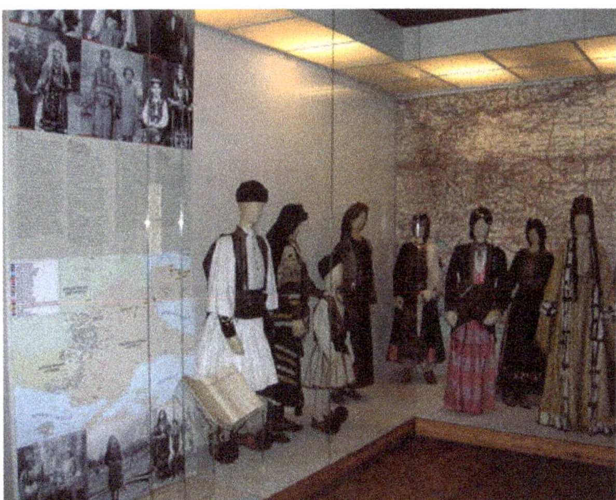

Figure 8: EMT: The Exhibition *Clothing, Men's and Women's Costumes.*

The huge body of recorded material of testimonies, historical events, songs, customs and other traditional narratives of the locals constituted the primary source for the creation of a considerable number of videos which accompany the displayed objects, and which are exhibits on their own. Developed and produced by experts, they present in a very vivid way stories and tales of different communities and elaborate themes such as *'Head-covering and Symbols'; 'Religious life in Thrace'; 'Calendar of Religious Festivities;, 'The History of Thrace'; 'The Natural Environment and Traditional Crops from Prehistoric Times to the Present Day'*; and *'Places of Worship in Evros Prefecture'*, to name but a few. Moving in the same direction, the museum has conducted (and still is conducting) research aiming to create four databases concerning: a) Historical events, dating from the era of the appearance of the Ottomans in Thrace to the Greek civil war, within the broader area of Thrace until 1922, and the historical events concerning Greek Thrace after 1922; b) Personalities living in the (extended) historical area of Thrace until 1922, and those in Greek Thrace after 1922; c) Nutrition, with various categories like devotional festivities, seasonal cycle, populations; d) Immigrants and displacement of populations after the Balkan wars. It is worth mentioning that one of the produced videos in the form of a documentary film titled '*The bride of the mirror*' was awarded the first prize in the 12th International Festival of Movies and Culture in Patra, Greece in 2010, underscoring the efforts of the museum to present Thracian history in a representative, intellectual and artistic way 'which is inspired by the primitive memory and light embedded in the culture of Thrace' (Giannakidou 2010)[185].

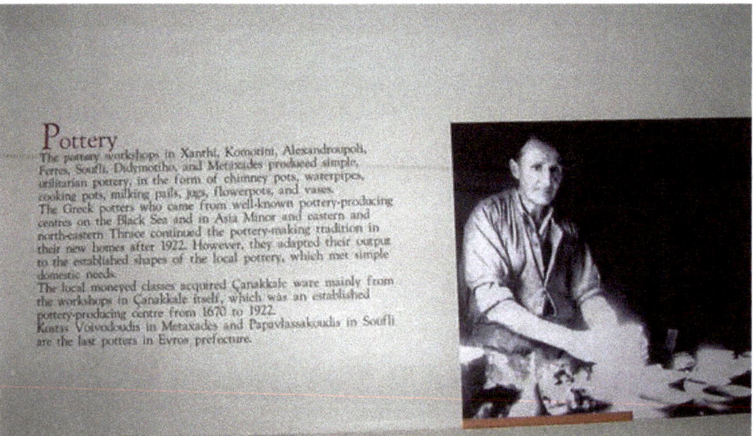

Figure 9: EMT: Panel from the Exhibition *Household*

The use of new technological digital means on the part of the museum is pursued extensively in an effort to present the cultures of the specific geographical area in multiple ways. The production of videos, we might say, constitutes an immediate and very vivid means of communication due to the combination of sound and

[185] The research and production for the film was done by A. Giannakidou and the producer D. Pantazi. Ελευθεροτυπία [*Eleutherotypia*] 13/10/2010 (digital edition).

picture, and also manages to evoke emotions and sentiments from the audience. Additionally, through the narration of stories and tales told by locals, it is made possible for the visitor to understand and conceive of this story-telling as an expression of elements and features which constitute the distinctive traits of different groups and communities, such as the language and linguistic forms created as part of their intangible heritage. Furthermore, the use of new technology tools in the management and the diffusion of the gathered information make it easier for the curator to adopt a more multidisciplinary approach to collection interpretation, as well as making the museum more open and democratic through increased public access to non-sensitive information.

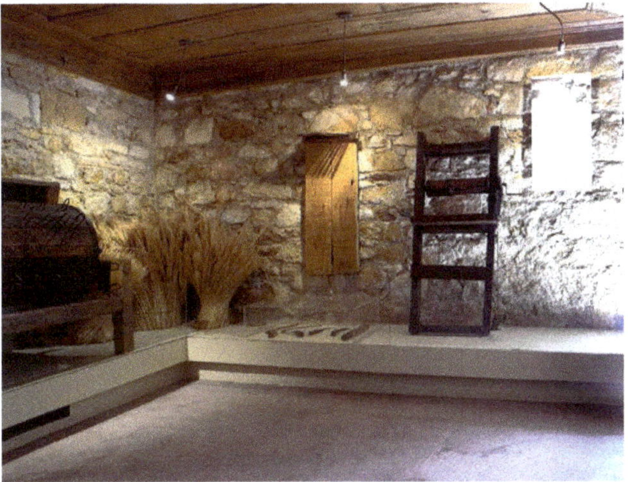

Figure 10: EMT: The Exhibition *Cultivation-Cereals*

Based on the last point, it should be noted that the collector, from the beginning of the collecting activity, recognized the significance of the intangible character of these communities and made many efforts to document (by recording) songs, customs, hymns and languages in order to safeguard them from extinction and to make them available for further research. For that purpose, the museum created a virtual library[186] through which the user can browse through the books and files on local history and tradition, catalogued in terms of themes, and pursue research or just to become better informed and obtain more insight on the area of interest. Added to the above, the museum's activities were enriched by an impressive educational museum curriculum consisting of numerous educational activities and learning processes addressed to a wide range of ages. These initiatives have been a particular priority among the collector's aims, who placed great emphasis on the principle that within the museum 'the child visitors' experiences, their social reference, and their critical thought should be fostered...they can find the opportunity to learn, decode and evaluate what socially and individually define

[186] Funded by the Information Society Project 2006.

themselves' (Giannakidou 2007)[187]. The Ethnological Museum of Thrace in Alexandroupolis, which was nominated and commended in 2005 as the European Museum of the year, represents a category of museums and collections in Greece which are making efforts to change and to adopt new roles and forms that reflect alternative approaches to heritage developing in local contexts. These new tendencies are contributing to the framework of new museum policies and contexts that are evolving in the Greek spectrum of archaeology and heritage management and which practitioners and museum people should take into consideration.

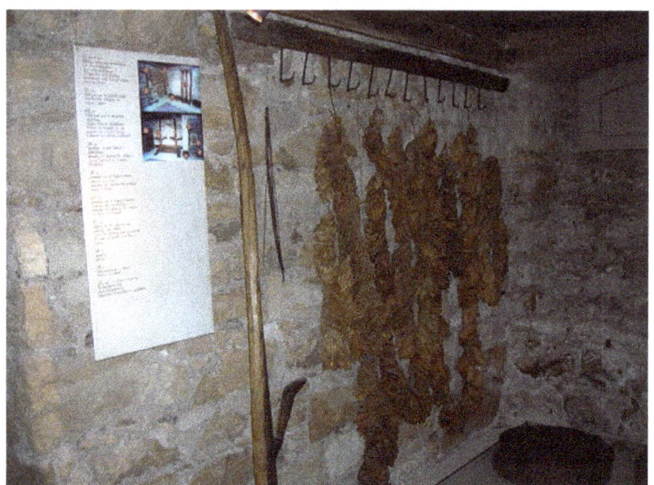

Figure 11: EMT. The Exhibition Tobacco

V. The Potential of Private Collections in Empowering Cultural Diversity and Intercultural Dialogue

It is important to understand, considering the above discussion of collecting and reflecting on the museum's potential to become a more inclusive place, that a democratization of the museum philosophy should be pursued. That recognition should be profoundly based on the vision of museums as places of representing different pasts, cultures and local communities, places of dialogue where the members of various cultures could 'sit well with each other' (Shelton 2003:192). The significance of that acceptance of diverse cultures and their expression in social places and institutions such as museums is underpinned by the principles defined by the UNESCO Universal Declaration on Cultural Diversity 2002 and extended in 2005 with the Convention on the Protection and Promotion of the Diversity of Cultural Expressions. In these principles, there is expressed the recognition that cultures should be approached as the 'common heritage of humanity' (UNESCO 2002) and it is of great importance to 'ensure harmonious interactions among people

[187] Personal interview with Mrs Giannakidou, Alexandroupolis 27/5/2007.

and groups with plural, varied and dynamic cultural identities as well as their willingness to live together' (ibid.). These official statements are also strengthened by the ICOM policy statement on museums and on cultural diversity which declares that 'museums have increasingly become forums for the promotion of community relations and peace' (ICOM 1997) and the Code of Ethics on the ethical duty of museums to work in close collaboration with the communities and to acquire 'a character beyond that of ordinary property, which may include strong affinities with national, regional, local, ethnic, religious or political identity' (ICOM 2006).

In the above statements, it is important to locate the efforts that are being made internationally to recognise the engagement of the community relations agenda, multiculturalism and diversity in museums, heritage and culture discussions (Crook 2007). To what extent the museums can become an arena and forum for the promotion of good relations, encouraging the principles of cultural diversity and multiculturalism, is a matter of concern for those modern experts and collectors who seek to implement a democratic and multivocal museum policy. This concept involves, on the one hand, the strategies and methods of decision-making management processes taken by the collectors or curators as an authorized agency to represent the material culture in museum exhibitions and, on the other, the members of the 'source communities' (the locals, the members of minorities), who are the 'guardians' of tangible and intangible elements of their heritage and the museum 'suppliers'. It is on the relationship and on the building of a framework of collaboration and close co-operation between these two agents that the attempt of the museums' exhibitions to become real communication bridges of an intercultural dialogue depends. It falls to museum professionals to establish a fundamental network of collecting and documentary activities which would respect the emotional and appropriation right of communities' attachment to their past, while at the same time promoting a museum context in which different and various pasts and backgrounds are able to have their say and play their part. In this way, the museum as an institution should follow new directions in developing its ability to re-create stories and meanings of the past. These directions could include a reassessment of the role of the curator as the dominant 'agent' within the museum context and the decisive involvement in the story-telling context of more voices.

In the case of Greece, it should be noted that the museum policy has been formed by the disciplinary approaches of the traditional views of archaeology (as has been discussed in earlier chapters) focusing mainly on the representation of a Greek sequence consisting of the ancient past or pasts and their evolution through time. Therefore, little room has been left for the formulation of a framework including alternative approaches, especially in the representation of the recent past and multiple heritages, as studied and researched by the disciplines of ethnography and anthropology. However, in recent years a remarkable shift, mainly in the ethnographic museums and those presenting facets of the recent past and cultures[188],

[188] Examples can be mentioned such as the museum of Asia Minor Culture Φιλιώ Χαιδεμένου in Athens or the Museum of Sarakatsanon (Σαρακατσάνων), the museum of Roma in Alexandroupolis and many ethnological museums all over the country which reflect mostly differences in customs and practices of a community rather than religious or ethnic diversities. It is also worth mentioning that the museum of

has been made in their attempts to represent various voices and local histories in a different, more inclusive way. As we have seen in the above cases, this practice is mostly promoted within the spectrum of private collections in which the administrative status can be considered more flexible and adaptive. However, a considerable tendency can also be observed within the framework of state museums to conduct research on private, individual collections related to early modern times, and to integrate them into the museological programme of the museum, thus introducing new approaches to interpreting and presenting the past. Thus, local communities, mostly in decentralized areas, are empowered to express their locality, their sense of belonging, and to define themselves within the present socio-cultural and political context through the biographies of the social system of objects which are carrying, on behalf of them, the communities' messages and identities. It is interesting to note at this point that the collected and displayed objects have ceased to be seen as objects of art but have turned into living memories and signifiers of identities, which are put in a museum context in order to produce intercultural interaction and dialogues. That aspect challenges the archaeologists, anthropologists and the museum people in Greece by forcing them to re-consider the role of the museum in modern society and demands that they pay attention to questions of how identity and difference are represented and approached within the museum environment.

Locating Identities

The examples of museum collections which have been discussed above illustrate the impacts that cultural distinctions and identities can have on the museum concept when it is used in different socio-cultural contexts and when it is adapted to pursuing the local community's benefit. In the example of the museum of Thrace it is interesting to reflect upon that concept, given the existence of communities with different religious and national backgrounds and heritages which define their identity in the present.

As discussed earlier in this chapter, the area of Thrace constitutes a palimpsest of heritage sites covering many periods and it is interesting to note that part of that heritage is associated with the Ottoman period, with which many of the present minorities are identified by the traces of the past that are expressed culturally and socially within the societies in which they live. These conditions automatically create a significant framework with respect to the way they perceive and locate their past and produce articulations of different facets of the past. So, Turkish or Muslim minorities living in the Greek Thracian territory live and experience the Ottoman traces in a different way from the past remains from the glorious periods of the Greek past and they produce and reproduce emotional attachment and significance in relation to these local heritages[189]. However, the duty of care and preservation of these traces is protected by the official heritage policy, according to the current

Asia Minor Culture in Athens has been the honored museum for the International Day of Museums 2011 in Greece, also indicating the considerable shift in museum policy and attitudes in Greece.

[189] For further discussion on these issues see Demetriou 2010.

Law, and many buildings from that period have been reconstructed in order to house museum collections or other cultural manifestations. It is worth mentioning here that the process of selection and the significance of the past is not merely an aspect or an attitude that can characterize the academic or official accounts of heritage management but one that can also be expressed within a local spectrum of ways of valuing and interpreting the past.

Recognizing the above, it is essential to stress the role of the museum and of local exhibitions in their capacity to empower the representation of cultural diversities and to reinforce the expression of many voices. In the case of Thrace, with its mosaic of cultures, the museum as an institution has to meet the challenge of conducting a cultural diversity policy and constituting a place of balancing conflicts and inequalities. That goal has been mostly reached by the museums of ethnographic cultures, where identities can be traced by the numerous personal collections. For the minority groups, these objects are endowed with identification features of their origins and location and with symbolic and religious values or with socio-political and national meanings. In any case, the museum objects are the markers of their identities, the elements with which they identify them in the past and locate themselves in the present. The museum as a democratic place of polyphony should recognize these needs of communities and should respond to the national and international call for openness and inclusion and the need 'to ensure harmonious interactions among people and groups with plural, varied and dynamic cultural identities as well as their willingness to live together' (UNESCO 2002).

VI. Conclusions

This chapter demonstrated that museums and heritage are engaged in a significant process to convey not only messages and stories of a fragmented institutionalized past but also to express community interests and perceptions. Based on the belief that the exploration and representation of culture is the *raison d'être* for museums, the chapter tried to illuminate different aspects and perspectives on seeing and approaching museum spaces. On one side was the perspective of locals, or 'source communities', who perceive the museums and local heritages as points of reference to symbolize their sense of belonging and to stress the sense of locality, and also as a means to communicate and interact with other members and those on the outside. And, on the other side were the perspectives of the collector and the authorized agent whom seek to explore and motivate new methods and strategies in the collecting process by pursuing close collaboration and continuing co-operation with locals and community groups in order to establish a link between official state management practices, private or individual collecting and local sources of information. For this attempt to succeed, what needs to be achieved is the recognition a) of the complexity and sensitivity of local communities towards 'their' local histories and b) the multiple ways by which communities and minority groups define and locate their identities in the present socio-political human landscape. These should be central issues in our assessment of museums and their purposes 'in order to take account of the dangers that lie in generalising, simplifying or even glorifying community' (Crook 2007:133).

The above considerations are elucidated in Greek territory mainly in the museums of ethnographic material and in regional private collecting activities. The case study of Alexandroupolis is representative of the shifting museum policies within a local spectrum, which attempt to introduce into a Greek context internationally recognized museum practices and theoretical pursuits that encourage and foster the relationships between local communities and museums. Given the socio-political and historical background of the area, a community-based museum policy has proven to be a challenge for the curator and for the locals as well and gave the museum the opportunity to include many voices and acquire multiple roles. It has become a pluralistic, memory-making and identity-expressing place charged with a constant dynamic. And it should be argued that in the last statement lies the future of the museums as an institution and as a place of making histories and meanings within the modern 'palimpsestal' (Olsen 2010) societies, considering that 'the past is not left behind but gathers and folds into the becoming present, enabling different forms of material memory' (Olsen 2010:126).

CHAPTER 6

Archaeological Discourses and Museum Representations of the Past: Conclusions

I. INTRODUCTION

In this chapter, an overall discussion of the issues addressed by this study will be undertaken, attempting to shed some light on the theoretical and practical complexities which have arisen in the research and the study of archaeology as a discipline and the museum as an institution in the meaning-making process. Thus, with reference to the aims and goals of this study, the central issues were to consider how and by whom the action of meaning-making, story-telling, or narrating past histories was produced in archaeological discourses and museum representations, and how the process of archaeology narrating multiple 'pasts' finds expression in the museum practice. We also consider what kinds of relationships and networkings were created by this process and how this defines the role of museum in modern society.

The above considerations are enriched by the recognition of the communicative potential of the agency to represent and interpret the tangible and intangible 'messages' of the past. Thus, the museum is an active, meaning-producing, and powerfully communicative and expressive place of rich dialectical means. An exploration of the roles of the actors, makers, or agents involved in the writing of past stories needs to be undertaken in order to highlight the alternative ways of *seeing*, *being in* and *acting* within a framework where the past remains are managed and projected into the present. So, in a museum context, the *seeing* is related to how we visually perceive and contemplate the traces of the past, the *being in* to how we experience them and *acting* to how we interact with them. Based on the above, we argue that within the museum's argumentative processes of the representation of the past a system of rhetoric is generated, and these persuasive strategies give the opportunity to multiple narratives to be expressed and participate in the communication and dissemination of information.

The chapter continues to stress the changing character of the museum in modern society, supporting the view that it is in a state of constant flux and transformation according to the needs and imperatives of the socio-political and cultural context in which it operates and which it serves. The changing attitudes and shifts in museum and heritage management, as have been observed in the Greek case studies, lead us to reflect on the multifarious possibilities of the museum place as a social institution to give expression to different voices, and on the discursive nature of archaeology as an authorised agency for the study and interpretation of past material. In Greece, there are no clear and distinctive lines between these two fields, and nor should there be, in my opinion; the relationship provides an opportunity for other perspectives and holistic alternatives to be investigated. This is the case for *in situ* museums and the development of 'museumscape' approaches which further progress the theoretical thinking of the museum's goals.

II. Looking at the Aims of the Study

This study explored Greek museum representations of the past in relation to the intellectual histories of the archaeological accounts involved in the investigation of material culture. It has been argued within this work that museums are places of 'power' and are a forum in which an understanding of the past is formulated, interpreted and presented to the public and re-presented and re-interpreted due to the multiple narratives created by multiple recipients and heritage consumers. However, what has been important for this investigation is to locate the mechanisms of how that power is generated and expressed, to identify the socio-politics of museum practices and the poetics of museum strategies, and to consider what kind of networkings and relationships are developed within this process. Focusing on the vast and stimulating amount of antiquities existing in the Greek territory, this study attempted to 'deconstruct' museum constructions by analyzing them in terms of a broad and interdisciplinary framework of studying and managing the past, on the one hand, and, on the other, to scrutinize the 'philosophy' of museum representations and how these can be influenced by various and multi-sided attitudes that relate to the past and the present. An essential concern for the study has been to illustrate the extent to which the Greek archaeological tradition of scholarship has governed the museum process of presenting the past and to define the room that is left for a new shift in thinking and alternative approaches to take to these past histories.

In this context, using the main case studies and various examples drawn from the Greek context, the writer has tried to unmask the process by which Greek museum exhibitions construct, represent and interpret different facets of the Greek past. Concern has mostly been taken to bring in cases from decentralized museums from the area of Northern Greece, in order to investigate museum practices and directions which have given new impetus to the formulation of museum policy in recent years in Greece. Charting the historical background of the genesis of the museums in Greece and defining the legislative and administrative contexts in which they operate, the study has explored the attitudes ascribed to the Greek past by examining its ideological and symbolic role in the shaping of historical framework. The investigation of the valuing of these multiple pasts—global, national, and local—in a Greek context has allowed us to define the socio-political framework within which archaeology, as a discipline of constructing an understanding of the past, and the museum, as a facilitator of disseminating this meaning, operate and produce a meaningful past. The politics of selectiveness that is expressed in any facet of museum and preservation practice indicates the ideological grounding of the archaeological field and the close interrelationship between the socio-politics of the past, the intellectual developments, and museum practice in Greece.

The exploration of case studies has proven revealing in bringing to the surface the theoretical and practical implications of exhibition processes and helping to formulate a basis for the construction of new articulations and dynamic relations between museum spaces/archaeological sites and the public. Thus, through a critical analysis of museum exhibitions, in the first group of case studies, the museum has been examined as an *institution*, as *architecture* and as *narrative*, as we seek to understand its multiple roles (educational, historical and symbolic) in modern society, which serve as social formulations of socio-cultural background. This extended analysis consisted of both practical (regulations and administrative principles) and theoretical considerations of the process of management decision-making, on the one side, and the process of the creating of meanings as conducted in the museum space, on the other. Close attention has been paid to the poetics of museum narratives and the rhetoric of story-telling construction, stressing the persuasive and rhetorical functioning of objects within the exhibition setting as communicative tools and creators of communication channels between the past and the present. Added to that, the concepts of the 'micro' and 'macro' spaces that the objects claim within a museum environment have been pointed out and analyzed in order to define the impact that the spatial narratives, as produced in the museum context, could have on the perception of past stories. Generally, the investigation of the first set of case studies of Greek museum exhibitions is related to the way that past experience is shaped and perceived in an administratively well-established museum institution which, based on its performative ability to present and tell stories, has as its primary goal the visualizing of the Greek past through the tradition of visual representation which is inherent to the discipline of archaeology. Added to that consideration, the administrative organization of the Greek museum, with the adoption of some new principles, is struggling to balance the issues of a) who has the ownership and b) who is responsible for the museums' exhibition planning, an issue that has created many tensions and conflicts within the community of archaeologists. The functioning of objects within the three museums has been based on this visualization of past cultures, where the objects as 'signatures' (Appadurai 2010) create visions of a glorious, emotive, symbolic, ideological and instructive Greek past. That visualization or 'visual expressionism' of the archaeological discipline, operating in different parts of the Greek historical territory, has found fertile ground in the museum's representational place and in its meaning-producing exhibition space.

The role of the archaeological landscape and *in situ* museum practice were concepts which were discussed in the next group of Greek case studies. The discussion emphasized the potentialities of site museums and the conception of the archaeological and historical place as a museum space. It advanced toward the creation of an inclusive framework within which theoretical approaches and intellectual developments of interpretation and representation of material culture, on the one hand, and museum practices and technologies, on the other, were entering into a dialogue where the visitor was not a passive recipient but rather an active one participating in that dialectical process. The narratives as produced in the museum environment can further take a decisively active role in the formation of archaeological discourse as they participate in forming interpretations of the archaeological material. The examination of the case studies was based on the above concept, which recognizes the multivocal and polysemic character of the landscapes (archaeological, historical) and the articulations and associations that have been developed through the inter-connections of museums as institutions and sites as 'referent systems'. The two cases evoke those features and elements that are endowed with historic, symbolic and political values embedded in specific constructions in the past but are projected and experienced under the socio-political conditions of the present. The way that these two cases produce meanings and are perceived by the wider public was highlighted through the exploration of the socio-political values ascribed to the past 'sacred' remains and the examination of the museum narratives produced in the exhibition process. To help this investigation, the introduction of the term 'museumscape' offered a method which could provide new holistic ways of thinking about and perceiving the museum and the archaeological and historical place, where the focus should move to being in a place and to how one can perceive and experience the dynamics of the place. That perspective challenges the traditional roles of the museum and allows the creation of a framework in which archaeological theoretical scholarship could adopt practices and strategies of writing the past which would stimulate and encourage the engagement of the public in the interpretation of the material culture of the past.

The last case considered the museums as memory-presenting places and institutions that are endowed with the task of presenting the tangible and intangible cultural heritage of diverse communities. The museum was examined in terms of its functions and methods which were adapted to suit the needs of a local context. The chosen museums have been investigated within the framework of the given socio-political and historical background of the area, and within the spectrum of private collecting as practiced (in legislative and administrative terms) in Greece. The focus was placed on the exploration of a community-based museum policy conducted by the collectors' management planning in concert with the engagement of the locals, the 'source communities' in the museum activities. These perspectives have proved to be a challenge for the curators, and for the locals as well, and have enabled the museum to become transformed into a pluralistic memory-making and identity-expressing place that is charged with a constant dynamic.

The analysis of all of the case studies was made on the basis of the three factors involved in the process of meaning-production and the interrelationships that are created between the socio-politics of the past, and the archaeological management and museum practice in Greece. The first is the authorized voice of the curator, archaeologist, historian or anthropologist, the story-teller, the narrator of tales of the past, the producer of meaning. The second is the object itself, whether tangible or intangible, whether comprised of buildings or sites, endowed with socio-political attributes and values of the past and present and capable of carrying significant meanings, through the semiotic power of the visual languages which create them. The third is the recipient, the consumer/producer of meaning, who, moving within a structured archaeological museum context, is acting by producing interrelationships and communicating messages between past and present. He/she was not considered by this study as passive but as fully active in receiving instructive information of the past and interacting with it by bringing his/her own cultural and social preconceptions of the material world. The next section discusses the roles of these factors in the shaping of archaeological representations and museum narratives in the Greek context.

III. ARCHAEOLOGICAL REPRESENTATIONS AND MUSEUM NARRATIVES RECONSIDERED

This study, in seeking to unmask the ways in which archaeological representations of the past and museum narratives are constructed in Greek archaeological and museological theoretical scholarship and practice, has placed an emphasis on the need to investigate the museum displays through the different factors that are involved in the communication discourse.

The 'Powerful' Narrator

Taking the museum as a trusted purveyor of the meaning of the past societies, the person who guarantees the objectivity and the relevance of this meaning is the exhibitor, the interpreter, the narrator. The archaeologist in Greece, as discussed in chapter II, represents the institutionalized aspect of archaeology in Greece; the person who, charged with administrative principles and legal guidelines, tries to articulate critical accounts and to produce interpretive approaches to the material culture of the past. His/her role as regulator of the legitimization of past meaning and dissemination through the writing and presenting of the traces of the past was recognized at the creation of the first organized archaeological services and museums in Greek territory (from the end of the 19th to the beginning of the 20th century), where the antiquities were conceived as national cultural capital. Their position has since been emblematic and definitive in the protection of the Greek glorious heritage and the profession of archaeologist has been recognized as a national profession at the service of the state and for the profit of the common good. In recent years, given the character of the museums, the archaeologists remain the sanctioned state agents who are privileged to study, conduct research and pursue interpretative approaches to the writing and presenting of the past. In museum work, one is empowered with the ability to select and assess or, to put it differently, to decide what to exclude from or include in the story-making, the archaeologist, or the excavator (in the case of Greece, the same person), the researcher, and the person involved in all stages of the uncovering of past remains, encounters the ideological and political character of the museum and of the discipline of archaeology itself. The exhibitor is charged with the mission to create and transmit the acquired understanding of past remains within a museum context and to re-produce and re-present it within a structured exhibition spatial context which will mediate, in turn, meaningful messages for the consumers. At this stage, the role of the curator is crucial and of high importance, as he/she is also part of a society and carries the socio-cultural and political values of a given societal framework. This has a considerable impact on the way that meaning is produced by the exhibition-maker as, apart from the historical scientific information relating to past artifacts and events, different values and ideologies can be attached to the traces of the past, transforming them so that they become more or less significant as seen and consumed by the wider audience. In the case of Greece, the dominance of Classical archaeology and its aesthetics has been decisive in the development of these kinds of attitudes and has prevailed in exhibitors' preference for main stories which celebrate the symbolic and glorious facets of the Greek heritage. However, in recent re-exhibitions, it should be noted that a shift in this attitude has been observed and that curators and archaeologists have started adopting approaches which include various aspects and different ways of reading past remains from different periods. Also, archaeologists are more aware of the need to become more open, socially-involved, and engaged with the audience in order to facilitate its ability to understand the complexities of the interpretation of the past. For instance, the 'hidden place' where meaning is produced can be made visible and accessible by the visitor in the case of in situ museum activities (as discussed in chapter IV), rendering the curator one among the various consumers of the messages created in the museum space.

Considering the above, it should be noted that within the museum environment the exhibitor is the key element and the narrator charged with the authority to tell persuasive stories of the past. He/she is the catalyst who seeks to create the framework and the appropriate nexus of relations between the past and the present in order to create meaning. To reach that goal, a number of museum technologies and architectonics are employed, and a structured and codified language is articulated so that the messages and the meaning of the past can easily be communicated. The curator uses a kind of argumentative parole, a persuasive way of making sure that the past stories will be heard by the visitor. The semiotic character of the exhibition's functioning has been recognized and taken into consideration by many museum theorists and scholars, who, positioning the museum among the powerful public media instruments that have emerged in recent years, are investigating its communication potentialities. This recognizes the interpretative mechanism arising from the discursive nature of archaeology and the influential impact of museums as vehicles of instruction and storytelling. The result of this complex mechanism is the production of a 'written' past, a narrated story that is made in order to be told, to be persuasive and to interest the public in engaging with the 'truth' about the past. This truth is authenticated by the displayed objects in a museum or in a structured past building environment, an archaeological site conceived as a set of 'signatures', verifications of the material culture that was once created in the past. But these stories can be more than one, as Shanks and Tilley have stated, 'material culture is polysemous—located along open systems of signified-signifiers or metacritical signs' (Shanks and Tilley 2007:92). So, given the plurality of levels and contexts in which the past remains once it has been created, it could be argued that the significance lies not in the story itself but rather in how that story is told and how it communicates with the present-day consumers. This is the key concept on which rests the poetic and rhetorical analysis of the museum narratives, focusing on an articulated, written and signified speech, a logos produced by the interpreters and translated into meanings and messages carrying past information in a present-day socio-cultural museum context. The structure and the forms that this logos can take is dependent also on the intrinsic and extrinsic values and meanings that the past remains inherently have or which they acquire when placed within a new framework for studying and understanding them.

It is interesting to recognize that the museum can become the place where all the above articulations of writing the past and the process of archaeology of narrating multiple pasts could find fruitful ground to be expressed. And this consideration is based on the recognition of the museum as a dynamic and vibrant place.

Objects Passive or Active?

In light of the above discussion about recognizing the multiple readings and interpretations of the material culture, one could argue that objects, tangible and intangible remains of the past, can take many forms and be 'translated' in different ways which are dependent on the socio-cultural context in which they are presented. It should be also recognized that the objects 'carry a twofold nature which embraces a continuing real or metonymic relationship to their own time and place and a metaphorical relationship to their original context, which arises from the process of selection and interpretation with which they have been involved' (Pearce 1992:141). In this study, emphasis has been placed on the relational positioning of the objects within the context in which they exist. The object, once removed from its original context and moved to another structured one, creates its own societal framework in which social and cultural meanings and associations are produced by its functioning and ideological symbolism. The concept that the production of meanings lies in the relations and networks created within a spatial-temporal and textual context through interaction and linkage has been the main concern of modern interpretative and social theories of material culture (Hodder 1986; Latour 2005; Tilley 1999; Renfrew 2001 etc.). In these theoretical accounts, great interest is taken in the extrinsic values and features of the objects, those which they have acquired in their new contextualized environment, which are transformed into museum means and which participate as signs in a system of communication. On the other side, the aspect that 'their significance actually depends on their intrinsic characteristics' (Olsen 2010: 157) has proved insightful for our attempt to understand and decode the way that heritage remains and relics of the past construct communication channels with the present and can have a decisive impact on people's perception of the material world. So, it is very important to consider that 'there are qualities immanent to the signifiers themselves, properties that are not accidental or only a product of their position in a relational web' (Olsen 2010:156). Based on the above, it should be noted that the investigation of the objects as producers of meanings and as communication carriers should recognize that the objects are conceived as having 'multiple ontologies' (Boast et al. 2007; Srinivasan 2007; Srinivasan and Huang 2005).

In this study, the objects have been seen from different perspectives and through multiple readings in order to unmask their functioning as 'vehicles' of Greek heritage. The plethora of archaeological remains from different periods of time, derived mostly from excavation activities, offers us the opportunity to adopt different approaches to the study of the material culture of the Greek past. It is beyond doubt that the objects coming from the traditional theorizing of classical antiquity share the most important characteristic of being conceived as forms of aesthetics, as works of art. The inherent qualities of those objects, confirmed, and signed by the historiography of the written sources of classical literature, are imposing and decisive for the way that they are perceived and interpreted by the wider public, bearing the intrinsic ability to attract the contemplation and to trigger the imagination of the visitors. These qualities are related also to the ancient landscaping from which the material remains derive, either still-standing indications of a 'ruined' glorious past, or uncovered by archaeologists, and prepared to be experienced by modern consumers. A kind of monumentality is generated, formed by different expressions and multiple layers of pastness which, in the case of Greece, is dominant in all facets of the interpretation and experience of the Greek heritage. Reflecting on this aspect, it might be also stressed that the meanings that the objects inherently possess can be experienced in different ways in a museum or by being placed in the original context. So, for example, a statue in a museum can be admired in terms of its artistic excellence as sculpture and as a proof of the ability of the artists of that era, but the same statue in a temple would be conceived in relation to the broader architectural and conceptual context of the human environment of the era. The same could be observed with the objects of sacredness such as a Byzantine icon which, when seen in a museum exhibition, has its artistic characteristics and properties stressed by the curator in order to mediate historical and typological information, but when seen in a Christian Byzantine church has ceased to be a work of art and acquires its original sacred meaning (as was discussed in the case of the museum of Byzantine culture and Mount Athos). Thus, the importance of the objects lies in their being and their being experienced in terms of 'in-place-ness' (Olsen 2010:160), in their original context, a positioning that makes them readable and conceivable by the people. Based on this, Greek archaeologists and curators have in recent years, as we saw in the cases of Vergina and the Museums of Thessaloniki, made extensive use of reconstructions and *in situ* preservation and formation of the museum environment, in order to create representations of the past in which material remains can be perceived and translated within their original social frame of production. In that way, the museum object's meaning is expressed through a process which is rooted in its emblematic and expressive properties relative to its maker, its origin or its provenance (Preziosi 2004:80).

On the other hand, the objects are made to serve many purposes, and this 'serviceability' (Olsen 2010:156) is dependent on the socio-political, economic and cultural context and the conditions in which they are valued and assessed. As has been discussed in the previous section, the objects become the main vehicles by which the curator or the archaeologist authenticates his/her storytelling about the past, but the same past evidence could be conceived and perceived by the wider public, by locals and by non-experts, in a different way which might ascribe a different system of values to the past remains. In the case of Greece (as was discussed in the case of Vergina and in the historical overview), the ruins from various periods have had an impact on the perception of people which is reflected in how they ascribe, for example, economic values in pursuing the economic regeneration of their area or symbolic values in celebrating a glorious past from which they derive pride and legitimation. In this case, the objects are turned into cultural capital for future investment in the socio-cultural regeneration of areas containing antiquities and archaeological sites.

What is worth noting, through the functioning of the object, as discussed above, seen as possessing either intrinsic or extrinsic values, is the fact that the meanings produced by this process are undergoing constant re-formulation and re-construction. The objects are considered to be very active, participating significantly in the dialectical process through which the communication activity proceeds. They are seen as actors that are endowed with codified messages and charged with the role of triggering the public's interest and engagement in the perception of the past. In this respect, one could argue that the museum constitutes not only a culturally differentiated space but also a place where a framework of culturally differentiating methods is constructed, aimed at unmasking the public's relations to sites and to objects associated with past societies.

Polyvocality and Inspired Recipients

If the challenge for museums, according to Merriman, 'lies in generating ways in which to give people an understanding of the process of interpretation in a way that is accessible and enables them to look at the source material in a critical way' (Merriman 2000:304), then one could argue that the public is challenged to participate in this process in order to fulfill the museum's aims as a socio-cultural and democratic institution empowering polyvocality and celebrating dialectical approaches. This aspect is based on the character of the museum as part of the mass media, as a socially constructed institution designed to produce and transmit meaning and to raise public awareness of the material world. But this can be accomplished only through a multi-directed policy of exchanging and negotiating ideas and concepts, even if these are rooted in the institutionalized and authorized generating network of the disciplines of history and archaeology. In that way, the recipients become participants in this network of meaning-making, and they produce and add their own conceptions to the museum storytelling. In recent years, this way of thinking has been increasing in museum theory and practice, arguing that audiences are anything but blank slates (Falk & Dierking 1992, 2000; Hooper Greenhill 1999; Karp & Lavine, 1991).

In the case of Greece, and in the examples that have been discussed, it is apparent that the message recipients in the form of non-experts (visitors, locals, groups and communities) were given only a limited voice in the museum making process as the role of the narrator-archaeologist, especially in the state museums, is dominant and he/she is recognized as the only regulator of the production of meaning of the distant past. However, in recent years, the necessity of involving other people in the museum process has gained significant traction among many Greek archeologists, who seek to enhance the museum communication policy in the Greek context[190] (Κωνστάντιος 2002, 2006; Βλάχου 2001). Despite the fact that visitor studies are still not a common practice in museum management and planning, a shift in the way of reading the public's behavior and the frequency of their attendance in the museums has started to emerge and to be incorporated into the priorities of museum evaluation activities. Accordingly, the curator or the archaeologist responsible for a site is more concerned with the idea of letting locals or 'source communities' get involved and have their say in the management and presentation of the related heritage. This is the case mostly in ethnographical museums (as discussed in chapter V), where the empowerment of collaboration and co-operation practices between the curator and the people from whom the information and the material derive has proved beneficial and remarkably effective for the museums' exhibition goals. Extending this practice to the general archaeological heritage and sites has begun to be recognized as a more decisive engagement of local communities in setting the archaeological agenda, based on the belief that archaeologists cannot continue to impose themselves as experts on local communities by means of their authoritative monologues in the form of publications, writings and presentations of exhibitions (Meskell & Preucel 2004; Stroulia & Sutton 2010). It is important to understand that the audience living and acting in present-day societies creates its own relations and emotional attachments to the cultural remains of the past, which means valuing and assessing them by projecting them into the present in order to find sustainable approaches to accommodating preservation movements and economic evolution. This is a challenge for the heritage practitioners and museum experts in Greece, where people living, literally, among vast quantities of past remains of different periods could become empowered and become inspired visitors, being allowed to participate by experiencing the creative process, which might be called approaching the story-telling of the past. This could give another dimension to the rather 'impersonal and distanced tone usually adopted by museum displays' (Merriman 2000:305).

The Museum as a Form of Public Speech

The above discussion has given us stimuli to consider the museum as a form of public speech in order to shed some light on the aspect of formulating and communicating messages and stories in the museum environment. What has become apparent through this study is that the museum, as a means created for and addressed to the public, constructs various facets of material culture through a network of museum technologies and written stories which are produced and designed by authorized experts and practitioners. A mechanism for constructing

[190] Kalamara 2009 (personal interview Athens, Ministry of Culture and Tourism 22/5/2009).

narratives of the past using a specific rhetorical language of persuasion has been developed in the museum context, with the aim of communicating their textual meanings. Building on this argument, we perceive the museum to function as a rhetorical public speech act and, following Aristotle's concepts in his *Rhetoric* (Anagnostopoulos 2009), thus to understand the extent of the museum's impact on the people's way of perceiving the past.

We can consider the museum as a place that employs a structured *logos*, consisting of argumentative features, textual or spatio-temporal, which are produced in order to make its messages understood by the public. In this way, it is transformed into a *persuasive milieu* in which a dialectical process is taking place involving three agents: the message-sender, the intermediate means-object and the recipient-consumer (as we have seen in the previous section). By emphasizing the dialectical nature of rhetoric, according to Aristotle, the three mechanical means of the art of rhetoric are the *ethos*, the *logos*, and the *pathos* (Rapp 2009), each one of which is addressed to the above three agents, and this allows us to understand the way in which they interact with each other. The *ethos* is addressed to the ability and the persuasive competence of the 'speaker' not only to construct an accurate sequence of facts from the past but also to raise the emotions and to stimulate the receptive channels of the hearer-audience. Translated into the terms of the museum process, this stresses that the archaeologist-curator, charged with the task of interpreting and writing past stories as part of a given present socio-political context, should take into account those stimulating means that can be applied not only in a methodology of the learning and teaching of a preconceived and fragmented past, but rather can create 'areas of experience' through a persuasive type of speech, inviting the viewer to add his/her own conceptual and emotional thinking on the material culture of the past.

The argumentative type of dialectical process is based on the way that logos is structured and articulated (as referred to above). The main elements of an argumentative speech, following Aristotle, are the *inductions* and *deductions*, where inductions are the examples (*paradeigma*), the references and the deductions are arguments in which certain things are been supposed (*syllogismos*, *enthymeme*[191]). Structured by these features, the aim of the speech would be the creation of a judgment (*krisis*) made by the audience after considering the way that the story is written and told by the speaker. That process is easily understood in museum terms when we consider that the museum as an institution creates its own *logos* consisting of various spatial, temporal and textual technologies. Through these properties (as analyzed variously in the case studies chapters), the museum tries to articulate not a static and monolithic speech but mainly a persuasive *parole*, which will motivate the audience and make them encounter past societies critically.

On the other hand, the persuasiveness of that *parole* is dependent also, according to Aristotle, on the condition of the 'listener', the '*pathos*', which in our case is the recipient who formulates his/her own versions of the received stories and makes his/her own judgments according to the emotional attachments and the

[191] Meaning 'to consider'.

system of values ascribed by him/her to the signs of the past (as discussed in the previous sub-section). It could be argued that the audience can be positioned in many ways towards the suggested interpretations (like or dislike) and could respond variously, leaving room for either rejection or approval of the sent messages. It is exactly on the basis of these considerations that the museum could become, as in recent years has come to be recognized, a place for the inclusion and expression of many voices, thus serving its democratic character (Macdonald 2011, Mason 2005, 2010, Hooper Greenhill 2004).

In the case of Greece, the persuasive nature of the museum and its management policy has begun to be well recognized by the archaeologists when they are called upon to reflect on the reasons for the limited numbers of visitors in recent years. 'We didn't manage to persuade,' confesses Dr P. Pantou[192], seeing the museum not only as an institution for telling authorized stories but one of telling persuasive stories, well-structured tales. 'It seems that we didn't manage to persuade the Greek people [to come to museums]. [We need] to "break" the established belief that in [museums] only the experts are able to conceive what they see.' She admits that the museum needs a more pluralistic approach and method in order to interpret and present the past. It has become a widespread belief among museum people and archaeologists that constructing sequenced stories and scientifically based writings presented as 'museumfied' fragments of the past is not enough to raise the public's interest and imagination, since they are looking for tales that are beautifully and persuasively told and presented. That was the case in Greece so many years ago, when most of the museums relied on the huge amounts of 'inherently' imposing traces of classical works of art which 'were speaking' only through an established and widely recognized tradition of classical archaeology. As Dr P. Pantou stated, 'all these years we have placed the ancient Greeks on a podium, and we were afraid of looking at it. No-one told the public that they [the ancient Greeks] were also like us'[193]. It is important to recognize that the attempt is being made by archaeologists to see the museum not as an 'elitist' place where a glorious past is kept but as a place of potentialities to incorporate different viewpoints These considerations have made Greek archaeologists realize that their role should become more interactive and more involved with the public's needs and expectations and that they should take the role of the narrator of tales within a museum or an archaeological place, attracting visitors to listen not to sterile and frozen fragmented stories of the past but to plotted tales which encourage their participation and diminish the distance between them and the story-makers. That goal has recently led to the initiative of creating a collaboration between experienced archaeologists and local communities to organize on the Greek island of Naxos an event entitled 'True tales of Naxos' under the auspices of the MONUMENTA movement and the 'Local Communities

---

192 Daily newspaper *Καθημερινή [Kathimerini]* 2/3/2008 Supplement Arts and Letters p.1. Dr. Pantou is an archaeologist and a former director of the directorate of Museum and Educational Programs of the Ministry of Culture.
193 Ibid.

and Monuments' project in order for archaeologists to 'narrate' archaeological histories and tales[194].

Reflecting on the above considerations, it should be noted that taking the museum as a form of public speech, drawing on philosophical arguments from the Rhetoric of Aristotle, could allow us to see and to investigate the museum not merely as a site for the construction and the dissemination of meaning but mainly as a place for producing dialogues. By embracing the idea of dialogue, the museum could be transformed from providing structured channels for transmitting 'myths' to providing sites where 'myths' can be critically evaluated and challenged, and thus places where communities can come together for mutual self-understanding. That gives us the opportunity to reconsider the roles of the museum and the ways in which these roles are formed and transformed under different perspectives and lenses of study and research.

IV. Changing Attitudes, Changing Aspirations: Looking Forward

It is widely recognized that in recent years the thinking on the study of heritage and museums has been undergoing change and is in a state of constant re-consideration. New international principles are emerging that will introduce new approaches which move away from traditional methods of theorizing and practicing heritage management assumptions (Fairclough 2008; Kerr 2008; Low 2008; McManamon 2008). These new approaches are introducing broader holistic and comprehensive attitudes and aspirations into the heritage and museum environment. They aim at creating a new framework for making archaeologists, practitioners and museum people revise their viewpoints and alter their angles of vision and how they see and interpret the past material. It is understood that at the core of effective heritage and museum management stands not a monolithic and one-sided policy focused only on the institutionalized and authorized protection of past cultures, but rather a more multi-sided and multi-routed theorizing of heritage and museum practices. This would include challenging attitudes and creating new alternative methods for approaching tangible and intangible past material, which was created in a given past socio-cultural context and is interpreted and presented in a different present one.

The case of Greece, with multiple examples and a diversity of archaeological material, has motivated this study aiming to trace the above observations and to put these new ideas into practice. A number of excavations, conservations, restorations and museum projects carried out in the last decade have given experts the opportunity to start re-considering and challenging the traditional methods and strategies by introducing views arising from these intellectual developments and interdisciplinary practices. As seen in chapter II, the formulation and introduction of a new legislative and administrative framework, consisting of a number of revolutionary principles, has been one of the most decisive steps forward in the cultural policy of the country, giving voice to skilled archaeologists-museologists in

[194] Newspaper *Το Βήμα [To Vima]* 23/2/2011 digital edition.

the study and planning of museum exhibitions. Stimuli for these changes have been provided by European funding projects regulated by a new regime of management and technical principles, obliging revisions to the administrative status of the official body of the archaeological service. The fundamental challenge in this new approach has been the pursuit of sustainability (cultural, social, economic, or political) in the preservation and presentation methods applied to the monuments and sites of the Greek landscape. The desire to maintain traditional approaches still characterizes aspects of archaeological and museum practices, but, despite the traditional way of thinking, rooted in a well-established disciplinary tradition, the body of Greek archaeologists has shown an ability to integrate new interdisciplinary theoretical and practical considerations. This willingness is exhibited not uncritically but taking into consideration the particularities of monuments, objects and landscapes which have been uncovered by the long-running process of the excavation of numerous sites, and additionally inspired and induced by these materials that they not only study but that they live among and interact with. The sustainability of the past landscape environment for future generations, one might say, depends upon meeting the challenge of selecting and identifying a value system in relation to the material culture of the past. In this framework, the challenge for the Greek archaeologist is both demanding and provoking, as he/she encounters many dilemmas derived from a theoretical and practical discussion of preservationist and modernizing aspects.

It should be stressed that in museum and heritage designation of recent policy-making projects, a tendency can be observed not to focus so much on isolated objects and monuments interpreted and presented in specific and traditionally established representational contexts, but rather attempt to broaden the interpretative methods of past material, placing them in their original provenance and landscaping context, combining museum and site potentialities, and most importantly highlighting their influential and creative impact by projecting the past remains into the present socio-cultural environment (as has been discussed in the case studies in relation to the term 'museumscape'). In that way, terms such as *localities*, *in situ museum practices,* and *local archaeologies* are starting to be incorporated into the national heritage and museum planning and a more holistic approach is being adopted, attitudes changing to incorporate different beliefs coming from ethno-museological directions or from the concept of the landscape as museum.

Furthermore, the introduction of information technology (IT) systems, with their applications for the field of archaeology and museum representations, has provided many possibilities in recent years for making museum collections and archaeological sites more engaging and more open to new challenges to their way of presenting and contextualising past stories. Many museums in Greece, making use of these opportunities, have developed digital collections and 3D reconstructions, incorporating them into the museological scenario of permanent exhibitions in order to become more accessible by encouraging interactivity in the experience of the past. These applications, as integrated and applied for example in the exhibitions of the AMT and MBC in Thessaloniki, in the form of a video presentation of experts narrating excavation stories (in the exhibition unit of Prehistory AMT) or in the form of a touch screen info-kiosk and video showing the conservation process of a vase in 3D modelling (MBC), could stimulate the visitors' interest in how the past is approached and interpreted in a museum context.

V. CONCLUSIONS

All the above discussions prove that the idea of the museum as an entity, limited in a constrained building, is under deconstruction, and the museum as an institution is being subjected to great changes which are being expressed through the creative process of the interpretation and representation of the past. Given that archaeology is 'an ongoing process of discussing the past which is, itself, an ongoing process' (McEnroe 2002:70), it is important for heritage practitioners and museum people to understand that the key element for an effective and essentially engaging museum and heritage policy is the multifaceted character of the museum itself as a social construction and the multiple meanings ascribed to the material culture of the past.

Summary

In chapter II, a legislative and administrative framework was provided in order to explore the museum operating as an *institution* in the Greek context. It is important for this study to shed light on every aspect that influences the way that the museum policy is constructed and why the museum exhibitions interpreting and presenting the Greek past have the form and the character that they do. So, it has been crucial to present a historical overview through which the prevailing attitudes towards the Greek past could be understood and to define a general framework based on which the idea of the museum has been constructed. Identifying the main characteristics of the first museums in Greece, as powerful instruments for the education and the ideological legitimization of the nation-identity construction, the study moved to trace some shifting in administrative and legislative terms, as illustrated by a new wave of developments in recent years that place the museum and the archaeological heritage in the forefront of the country's cultural policy. This investigation looks critically at these theoretical and practical considerations, formed at an international, national and local level, from the perspective of heritage management. Focusing on museums, an attempt is made to explore management practices, through the examination of recent museum projects, which reveal the complexities, the potentialities and the future perspectives on Greek museums' role in representing the past.

Of critical importance, there is also the examination of attitudes to Greek archaeological heritage and the presentation of the prevailing concepts governing the evaluation of the past. I attempted to formulate a theoretical framework within which ideological and social attitudes and perceptions towards the Greek past can be examined. A discussion of the ideological use of Greek remains as symbolic and national emblems was provided in order to clarify the socio-political context in which archaeology proceeded and museums were formed in Greece. This discussion was pursued in order to reveal how archaeology and museum objects can represent symbolic meanings and associations used to legitimize stories and narratives and to create an emotional attachment to the remote past. That discussion led to the recognition that multiple pasts are selected to be represented and assigned meanings in the museum environment on the basis of an evaluation, and that this creates the conditions for the use and abuse of that past.

Having established the theoretical and practical framework, the study then investigated, through the case studies in chapters III, IV, and V, the museum as a social product and a communicative instrument which affects people's understandings. It has been deconstructed in order to provide us with various kinds of theoretical and practical thinking on how that knowledge is created and by whom, what kinds of spatio-temporal relations are constructed through the museum's interpreting technologies, and how these affect the public's perception of the past. One of the primary aims of the study has been to stress the multiplicity of approaches, theorizations and diverse perspectives. Thus, the museums are considered in different categories which expose different facets of this process: 1) Museums with exhibitions which cover all the periods (Prehistory, Classical Byzantine and early modern times) are considered in order to locate differentiations in the way that the 'pasts' are presented according to the theoretical archaeological thinking which supports these various disciplinary expressions of the field. 2) Site museums and archaeological-historical places are examined as museum spaces to investigate their potentialities and aspects that challenge the traditional image of the museum as the 'keeper' and 'guardian' of valuable things and focus rather on the recognition of the socio-cultural role of the museum within modern society and the perception of an archaeological and historical landscape as a place of social action (past and present) that creates layers of relations. 3) Museums with private collections are discussed to examine a more local context, to address issues of multivocality, and to explore museum exhibitions as *aides-mémoires*, as memory-spaces, places where memories are re-created and where the empowering of a cultural diversity and a process of intercultural dialogue are ongoing and in constant flux. That dialogue cannot easily be accomplished, as it is subjected to different socio-cultural conditions which affect decisively and variously the way in which the past is interpreted and consumed, putting it in a constant state of re-creation and re-interpretation. And that is in my opinion the most challenging feature of the museological *praxis*.

Final Thoughts

It was in such a spirit that I had once remarked that a landscape is not, as some perceive it, simply a mass of earth, plants and water; it is the projection of a people's soul on matter.

I want to believe—and this belief of mine always comes out on top in its struggle with knowledge—that, however we look at it, the age-old presence of Hellenism in the here and there of the Aegean world has come to establish an orthography, in which every omega, every upsilon, every acute and every subscript is but a cove, a declivity, a sheer rock against the curved stern of a vessel, undulating vineyards, church lintels and, here and there, whites and reds, dovecotes and pots of geraniums

(Elytis 1999:65-74)

The primary focus of this study was to focus on the aspect of a changing museum philosophy and practice within a broader framework of the exploration of archaeological heritage management. Recent initiatives in the Greek context have provided me with fertile material to reflect on the museum's representations of the past and to unmask the socio-politics and the poetics of museum narratives. It can be said that the museums are going through a revolutionary era, as has been stated by Knell, MacLeod and Watson in their book *Museum Revolutions* (Knell, MacLeod and Watson 2007: xix-xxvi), an era characterized by a plethora of new museums demonstrating new ways of presenting the cultural or physical world using modern conceptions of the living, eco-digital or post-museum (ibid: xix). The museum is under re-theorization and as a product of modern society it is being subjected to those influential forces which are transforming it into a dynamic and shaping place of perceptions of past societies.

On the other hand, it can be argued that the museums, despite these recognized changing features, are getting more 'skeptical', more reflective, in their ability to present and tell past stories. By recognising their persuasive character and their impact on the public's views on the past remains they are trying to find those languages and channels of communication, including concepts such as polyphony and multiplicity of meaning, that will create the conditions to enable the museum to serve its social character. To do that, we need both a re-consideration and a re-theorization of the main aims of the museum as an institution and of archaeology as a discipline which studies and produces interpretative instruments to understand the past. The case of Greece showed the route of the above re-theorization through an ongoing articulation of modern Greek choices revealing an experimentation and a mode of reflective thinking in the area of museums' representations.

The above skepticism derives from the fact that the archaeological heritage in Greece, with its multiplicity and its 'palimpsestal' character, provides a fertile ground, a starting point, for a challenging discussion of the way that museum narratives are produced. The domination of aesthetics and of 'fetishized' objects is being challenged and their museum primacy is being revised with the aim of presenting a more holistic image of past societies and getting a better understanding of the past by projecting it into the present. By seeking to accomplish that aim, Greek archaeologists are becoming skeptical not only in challenging the monumentality of classical objects and sites but mainly to shift into a more multi-sided perception of culture which is fully supported by the scientific aspirations of archaeology as a social discipline and the museum as a re-presentational place. That shift, as has been argued by this study, has already started in the museum realm, where the archaeologists have found the stimuli needed to express the multiplicity of archaeological narratives and to re-examine the museum's role within modern society. To this purpose, emphasis has been placed on the way that the archaeological landscape can become involved in the museum dialogue-making process and new approaches are posited, such as the idea of 'museumscape', for perceiving the past as an active entity promoting multiple possibilities of experiencing it. On the other hand, seeing the museum as a performative and persuasive place for the creation of textual narratives dictates the reconsideration of ways of writing and communicating the past by using functioning tools from the disciplines of linguistics and sociology. Also, the changing approach of museums recognizes them as places of intercultural dialogue and as loci of interaction where many voices are encouraged to be expressed and where individual memories can be re-created.

All the above considerations and pursuits aimed at the broadening of the concept of the museum from just a place of education and instruction to a dynamic space providing a variety of perspectives and potentials. In that way, the museum is becoming more involved in the society of which it is at once the product and the producer, involved in the continuous process of the creation of interrelationships among the participants and consumers of the messages of the past. That energetic and dynamic relation defines a new framework within which the new museum is perceived not merely as a space for creating meanings, but rather as a place for producing dialogues.

Appendix

The official document issued on the 7th October 1829, by which the first Greek museum, 'Mouseion', was established in the Greek island of Aigina. It was provided the first definition of the museum as an institution and its aims and goals were defined for the first time.

Source: Πρωτοψάλτης 1967:no 82

Bibliography

The resources for this study fall within five distinct categories, which are listed by category for reasons of clarity and of convenience.

Archival Material, Reports and Official Documents

Archives-Reports

Guidelines Book, (reports) Section B', Specifications of Archaeological Works Studies. 2009. Archive of General Directorate of Antiquities and Cultural Heritage. Ministry of Culture and Tourism

Επιχειρησιακό Πρόγραμμα Πολιτισμός. Κοινοτικό Πλαίσιο Στήριξης, 2000-2006.Υπουργείο Πολιτισμού [European Funding Framework 2000-2006. Ministry of Culture]

Έργα Πολιτισμού στο Β' Κοινοτικό Πλαίσιο Στήριξης. Υπουργείο Πολιτισμού [Heritage Works funded by the 2nd European Funding Framework. Ministry of Culture]

Πολιτιστική Ολυμπιάδα 2001-2004. Για Έναν Πολιτισμό των Πολιτισμών. Υπουργείο Πολιτισμού- Α.Ε. Προβολής της Ελληνικής Πολιτιστικής Κληρονομιάς [Cultural Olympics 2001-2004. Ministry of Culture-Organisation of Promotion of Cultural Heritage]

Museological scenario-study for the exhibitions of the Archaeological Museum of Thessaloniki. Archive of Directorate of Museums, Exhibitions and Educational Programmes. Department of State Museums. Ministry of Culture and Tourism. Athens [Μουσειολογική Μελέτη των εκθέσεων του Αρχαιολογικού Μουσείου Θεσσαλονίκης. Αρχείο της ΔΜΕΕΠ. Τμήμα δημόσιων μουσείων. ΥΠΠΟΤ. Αθήνα].

Catalogues of objects and forms of thematics and sections of the exhibitions of the Archaeological Museum of Thessaloniki. Archive of Directorate of Museums, Exhibitions and Educational Programmes. Department of State Museums. Ministry of Culture and Tourism. Athens [Κατάλογοι αντικειμένων και δελτία εκθεσιακού υλικού των εκθέσεων του Αρχαιολογικού Μουσείου Θεσσαλονίκης. Αρχείο της ΔΜΕΕΠ. Τμήμα δημόσιων μουσείων. ΥΠΠΟΤ. Αθήνα]

Museographical plan-study. for the exhibitions of the Archaeological Museum of Thessaloniki. Archive of Directorate of Museums, Exhibitions and Educational Programmes. Department of State Museums. Ministry of Culture and Tourism. Athens [Μουσειογραφική και των εκθέσεων του Αρχαιολογικού Μουσείου Θεσσαλονίκης. Αρχείο της ΔΜΕΕΠ. Τμήμα δημόσιων μουσείων. ΥΠΠΟΤ. Αθήνα].

Architectural plan-study. of the Archaeological Museum of Thessaloniki. Archive of Directorate of Museums, Exhibitions and Educational Programmes. Department of State Museums. Ministry of Culture and Tourism. Athens [Αρχιτεκτονική Μελέτη του Αρχαιολογικού Μουσείου Θεσσαλονίκης. Αρχείο της ΔΜΕΕΠ. Τμήμα δημόσιων μουσείων. ΥΠΠΟΤ. Αθήνα]

Museological scenario-study for the exhibitions of the Museum of Byzantine Culture, Thessaloniki. Archive of Directorate of Museums, Exhibitions and Educational Programmes. Department of State Museums. Ministry of Culture and Tourism. Athens [Μουσειολογική Μελέτη των εκθέσεων του

Μουσείου Βυζαντινού Πολιτισμού Θεσσαλονίκης. Αρχείο της ΔΜΕΕΠ. Τμήμα δημόσιων μουσείων. ΥΠΠΟΤ. Αθήνα]

Museological scenario-plan and exhibition program of the Museum of Byzantine Culture, Thessaloniki 'On the exhibition in Gallery10 and 11' Archive of Directorate of Museums, Exhibitions and Educational Programmes. Department of State Museums. Ministry of Culture and Tourism. Athens. [Μουσειολογική Μελέτη των εκθέσεων 10 και 11 του Μουσείου Βυζαντινού Πολιτισμού Θεσσαλονίκης. Αρχείο της ΔΜΕΕΠ. Τμήμα δημόσιων μουσείων. ΥΠΠΟΤ. Αθήνα]

Catalogues of objects and forms of thematics and sections of the exhibitions of the Museum of Byzantine Culture, Thessaloniki. Archive of Directorate of Museums, Exhibitions and Educational Programmes. Department of State Museums. Ministry of Culture and Tourism. Athens [Κατάλογοι αντικειμένων και δελτία εκθεσιακού υλικού των εκθέσεων του Μουσείου Βυζαντινού Πολιτισμού Θεσσαλονίκης. Αρχείο της ΔΜΕΕΠ. Τμήμα δημόσιων μουσείων. ΥΠΠΟΤ. Αθήνα]

Museographical plan-study for the exhibitions of the Museum of Byzantine Culture, Thessaloniki. Archive of Directorate of Museums, Exhibitions and Educational Programmes. Department of State Museums. Ministry of Culture and Tourism. Athens [Μουσειογραφική Μελέτη των εκθέσεων του Μουσείου Βυζαντινού Πολιτισμού Θεσσαλονίκης. Αρχείο της ΔΜΕΕΠ. Τμήμα δημόσιων μουσείων. ΥΠΠΟΤ. Αθήνα]

Museological reports and plans for the exhibitions of the Ethnological Museum of Thrace. Archive of Ethnological Museum of Thrace. Alexandroupolis. [Μουσειολογικές αναφορές για τις εκθέσεις του Εθνολογικού Μουσείου Θράκης. Αρχείο Εθνολογικού Μουσείου Θράκης. Αλεξανδρούπολη]

Museological scenario-study for the exhibitions of the Ouranoupolis Museum, Chalkidiki. Archive of 10th Ephorate of Byzantine Antiquities. Ministry of Culture and Tourism. Thessaloniki. [Μουσειολογική Μελέτη των εκθέσεων του Μουσείου Ουρανούπολης. Αρχείο 10^{η} Εφορεία Βυζαντινών Αρχαιοτήτων. ΥΠΠΟΤ.Θεσσαλονίκη].

Museographical plan-study of the Ouranoupolis Museum, Chalkidiki. Archive of 10th Ephorate of Byzantine Antiquities. Ministry of Culture and Tourism. Thessaloniki. [Μουσειογραφική Μελέτη των εκθέσεων του Μουσείου Ουρανούπολης. Αρχείο 10^{η} Εφορεία Βυζαντινών Αρχαιοτήτων. ΥΠΠΟΤ.Θεσσαλονίκη].

Museological reports of the Project 'The Ouranoupolis Museum-Exhibitions'. 3rd Funding Framework Project of EU. Archive of 10th Ephorate of Byzantine Antiquities. Ministry of Culture and Tourism. Thessaloniki. [Μουσειολογικές αναφορές για τις εκθέσεις του Μουσείου Ουρανούπολης. Αρχείο 10^{η} Εφορεία Βυζαντινών Αρχαιοτήτων. ΥΠΠΟΤ.Θεσσαλονίκη]

Technical Reports of the Project 'The Ouranoupolis Museum-Exhibitions'. 3rd Funding Framework Project. Archive of 10th Ephorate of Byzantine Antiquities. Ministry of Culture and Tourism. Thessaloniki. [Τεχνικά Δελτία του έργου 'Μουσείο Ουρανούπολης'. Γ' Κοινοτικό Πλαίσιο Στήριξης (ΚΠΣ). Αρχείο 10^{η} Εφορεία Βυζαντινών Αρχαιοτήτων. ΥΠΠΟΤ.Θεσσαλονίκη]

Supervision Reports of the Project 'The Ouranoupolis Museum-Exhibitions'. 3rd Funding Framework Project. Archive of 10th Ephorate of Byzantine Antiquities. Ministry of Culture and Tourism. Thessaloniki. [Δελτία παρακολούθησης του έργου 'Μουσείο Ουρανούπολης'. Γ' Κοινοτικό Πλαίσιο Στήριξης (ΚΠΣ). Αρχείο 10^{η} Εφορεία Βυζαντινών Αρχαιοτήτων. ΥΠΠΟΤ.Θεσσαλονίκη]

Evaluation reports of the Project 'The Ouranoupolis Museum-Exhibitions'. 3rd Funding Framework Project of EU. Archive of 10th Ephorate of Byzantine Antiquities. Ministry of Culture and Tourism. Thessaloniki. [Εκθέσεις Αξιολόγησης του έργου 'Μουσείο Ουρανούπολης'. Γ' Κοινοτικό Πλαίσιο Στήριξης (ΚΠΣ). Αρχείο 10η Εφορεία Βυζαντινών Αρχαιοτήτων. ΥΠΠΟΤ.Θεσσαλονίκη]

Museological reports of the Project 'Justinian. Centre of Byzantine Culture'. 3rd Funding Framework Project of EU. Archive of 10th Ephorate of Byzantine Antiquities. Ministry of Culture and Tourism. Thessaloniki. [Μουσειολογικές αναφορές του έργου 'Ιουστινιανός. Κέντρο Βυζαντινού Πολιτισμού'. Γ' Κοινοτικό Πλαίσιο Στήριξης (ΚΠΣ) Αρχείο 10η Εφορεία Βυζαντινών Αρχαιοτήτων. ΥΠΠΟΤ.Θεσσαλονίκη]

Technical Reports of the Project 'Justinian. Centre of Byzantine Culture'. 3rd Funding Framework Project. Archive of 10th Ephorate of Byzantine Antiquities. Ministry of Culture and Tourism. Thessaloniki. [Τεχνικά Δελτία του έργου 'Ιουστινιανός. Κέντρο Βυζαντινού Πολιτισμού'. Γ' Κοινοτικό Πλαίσιο Στήριξης (ΚΠΣ). Αρχείο 10η Εφορεία Βυζαντινών Αρχαιοτήτων. ΥΠΠΟΤ.Θεσσαλονίκη]

Supervision Reports of the Project 'Justinian. Centre of Byzantine Culture'. 3rd Funding Framework Project. Archive of 10th Ephorate of Byzantine Antiquities. Ministry of Culture and Tourism. Thessaloniki. [Δελτία παρακολούθησης του έργου 'Ιουστινιανός. Κέντρο Βυζαντινού Πολιτισμού'. Γ' Κοινοτικό Πλαίσιο Στήριξης (ΚΠΣ). Αρχείο 10η Εφορεία Βυζαντινών Αρχαιοτήτων. ΥΠΠΟΤ.Θεσσαλονίκη]

Restoration reports of the Project 'Justinian. Centre of Byzantine Culture'. 3rd Funding Framework Project of EU. Archive of 10th Ephorate of Byzantine Antiquities. Ministry of Culture and Tourism. Thessaloniki. [Μελέτες αναστήλωσης του έργου 'Ιουστινιανός. Κέντρο Βυζαντινού Πολιτισμού'. Γ' Κοινοτικό Πλαίσιο Στήριξης (ΚΠΣ). Αρχείο 10η Εφορεία Βυζαντινών Αρχαιοτήτων. ΥΠΠΟΤ.Θεσσαλονίκη]

Evaluation reports of the Project 'Justinian. Centre of Byzantine Culture'. 3rd Funding Framework Project of EU. Archive of 10th Ephorate of Byzantine Antiquities. Ministry of Culture and Tourism. Thessaloniki. [Εκθέσεις Αξιολόγησης του έργου 'Ιουστινιανός. Κέντρο Βυζαντινού Πολιτισμού'. Γ' Κοινοτικό Πλαίσιο Στήριξης (ΚΠΣ). Αρχείο 10η Εφορεία Βυζαντινών Αρχαιοτήτων. ΥΠΠΟΤ.Θεσσαλονίκη]

Conservation feasibility studies of the Project 'The Mount-Athos Conservation Project'. 3rd Funding Framework Project of EU. Archive of 10th Ephorate of Byzantine Antiquities. Ministry of Culture and Tourism. Thessaloniki. [Μελέτες συντήρησης του έργου 'Συντήρηση κειμηλίων Αγίου Όρους'. Γ' Κοινοτικό Πλαίσιο Στήριξης (ΚΠΣ). Αρχείο 10η Εφορεία Βυζαντινών Αρχαιοτήτων. ΥΠΠΟΤ.Θεσσαλονίκη]

Technical Reports of the Project 'The Mount-Athos Conservation Project'. 3rd Funding Framework Project. Archive of 10th Ephorate of Byzantine Antiquities. Ministry of Culture and Tourism. Thessaloniki. [Τεχνικά Δελτία του έργου 'Συντήρηση κειμηλίων Αγίου Όρους'. Γ' Κοινοτικό Πλαίσιο Στήριξης (ΚΠΣ). Αρχείο 10η Εφορεία Βυζαντινών Αρχαιοτήτων. ΥΠΠΟΤ.Θεσσαλονίκη]

Supervision Reports of the Project 'The Mount-Athos Conservation Project'. 3rd Funding Framework Project. Archive of 10th Ephorate of Byzantine Antiquities. Ministry of Culture and Tourism. Thessaloniki. [Δελτία παρακολούθησης του έργου. 'Συντήρηση κειμηλίων Αγίου Όρους'. Γ' Κοινοτικό Πλαίσιο Στήριξης (ΚΠΣ). Αρχείο 10η Εφορεία Βυζαντινών Αρχαιοτήτων. ΥΠΠΟΤ. Θεσσαλονίκη]

Restoration reports of the Project 'The Mount-Athos Conservation Project'. 3rd Funding Framework Project of EU. Archive of 10th Ephorate of Byzantine Antiquities. Ministry of Culture and Tourism. Thessaloniki. [Μελέτες αναστήλωσης του έργου 'Συντήρηση κειμηλίων Αγίου Όρους' Γ' Κοινοτικό Πλαίσιο Στήριξης (ΚΠΣ). Αρχείο 10η Εφορεία Βυζαντινών Αρχαιοτήτων. ΥΠΠΟΤ. Θεσσαλονίκη]

Evaluation reports of the Project 'The Mount-Athos Conservation Project'. 3rd Funding Framework Project of EU. Archive of 10th Ephorate of Byzantine Antiquities. Ministry of Culture and Tourism. Thessaloniki. [Εκθέσεις Αξιολόγησης του έργου. 'Συντήρηση κειμηλίων Αγίου Όρους'. Γ' Κοινοτικό Πλαίσιο Στήριξης (ΚΠΣ). Αρχείο 10η Εφορεία Βυζαντινών Αρχαιοτήτων. ΥΠΠΟΤ. Θεσσαλονίκη]

Official Documents-Decisions

ΥΠΠΟ/ΑΡΧ/Β2/Φ21/18240/340/13.4.1993
ΥΠΠΟ/ΓΔΑΠΚ/ΑΡΧ/Γ1/Φ21-ΓΕΝ/99931/1388/23.10.2007
ΥΠΠΟ/ΓΔΑΠΚ/ΔΜΕΕΠ/Γ1/Φ21-ΓΕΝ/99797/1387/23.10.2007
ΥΠΠΟ/ΔΙΑΛΑΠ/Γ/4403/65150/8.12.2000
ΥΠΠΟ/ΓΔΑΠΚ/ΔΜΕΕΠ/Γ1/Φ21/54590/340/16.10.2003
ΥΠΠΟ/ΓΝΟΣ/50304/25.10.1999
ΥΠΠΟ/ΔΙΛΑΠ/Γ/3142/55420/19.10.2001
ΥΠΠΟ/ΑΡΧ/Β2/Φ21/18240/340/13.4.1993

Codified Statute of founding the 'Ethnological Museum of Thrace-Aggeliki Giannakidou'. Archive Ethnological Museum of Thrace. Alexandroupolis. [Κωδικοποίηση του Καταστατικού της Αστικής Εταιρείας Μη κερδοσκοπικού χαρακτήρα με την επωνυμία 'Εθνολογικό Μουσείο Θράκης-Αγγελική Γιαννακίδου' και ενσωμάτωση του εσωτερικού κανονισμού λειτουργίας του μουσείου. Αρχείο Εθνολογικό Μουσείο Θράκης. Αλεξανδρούπολη.

Legislation

National Legislative Regulations

Νόμος 2557/1997, ΦΕΚ Α' 271/24.12.1997 'Θεσμοί, Μέτρα και Δράσεις της Πολιτιστικής ανάπτυξης [Law 2557/1997 Greek Government Gazette No. 271, 24 December 1997 'Institutions, Measures and Actions']

Νόμος 5081/1931 'Περί Ιδρύσεως Μουσείων Πόλεως' ΦΕΚ Α' 186/7.7.1931
[Law 5081/1931 'On the Foundation of City Museums' Greek Government Gazette No. 186/ 7 July 1931]

Νόμος 10/ 22 Μαΐου 1834 'Περί των Επιστημονικών και Τεχνολογικών Συλλογών, περί Ανακαλύψεως και Διατηρήσεως των Αρχαιοτήτων και της Χρήσεως αυτών' ΦΕΚ 22/ 16 Ιουνίου 1834
[Law of 10/22 May 1834 'Concerning the Scientific and Technological collections and the Retrieval and Conservation of Antiquities and their Use' Greek Government Gazette No. 22, 16 June 1834]

Νόμος ΒΧΜΣΤ 24.7.1899 'Περί Αρχαιοτήτων' ΦΕΚ Α' 158/ 27 Ιουλίου 1899
[Law ΒΧΜΣΤ' 'On Antiquities' Greek Government Gazette No. 158 A, 27 July 1899]

Προεδρικό Διάταγμα (ΠΔ) 941/1977 ' Οργανισμός του Υπουργείου Πολιτισμού' ΦΕΚ Α' 320/17.10.1977
[PD 941/1977 'Organization of the Ministry of Culture, Government Gazette No. 320, 17 October 1977]

Σύνταγμα της Ελλάδος 1975, άρθρα: 24 και 18
Greek Constitution 1975, articles 24 and 18

Νόμος 3028/2002 'Για την Προστασία των Αρχαιοτήτων και εν γένει της Πολιτιστικής Κληρονομιάς' ΦΕΚ Α' 153/28.06.2002
[Law 3028/2002 'On the Protection of Antiquities and Cultural Heritage in general' Government Gazette No. 153 A, 28 June 2002.

Προεδρικό Διάταγμα 191/2003 'Οργανισμός του Υπουργείου Πολιτισμού' ΦΕΚ Α' 146/ 13.06.2003
Presidential Decree 191/2003 Organisation of the Ministry of Culture, Government Gazette 146 A, 13 June 2003

Νομοθετικό Διάταγμα 10/16 Σεπτεμβρίου 1926 'Περί Καταστατικού Χάρτου του Αγίου Όρους'
Legislative Decree 10/16 September 1926 'On Constitutional Charter of the Greek Church'

Νόμος 590/1977 'Περί του Καταστατικού Χάρτου της Εκκλησίας της Ελλάδος' ΦΕΚ Α' 146/31.05.1977
[Law 540/1977 'On Constitutional Charter of the Greek Church' Greek Government Gazette No.146, 31 May 1977]

Κωδικοποιημένος Νόμος 5351/1932 'Περί Αρχαιοτήτων' ΦΕΚ Α' 93/28.03.1932
[Codified Law 5351/1932 'On Antiquities' Greek Government Gazette No. 93, 28 March 1932]

Νόμος 4823/1930 'Περί Ανεγέρσεως, Επισκευής και Συντηρήσεως Αρχαιολογικών Μουσείων' ΦΕΚ Α' 245/18.07.1930
[Law 4823/1930 'On Foundation, Renovation and Conservation of Archaeological Museums' Greek Government Gazette No. 245, 18 July 1930]

Νόμος 401/1914 'Περί Ιδρύσεως Βυζαντινού και Χριστιανικού Μουσείου' ΦΕΚ Α' 347/27.11.1914
[Law 401/1914 'On Foundation of Byzantine and Christian Museum' Greek Government Gazette No. 347, 27 November 1914]

Νόμος 1469/1950 'Περί Προστασίας Ειδικής Κατηγορίας Οικοδομημάτων και Έργων Τέχνης Μεταγενέστερων του 1830' ΦΕΚ Α' 169/7.08.1950
[Law 1469/1950 'On Protection of Special Division Establishments and Works of Art dated later than 1830' Greek Government Gazette No. 169, 7 August 1950]

Νόμος 1958/1991 art. 81 par.1 'Τρόπος Εκτέλεσης Αρχαιολογικών Έργων' ΦΕΚ Α' 122/05.08.1991
[Law 1958/1991 art. 81 par. 1 'Implementation ways of Archaeological Works' Greek Government Gazette No.122/5 August 1991]

Προεδρικό Διάταγμα 99/1992 'Μελέτη και Εκτέλεση Αρχαιολογικών εν γένει Έργων' ΦΕΚ Α' 46/23.03.1992
[Presidential Decree 99/1992 'Study and Implementation of Archaeological Works in general' Greek Government Gazette No. 46, 23 March 1992]

International Norms and Standards

UNESCO. 2003. *Convention for the Safeguarding of Intangible Cultural Heritage* Paris: UNESCO

UNESCO 2002 *Universal Declaration on Cultural Diversity*. Paris: UNESCO. Available at www.unesco.org/culture

UNESCO 2005. *Convention on the Protection and Promotion of the Diversity of Cultural Expressions.* Paris: UNESCO

ICOM. 1986. (2004 revised) *Code of Ethics for Museums.* Paris: International Council of Museums

ICOM. 1997. *Museums and Cultural Diversity*. Policy Statement. Paris: ICOM

ICOMOS. 1964. International Charter for the Conservation and Restoration of Monuments and Sites. Paris: ICOMOS (The Venice Charter)

ICOMOS. 1990. Charter for the Protection and Management of the Archaeological Heritage. Paris: ICOMOS

ICOM. 1997. *Museums and Cultural Diversity*: Policy Statement. Paris, ICOM

ICOM. 2006. *Code of Ethics for Museums*. Paris, ICOM

COUNCIL REGULATION (EC) No 1260/1999 of 21 June 1999, "General Provisions on the Structural Funds". *Official Journal of European Communities.* 26.6.1999. (http://eur-lex.europa.eu/LexUriServ)

Council of Europe. European Convention on the Protection of the Archaeological Heritage (Revised). Valetta, 16/1/1992

Council of Europe. European Convention on the Protection of the Archaeological Heritage. London, 6/5/1969

Newspapers

Kathimerini [Καθημερινή] 2/3/2008 Supplement Arts and Letters
Kathimerini [Καθημερινή] 12/4/2009
Kathimerini [Καθημερινή] 24/1/2010
Kathimerini [Καθημερινή] 27/6/2010
Kathimerini [Καθημερινή] 15/6/2008
Kathimerini [Καθημερινή] 17/7/1993
Kathimerini [Καθημερινή] 26/10/2008 supplement on Arts and Letters
Kathimerini [Καθημερινή] 29/3/2009 supplement on Arts and Letters
Kathimerini [Καθημερινή]23/2/11 digital edition

Ependytis [Επενδυτής- Ο Κόσμος του Επενδυτή] 10/5/2008
Ependytis [Επενδυτής- Ο Κόσμος του Επενδυτή] 16/8/2009

To Thema [Το Θέμα] 21/6/2009

Aggelioforos [Αγγελιοφόρος] 12/7/2009

To Vima [Το Βήμα] 1/7/1990
To Vima [Το Βήμα] 23/2/2011 digital edition
To Vima [Το Βήμα] 25/11/1977

Eleutherotypia [Ελευθεροτυπία] 24/6/1993
Eleutherotypia [Ελευθεροτυπία] 21/7/1993
Eleutherotypia [Ελευθεροτυπία] 13/10/2010 (digital edition)

Thessaloniki [Θεσσαλονίκη] 20/7/1993
Thessaloniki [Θεσσαλονίκη] 21/7/1993

Thessaloniki [Θεσσαλονίκη] 24/11/1977
Thessaloniki [Θεσσαλονίκη] 25/11/1977

Ta Nea [Τα Νέα] 21/7/1993

English Publications

Anagnostopoulos, G. (ed.) 2009. *A Companion to Aristotle.* UK: Blackwell

Alcock, S. E. 2002. *Archaeologies of the Greek Past. Landscapes, Monuments, and Memories.* Cambridge: Cambridge University Press

Alpers, S. 1991. The Museum as a Way of Seeing, in S. D. Lavine and I. Karp (ed.), *Exhibiting Cultures. The Poetics and Politics of Museum Display:* 25-32. Washington, DC: Smithsonian Institution Press.

Ames, M. A. 1990. Cultural Empowerment and Museums: Opening up Anthropology through Collaboration, in S. Pearce (ed.), *Objects of Knowledge:* 158-173. The Athlone Press.

Anderson, B. 1991. *Imagined Communities.* London: Verso

Andronikos, M. 1986. Thessalonike Museum: A New Guide to the Archaeological Treasures [translation: L. Turner] Αθήνα: Εκδοτική Αθηνών

Appadurai, A. and C. A. Breckenridge. 1992. Museums are Good to Think: Heritage on View in India, in I. Karp, C. Mullen Kreamer and S. D Lavine (ed), *Museums and Communities: The Politics of Public Culture:* 34-55. Washington, DC and London: Smithsonian Institution Press

Appadurai, A. (with A. Chadha, I. Hodder, T. Jachman and C. Witmore). 2008. The Globalization of Archaeology and Heritage: A Discussion with Arjun Appadurai in G. Fairclough, R. Harrison, J.H. Jameson Jnr and J. Schofield (eds), *The Heritage Reader:* 209-218. London and New York: Routledge

Ashmore W. and A. B., Knapp (eds). 1999. *Archaeologies of Landscape. Contemporary Perspectives.* Oxford: Blackwell Publishers Ltd

Ashmore W. and Knapp A. B. 1999. Archaeological Landscapes: Constructed, Conceptualized, Ideational in W. Asmore and A. B. Knapp (eds), *Archaeologies of Landscape. Contemporary Perspectives*: 1-30. Oxford: Blackwell Publishers Ltd

Avgouli, M. 1994. The First Greek Museums and National Identity in F. Kaplan (ed) *Museums and the Making of 'Ourselves': The Role of Objects in National Identity*: 246-266. London: Leicester University Press

Bal, M. 1996. *Double Exposures: The Subject of Cultural Analysis.* London and New York: Routledge

Barrett, J., Brandley, R., and Green, M. 1991: *Landscape, Monuments and Society: The Prehistory of Cranborne Cbase.* Cambridge: Cambridge University Press

Baxandall, M. 1991. Exhibiting Intention: Some Preconditions of the Visual Display of Culturally Purposeful Objects, in S. D. Lavine and I. Karp (eds.), *Exhibiting Cultures. The Poetics and Politics of Museum Display:* 33-41. Washington, DC: Smithsonian Institution Press.

Bender, B. (ed) 1993. *Landscape: Politics and Perspectives.* Oxford: Berg

———. 1998. *Stonehenge: Making Space.* Oxford: Berg

———.2002. Landscape and Politics in Victor Buchli (ed.), The Material Culture Reader: 135-174. Oxford: Berg

Bennett, T. 1998. Pedagogic Objects, Clean Eyes, and Popular Instruction: On Sensory Regimes and Museum Didactics, *Configurations* 6: 345-371, Number 3

Boast, R. 1997. A Small Company of Actors: A Critique of Style, *Journal of Material Culture* 2(2):173-198

Boast, R., S. Guha and A. Herle. 2001. *Collecting Sights: The Photographic Collections of the Museum of Archaeology and Anthropology, 1850-1970*. Cambridge: Museum of Archaeology and Anthropology, Cambridge University Press

Boast, R., M. Bravo, and R. Srinivasan. 2007. Return to Babel: Emergent Diversity, Digital Resources, and Local Knowledge, *The Information Society* 23(5):395 –403.

Buchli, V. 2002. Introduction. In V. Buchli, *The Material Culture Reader*. Oxford: Berg.

Carman, J. 1996. *Valuing Ancient Things. Archaeology and Law*. London and New York: Leicester University Press

———. 1996. Valuing Ancient Things.Archaeology and Law. London: Leicester University Press

———. 2002. *Archaeology and Heritage. An Introduction*. London: Continuum

Clifford, J. 1997. *Routes: travel and translation in the Late of Twentieth Century* Cambridge, Massachusetts: Harvard University Press

Clifford, S. 2011. Local Distinctiveness: Everyday Places and How to Find Them in J. Schofield and R. Szymanski (eds), *Local Heritage, Global Context. Cultural Perspectives on Sense of Place:*13-32. UK: Ashgate

Corsane, G.(ed) 2005. *Heritage, Museums and Galleries: An Introductory Reader*. USA and Canada: Routledge

Coxal, H. 1991. How Language means: An Alternative View of Museums Text in Kavanagh G. (ed) *Museum Languages: Objects and Texts*: 85-99. Leicester: Leicester University Press

Crew, S. R. and J. E. Sims. 1991. Locating Authenticity: fragments of a dialogue, in S. D. Lavine and I. Karp (eds), *Exhibiting cultures. The Poetics and Politics of Museum Display:* 159-175. Washington, DC: Smithsonian Institution Press.

Crooke, E. 2007. *Museums and Communities. Ideas, Issues and Challenges*. London and New York: Routledge

———. 2011. Museums and Community in S. Macdonald (ed), *A Companion to Museum Studies*: 170-185. UK: Blackwell Publishing

Daniels, S and D. E. Cosgrove. 1988. Introduction: iconography and landscape in D. E Cosgrove and S. Daniels (eds), *The Iconography of Landscape. Essays on the Symbolic Representation, Design and Use of Past Environments:* 1-10. Cambridge: Cambridge University Press.

Demacopoulos, J. E. 1995. *A Shelter in the Style of a Tumulus. Vergina. An Underground Archaeological Site and Museum in the Type of a Crypt*. Athens: Ministry of Culture, Archaeological Receipts Fund.

Demetriou, O. 2010. The Cyclops, the Sultan, and the Empty Post: Sites and Histories in Turkish (Re)appropriations of the Thracian Past, in A Stroulia. and S Buck Sutton. (eds) *Archaeology in Situ. Sites, Archaeology and Communities in Greece*: 221-239. United States: Lexington Books

Diaz-Andreu, M. and T. Champion, (eds.) 1996. *Nationalism and Archaeology in Europe*. London: UCL Press

Drougou, S. and Ch. Saatsoglou Paliadeli. 2008. *Vergina. Wandering through the Archaeological Site*. Hellenic Ministry of Culture. Archaeological Receipts Fund

Dudley, S. (ed.). 2010. *Museum Materialities. Objects, Engagements, Interpretations*. London and New York: Routledge

Duncan, C. 1991. Art Museums and the Ritual of Citizenship, in S. D. Lavine and I. Karp (eds), *Exhibiting Cultures. The Poetics and Politics of Museum Display:* 88-103. Washington, DC: Smithsonian Institution Press.

———. 2005. The Art Museum as Ritual in G. Corsane (ed.) *Heritage, Museums and Galleries. An introductory Reader*. 78-88 London New York: Routledge

Elsner, J. and R. Cardinal. (eds) 1994. *The Cultures of Collecting*. London: Reaktion Books

Elytis, O. 1999. Things Public and Private *in Carte Blanche. Selected Writings*. Translated by David Connolly: 65-74. The Netherlands: OPA:65

Evans, J. and S. Hall 1999. *Visual Culture: A Reader*. London: Sage Publications

Fairclough, G. 2008. New Heritage, an Introductory Essay-People, Landscape and Change, in G. Fairclough et al. (eds), *The Heritage Reader*: 297-312. London and New York: Routledge

Falk, J. and L. Dierking. 1992. *The Museum Experience*. Washington: Whalesback

———. 2000. *Learning from Museums: Visitor Experiences and the Making of Meaning*. Walnut Reek: Altamira

Friedman, J. 1992. The Past in the Future: History and Politics of Identity, *American Anthropologist* 4: 837-859

Fyfe, G. 2011. Sociology and the Social Aspects of Museums in S. Macdonald (ed), *A Companion to Museum Studies*: 33-49. UK: Blackwell Publishing

Gathercole, P. 1989. The Fetishism of Artifacts, in S. Pearce (ed.) *Museum Studies in Material* Culture: 73-81. Leicester: Leicester University Press.

Gellner, E. 1987. *Cutlture, Identity and Politics*. Cambridge: Cambridge University Press

Gothóni, R. 1993 *Paradise within Reach. Monasticism and Pilgrimage on Mount Athos*. Helsinki: Helsinki University Press

Gregory, K. and A. Witcomb. 2007. Beyond Nostalgia. The Role of Affect in generating Historical Understanding at Heritage Sites, in S. J. Knell, S. MacLeod and S. Watson (eds.), *Museums Revolutions. How Museums change and are changed*: 263-275. London and New York: Routledge

Hamilakis, Y. and E. Yalouri. 1996. Antiquities as Symbolic Capital in Modern Greek Society, *Antiquity* 70: 117-129

Hamilakis, Y. 2007. *The Nation and its Ruins: Antiquity, Archaeology, and National Imagination in Greece*. Oxford: Oxford University Press,

Hatzinikolaou, N. 2005. Distinctive Features of Athonite Spirituality in D. Conomos and G. Speake (eds) *Mount Athos the Sacred Bridge. The Spirituality of the Holy Mountain:* 17-47. Germany: Peter Lang

Herle, A. 2003. Objects, Agency and Museums. Continuing dialogues between the Torres Strait and Cambridge, in C. Peers and A. Brown (eds), *Museum and Source Communities*: 194-207. London: Routledge

Hodder, J. 1994. The Contextual Analysis of Symbolic Meanings in S. Pearce (ed.) *Interpreting Objects and Collections*: 12. London: Routledge

Hodder, I. 1986. *Reading the Past: Current Approaches to Interpretation in Archaeology*. Cambridge: Cambridge University Press.

Hooper Greenhill, E. 1999. *The Educational Role of the Museum*. London: Routledge

———. 2004. Changing Values in the Art Museum: Rethinking Communication and Learning in B. M. Carbonell (ed), *Museum Studies. An Anthology of Contexts:*556-575. Oxford: Blackwell

Hoskins, J. 1998. *Biographical Object: How Things tell the Stories of People's Live*. London and New York: Routledge

Kadas S. 1987. *Mount Athos An Illustrated Guide to the Monasteries and their History*. Athens: Ekdotiki Athenon S. A.

Karp, I. 1992. Introduction: Museums and Communities: The Politics of Public Culture, in I. Karp, C. Mullen Kreamer and S. D Lavine (eds), *Museums and Communities: The Politics of Public Culture:* 1-17. Washington, DC and London: Smithsonian Institution Press

———. 1991. Culture and representation, in S. D. Lavine and I. Karp (eds), *Exhibiting cultures. The Poetics and Politics of Museum Display:*11-24. Washington, DC: Smithsonian Institution Press.

Karp, I. and Lavine, S. (eds.). 1991. *Exhibiting Cultures: The Poetics and Politics of Museum Display*. Washington, DC: Smithsonian Institution Press

Kavanagh, G. (ed) 1991. *Museum languages: Objects and Texts*. Leicester University Press

Kazantzakis, N. 1965. *Journey to the Morea*. Translated from Greek by F.A. Reed. New York: Simon and Shuster

Keeley E. and P. Sherrard.1982. *Seferis George. Collected Poems*. Great Britain: Anvil Press Poetry.

Kerr, J. S. 2008. The Conservation Plan, in G. Fairclough et al. (eds), *The Heritage Reader:*322-330. London and New York: Routledge

Kirshenblatt-Gilbert, B. 1998. *Destination Culture: Tourism, Museums, and Heritage*. Berkeley: University of California Press

Knapp, A. B. 1999. Ideational and Industrial Landscape on Prehistoric Cyprus, in W. Ashmore and A. B. Knapp (eds) *Archaeologies of Landscape. Contemporary Perspectives*: 229-252. Oxford: Blackwell Publishers Ltd

Knell, S.J. (ed.) 2007. *Museums in the Material World*. Leicester Readers in Museum Studies. London: Routledge.

Knell, S. J., S. MacLeod and S. Watson. 2007. Introduction, in S. J. Knell, S. MacLeod, and S. Watson (eds), *Museum Revolutions. How Museums change and are changed*: xix-xxvi. London and New York: Routledge

Kohl, P. L. and C. Fawcett (eds) 1995. *Nationalism, Politics and the Practice of Archaeology*. Cambridge: Cambridge University Press

Kopytoff, I. 1986. The Cultural Biography of Things: Commoditization as process, in A. Appadurai (ed) *The Social Life of Things: Commodities in Cultural Perspective:* 64-61. Cambridge: Cambridge University Press

Kottaridi, A. 2003. *The Museum of Royal Graves of Aiges. Seeking the Lost Memory*. 17th Ephorate of Prehistorical and Classical Antiquities

Kotsakis, K. 1991. The Powerful Past: Theoretical Trends in Greek Archaeology, in I. Hodder (ed.), *Archaeological Theory in Europe: The Last Three Decades:* 65-90 London and New York: Routledge.

———. 1998. The Past is Ours: Images of Greek Macedonia, in L. Meskell (ed.), *Archaeology Under Fire*: 44-67. London and New York: Routledge.

———. 2003. Ideological Aspects of Archaeology in Greece in M. Haagsma, P. Den Boer and E. M. Moorman (eds) *The Impact of Classical Greece on European and National Identities*, Proceedings of an International Qolloquium held at the Netherlands Institute at Athens 2-4 October 2000: 55-70 Amsterdam: J.S Gieben Publisher

Kotsakis, K. 2005. Across the Border: Unstable Dwellings and Fluid Landscapes in the Earliest Neolithic of Greece, in D. Bailey, A. Whittle and V. Cummings (eds), *(Un)settling the Neolithic*. Oxford: Oxbow.

Latour, B. 2005. *Reassembling the social: An Introduction to Actor-Networking Theory*. Oxford: Oxford University Press

Lawrence, G. 1990. Object Lessons in the Museum Medium, in S. Pearce (ed.), *Objects of Knowledge:* 103-124. The Athlone Press.

Lidchi, H. 1997. The Poetics and Politics of Exhibiting Other Cultures, in S. Hall (ed.), *Representation*: 151-222. London: Sage.

Lowenthal, D. 1985. *The Past is a Foreign Country*. Cambridge: Cambridge University Press

Low, S. M. 2008. Social Sustainability. People, History, and Values, in G. Fairclough et al. (eds), *The Heritage Reader:* 392-404. London and New York: Routledge

Low, S. M. and D. Lawrence-Zuniga (eds). 2003. *The Anthropology of Space and Place: Locating Culture*. Oxford: Blackwell

Lumley, R. 1988. *The Museum Time Machine*. London: Comedia/Routledge

Macdonald, G. F. 1992. Change and Challenge: Museums in the Information Society, in I. Karp, C. Mullen Kreamer and S. D Lavine (ed), *Museums and Communities: The Politics of Public Culture:* 158-181. Washington, DC and London: Smithsonian Institution Press

Macdonald, S. 1996. Introduction in S. Macdonald and G. Fyfe (eds), *Theorizing Museums. Representing Identity and Diversity in a Changing World:* 1-18. Oxford: Blackwell/The Sociological Review

———. (ed.) 1998. *The Politics of Display. Museums, Science, Culture.* London and New York: Routledge.

———. 2005. A People's Story: Heritage, Identity and Authenticity, in G. Corsane (ed), *Heritage, Museums and Galleries*: 272-290. London and New York: Routledge

———. 2006. Expanding Museum Studies: An Introduction, in S. Macdonald (ed), *A Companion to Museum Studies*: 1-12. UK: Blackwell Publishing

———. 2011. Expanding Museum Studies: An Introduction, in S. Macdonald (ed.), *A Companion to Museum Studies*: 1-12. UK: Blackwell Publishing

Macdonald, S. and G. Fyfe (eds) 1996. *Theorizing Museums. Representing Identity and Diversity in a Changing World.* Oxford: Blackwell/The Sociological Review

MacLeod, S. 2005. Introduction in S. MacLeod (ed.), *Reshaping Museum Space: Architecture, Design, Exhibition:* 1-5. London: Routledge

Marshall, G.(ed). 1998. *A Dictionary of Sociology*. Oxford and New York: Oxford University Press

Mason, R. 2010. Assessing Values in Conservation Planning: Methodological issues and Choices in G. Faiclough et al (eds), *Heritage Reader*: 99-124. London and New York: Routledge

———. 2005. Museums, Galleries and Heritage: Sites of Meaning-Makingand Communication in G. Corsane (ed), *Heritage, Museums and Galleries*: 200-214. London and New York: Routledge

McEnroe, J. 2002. Cretan Questions: Politics and Archaeology 1898-1903, in Y. Hamilakis (ed.), *Labirynth Revisisted: Rethinking 'Minoan' Archaeology*: 59-72 Oxford: Oxbow

McManamon, F. P. 2008. Archaeological Messages and Messengers, in G. Fairclough et al. (eds), *The Heritage Reader:* 457-481. London and New York: Routledge

Merriman, N. 2000. The Crisis of Representation in Archaeological Museums in F.P. McManamon and A. Hatton (eds) *Cultural Resource Management in Contemporary Society. Perspectives on Managing and Presenting the Past*: 300-309. London and New York: Routledge

Merimman, N. 1995. Looking at the People Behind the Objects. *Curator. The Museum Journal*, 38: 6-8

Meskell, L. (ed.) 1998. *Archaeology Under Fire*. London and New York: Routledge

Meskell, L. and R. Preucel, (eds). 2004. *A Companion to Social Archaeology*. Cambridge: Cambridge University Press

Mgomezulu, G. 2004. *UNESCO, Museum International*, no. 223 (vol. 56, no.3, 2004). London: Blakwell Publishing,

Mora, J. and M. Smith. 2006. *Visual Culture: Critical Concepts in Media and Cultural Studies*. Abingdon: Routledge

Morris, I. 1994. Archaeologies of Greece in I. Morris (ed) *Classical Greece: Ancient Histories and Modern Archaeologies*: 8-47. Cambridge: Cambridge University Press.

Mullen Kreamer, C. 1992. Defining Communities through Exhibiting and Collecting, in I. Karp, C. Mullen Kreamer and S. D Lavine (ed), *Museums and Communities: The Politics of Public Culture:* 367-381. Washington, DC and London: Smithsonian Institution Press

Nixon, T.1995.Rocking the Boat: Project Management means Change, in M. A. Cooper, A. Firth, John Carman and D. Wheatley (eds), Managing Archaeology: 216-223. London and New York: Routledge

Olsen, B. 2010. In *Defence of Things. Archaeology and the Ontology of Objects*. UK: Altamira Press

Papantoniou, J.1983. The Pelloponessian Folklore Foundation, *Museum* 139:168-172

Pearce, S. 1990. Introduction, in S. Pearce (ed.), *Objects of Knowledge*: 1-5. The Athlone Press.

———. 1990. Objects as Meanings. Or narrating the past, in S. Pearce (ed.), *Objects of Knowledge:*125-140. The Athlone Press.

———. 1992. *Museums, Objects and Collections: A Cultural Study*. Leicester and London: Leicester University Press

———. (ed) 1994. *Interpreting Objects and Collections*. London: Leicester Readers in Museum Studies: Routledge

———. 1995. *On Collecting. An Investigation into Collecting in the European Tradition*. London and New York: Routledge

Peers, C. and A. Brown. 2003. Introduction in C. Peers and A. Brown (eds.) *Museum and Source Communities*: 1-16. London: Routledge

Plantzos, D. 2008. Introduction. Archaeology and Hellenic identity, 1896-2004: The Frustrated Vision, in D. Damaskos and D. Plantzos (eds.), *A Singular Antiquity. Archaeology and Hellenic Identity in twentieth century Greece:* 11-30. Athens: Mouseio Benaki 3rdSupplement.

Polyzoudi, A. 1999. Recent Approaches to Archaeological Heritage Management in Greece: The Case Study of Ancient Theatres. Unpublished Mphil dissertation. University of Cambridge.

Polyzoudi, A. and K. Nikolaidou. 2005. Choice and Inspiration: Content for Audio and Multimedia Guiding Systems. Paper presented at the CAA International Conference, Tomar, 21-24 March 2005

Polyzoudi, A. and A. Chatzoglou. 2007 The Power of Museum and Archaeological Space in Greece in the Interpretive Process of Archaeological Narratives. Paper presented at the 29th International Conference TAG, York, 14-16 December 2007

Pomian, K. 1990. *Collectors and Curiosities: Paris and Venice, 1500-1800* (trans. Elizabeth Wiles-Portier). Cambridge: Polity Press

Preziosi, D. 2004. Brain of the Earth's Body. Museums and the Framing of Modernity, in B. M. Carbonell (ed.), *Museum Studies. An Anthology of Contexts*: 71-84. Oxford: Blackwell

Prott, L. V. and P. J. O' Keefe. 1984. *Law and the Cultural Heritage, I: Discovery and Excavation.* London: Abingdon

Rapp, C. 2009. The Nature and Goals of Rhetoric, in G. Anagnostopoulos (ed.) A *Companion to Aristotle*: 579-596. UK: Blackwell

Renfrew, C. 1980. The Great Tradition versus Great Divide. Archaeology as Anthropology? *American Journal of Archaeology* 84:287-298

———. 2001. Symbols before Concept: Material Engagement and the early Development of Society, in I. Hodder (ed.), *Archaeological Theory today*. Cambridge: Polity Press

Ritchie, I. 1994. An Architect's View of Recent Developments in European Museums in R. Miles and L. Zavala (eds) *Towards the Museum of the Future. New European Perspectives*: 7-30. London and New York: Routledge

Rose, G. 2007. *Visual Methodologies: An Introduction to the Interpretation of Visual Materials.* London: Sage Publications

Saunders, N. J. 2002. Memory and Conflict, in V. Buchli (ed.), *The Material Culture Reader*: 175-206. Oxford and New York: Berg

Schirato, T. and J. Webb, 2004. *Understanding the Visual.* London: Sage Publications

Schofield, J and R. Szymanski. 2011. Sense of place in a Changing World, in J. Schofield and R. Szymanski *Local Heritage, Global Context. Cultural Perspectives on Sense of Place:*1-11. UK: Ashgate

Shanks, M. and C. Tilley. 1992 (2nd ed). *Re-constructing Archaeology*. Cambridge: Cambridge University Press

Shanks, M. and I. Hodder. 1995. Processual, Postprocessual and Interpretive Archaeologies, in M. Shanks, I. Hodder, A. Alexandri, V. Buchli, J. Carman, J. Last and G. Lucas (eds), *Interpreting Archaeology. Finding Meaning in the Past*: 3-29. London and New York: Routledge.

Shanks, M. and C. Tilley. 2007. Material Culture in Knell S. (ed.) *Museums in the Material World*: 79-93. London and New York: Routledge

Shelton, A. 1990. In the Lair of the Monkey: Notes Towards a Post-Modernist Museography, in S. Pearce (ed.), *Objects of Knowledge:* 79-102. The Athlone Press.

———. 2003. Curating African Worlds, in C. Peers and A. Brown (eds), *Museum and Source Communities*: 181-193. London: Routledge

Sherman, J. D. and I. Rogoff. (eds) 1994. Introduction: Frameworks for Critical Analysis, in J. D. Sherman and I. Rogoff. (eds) *Museum Culture. Histories, Discourses, Spectacles:* ix-xx. London: Routledge

Silberman N. A. 1989. *Between Past and Present: Archaeology, Ideology and Nationalism in the Modern Middle East*. New York: H. Holt

Silverstone, R. 1994. The Medium is the Museum: On Objects and Logics in Times and Spaces, in R. Miles and Zavala L. (eds), *Towards the Museum of the Future. New European Perspectives*:161-176. London and New York: Routledge

Smiles, S. and S. Moser. (eds). 2005. *Envisioning the Past: Archaeology and the Image.* Malden, MA: Blackwell Press

Smith, L. 2006. *Uses of Heritage*. London and New York: Routledge

Smith, L. and E. Waterton. 2009. *Heritage, Communities and Archaeology*. London: Duckworth

Snodgrass, A. 1987. *An Archaeology of Greece. The Present State and the Future Scope of a Discipline.* Berceley, Los Angeles, London: University California Press

Sørensen, S. M. 1996. The Fall of a Nation the Birth of a Subject. The National use of Archaeology in Nineteenth-Century in Denmark in M. Diaz-Andreu and T. Champion (eds) 1996. *Nationalism and Archaeology in Europe*: 24-47. London: UCL Press

Srinivasan, R. and J. Huang. 2005 Fluid Ontologies for Digital Museums, *International Journal on Digital Libraries* 5(3):193–204.

Srinivasan, R. 2007. Ethnomethodological Architectures: Information Systems driven by Cultural and Community Visions, *Journal of the American Society for Information Science and Technology* 58(5):723 –733.

Stroulia, A. and S. Buck Sutton (eds) 2010. *Archaeology in Situ. Sites, Archaeology and Communities in Greece*. United States: Lexington Books

Swain, H. 2007. *An Introduction to Museum Archaeology*. Cambridge: Cambridge University Press

Taborsky, E. 1990. The Discursive Object, in S. Pearce (ed.), *Objects of knowledge:* 51-77. The Athlone Press.

Tapsell, P. 2003. Afterword. Beyond the Frame, in C. Peers and A. Brown (eds), *Museum and Source Communities*: 242-251. London: Routledge

Tilley, C. (ed) 1993. Introduction: Interpretation and a Poetics of the Past, in *Interpretative Archaeology*: 1-27. Oxford: Berg, Providence,

———. 1994. *A Phenomenology of Landscape*. London: Berg

———. 1999. *Metaphor and Material Culture*. Oxford: Blackwell

———. 2002. Metaphor, Materiality and Interpretation in Victor Buchli (ed.), *The Material Culture Reader*: 23-26. Oxford: Berg

———. 2006. Introduction. In Chris Tilley, Webb Keane, Susanne Küchler, Mick Rowlands and Patricia Spyer. *Handbook of Material Culture*. London: Sage

Uzzell, D. and R. Ballantyne. 1998. Heritage that hurts: Interpretation in a Post-Modern World in D. Uzzell and R. Ballantyne (eds) *Contempotrary issues in Heritage and Environmental interpretation. Problems and Prospects*: 152-17. London: Stationery Office Books

Van Mench, P. 1990. Methodological Museology; or Towards a Theory of Museum Practice, in S. Pearce (ed), *Objects of Knowledge:* 141-157. The Athlone Press.

Vergo, P. 1989. *The New Museology*.London: Reaktion Books

———. 1994. The rhetoric of Display, in R. Miles and L. Zavala (eds), *Towards the Museum of the Future. New European Perspectives:*149-159. London and New York: Routledge

Voudouri, D. 2010. Law and the Politics of the Past: Legal Protection of Cultural Heritage in Greece, *International Journal Cultural Property* 17: 547-568.

Walsh, K. 1992. *The Representation of the Past. Museums and Heritage in the Post-modern world.* London and New York: Routledge

Waterton, E. and Watson, S. 2010. Introduction: A Visual Heritage, in E. Waterton, and S. Watson (eds.) *Culture, Heritage and Representation. Perspectives on Visuality and the Past*:1-16 UK: Ashgate

Yalouri, E. 2001. *The Acropolis: Global Flame Local Claim.* Oxford: Berg

———. 2010. Between the Local and the Global in Stroulia, A. and S. Buck Sutton (eds) *Archaeology in Situ. Sites, Archaeology and Communities in Greece.* 131-158. United States: Lexington Books

Žaknić, I. (ed) 1987. *Le Corbusier 1887-1965.* Journey to the East / Le Corbusier (Charles-Edouard *Jeanneret)*, translated by Ivan Žaknić in collaboration with Nicole Pertuiset. Cambridge Mass. and London: MIT Press.

Greek Publications

Ανδρεάδης, Γ. 2010. *Επιστροφή στα παιδιά της Αντιγόνης.* Αθήνα: Καστανιώτης

Ανδρόνικος Μ. 2006 (β'εκδ.) *Το Χρονικό της Βεργίνας. Μορφωτικό.* Αθήνα: Ίδρυμα Εθνικής Τράπεζας.

Ανδρόνικος, Μ. 1990. Η Αρχαιολογική Υπηρεσία, ένα μείζον πρόβλημα. *Το Βήμα.*

Αντζουλάτου-Ρετσίλα, Ε. 2005.Πολιτιστικά και Μουσειολογικά Σύμμεικτα. Αθήνα: Παπαζήση

Αρβανίτη-Κρόκου, Λ. 2002. Διαρκής Αναζήτηση. *Καθημερινή, Επτά Ήμερες.4,5 Μαΐου*

Αρβελέρ-Γλύκατζη, Ε. 2009. *Γιατί το Βυζάντιο.* Αθήνα: Ελληνικά Γράμματα

Αρχοντίδου, Α. 2001 Ελληνική Αρχαιολογική Υπηρεσία και Μουσειολογία: Πραγματικότητα και Προοπτικές, στο Μ. Σκαλτσά (επιμ.) *Η Μουσειολογία στον 21° αιώνα. Θεωρία και Πράξη*:183-185. Πρακτικά Διεθνούς Συμποσίου, 21-24 Νοεμβρίου 1997. Θεσσαλονίκη:ΥΠΠΟ, ICOM, ΑΠΘ

Βενιζέλος, Ε. 2002. *Για έναν πολιτισμό των πολιτισμών. Ελληνικότητα και Οικουμενικότητα* Αθήνα: Καστανιώτης

Βλαχογιάνης, Ι. (επιμ.) 1947. Μακρυγιάννης Ι.: Στρατηγού Μακρυγιάννη Απομνημονεύματα. Αθήνα

Βλάχου, Ε. 2001. Επικοινωνώντας με τους Επισκέπτες: Δύσκολη δουλειά αλλά κάποιος πρέπει να την κάνει (και στην Ελλάδα)! στο Μ. Σκαλτσά (επιμ.), *Η Μουσειολογία στον 21° αιώνα: Θεωρία και πράξη* :61-65. Πρακτικά Διεθνούς επιστημονικού Συμποσίου, 21-24 Νοεμβρίου 1997. Θεσσαλονίκη: Εντευκτήριο.

Βοκοτοπούλου, Ι. 1986. Τα Πρώτα 50 χρόνια της Εφορείας Κλασσικών Αρχαιοτήτων Θεσσαλονίκης, στο *Η Θεσσαλονίκη μετά το 1912*, Συμπόσιο 1-3 Νοεμβρίου 1986. Θεσσαλονίκη

Βουδούρη, Δ., 2003. *Κράτος και μουσεία. Το Θεσμικό πλαίσιο των Αρχαιολογικών Μουσείων.* Αθήνα-Θεσσαλονίκη: Σάκκουλα,.

Γερούση, Ε. και Μ. Πάντου. 2002. Η Αδυναμία Διαχείρισης του Αρχαιολογικού Έργου και οι Συνέπειές της, στο *Το Μέλλον του Παρελθόντος μας. Ανιχνεύοντας τις Προοπτικές της Αρχαιολογικής Υπηρεσίας και της Ελληνικής Αρχαιολογίας,* Πρακτικά 4^{ου} Συνεδρίου 24-26 Νοεμβρίου 2000: 49-52. Αθήνα: Ένωση Ελλήνων Αρχαιολόγων. [4th Conference Proceedings of the Archaeological Society of Greece 24-26 November 2000, Athens]

Γιαννακίδου, Α. 2002. Κατάλογος μουσείου Εθνολογικό Μουσείο Θράκης. Αλεξανδρούπολη: εκδόσεις Εθνολογικό Μουσείο Θράκης

Γιακουμάτος, Α.2002. *Καθημερινή, Επτά Ήμερες. 4,5 Μαΐου*

Γκαζή Α. 1999 Η έκθεση των αρχαιοτήτων στην Ελλάδα (1829-1909) Ιδεολογικές αφετηρίες- πρακτικές προσεγγίσεις, *Αρχαιολογία και Τέχνες* 73: 45-53

Γραμμένος, Δ. 2004. Το Αρχαιολογικό Μουσείο Θεσσαλονίκης. Τράπεζα EFG Eurobank Ergasias A.E. / Κοινωφελές Ίδρυμα Ιωάννη Σ. Λάτση: Ολκός

Νικηφορίδου, Α. και Α. Γκαζή. 2006. Οπτικοακουστικές Εφαρμογές στην Επανέκθεση του Αρχαιολογικού Μουσείου Θεσσαλονίκης. Η Μουσειολογική Προσέγγιση, *Το Αρχαιολογικό Έργο στη Μακεδονία και Θράκη*, 20:368-379

Γκαλινίκη, Σ., Ε. Κεφαλίδου, Α. Κουκουβού, Ε. Μέλλιου, Κ. Ξανθοπούλου και Κ. Σουέρεφ. 2006. Οι Νέες Εκθέσεις του Αρχαιολογικού Μουσείου Θεσσαλονίκης: Οι Ιστορικοί Χρόνοι, Το *Αρχαιολογικό Έργο στη Μακεδονία και Θράκη*, 20:404-409

Γκότσης, Στ., Λέκκα, Α., και Σακαλή, Ο. 2002 Υλικός πολιτισμός, τοπικές κοινωνίες και ερμηνευτικές δράσεις στο *Το Μέλλον του Παρελθόντος μας. Ανιχνεύοντας τις προοπτικές της Αρχαιολογικής Υπηρεσίας και της Ελληνικής Αρχαιολογίας,* Πρακτικά 4[ου] Συνεδρίου 24-26 Νοεμβρίου 2000:298-304. Αθήνα: Ένωση Ελλήνων Αρχαιολόγων. [4th Conference Proceedings of the Archaeological Society of Greece 2000, Athens]

Γραμμένος, Δ. 2004. *Το Αρχαιολογικό Μουσείο Θεσσαλονίκης*. Τράπεζα EFG Eurobank Ergasias A.E. / Κοινωφελές Ίδρυμα Ιωάννη Σ. Λάτση. Αθήνα: Ολκός

Δούλκερη-Ιντζεσίλογλου, Α.1987. Τοπικά Συμβούλια Μνημείων στο Γκράτζιου Ο., Παπαγγελή Π., Σπαθάρη Ε. (επιμ.) *Εργο και Λειτουργία μιας Υπηρεσίας για την Προστασία των Μνημείων Σήμερα,* Πρακτικά Έκτατου Συνεδρίου Συλλόγου Αρχαιολόγων για τον Οργανισμό της Αρχαιολογικής Υπηρεσίας, 9-13 Μαρτίου 1984:475-482. Αθήνα:ΥΠΠΟ-ΤΑΠΑ [Conference Proceedings of the Archaeological Society of Greece 1987, Athens]

Δωρής, Ε. 1985. *Το Δίκαιον των Αρχαιοτήτων. Νομοθεσία, Νομολογία, Ερμηνεία.* Αθήνα-Κομοτηνή: Σάκκουλας,

Ζέπος, Ρ. 1966. Ζητήματα από την Ισχύουσα Νομοθεσίαν περί Αρχαιοτήτων, στο *Χαριστήριον εις Αν. Κ. Ορλάνδον*, Γ' Βιβλιοθήκη της εν Αθήναις Αρχαιολογικής Εταρείας. Αθήνα. Vol. 3

Καββαδίας, Π. 1900. *Ιστορία της Αρχαιολογικής Εταιρείας από της εν έτει 1837 Ιδρύσεως αυτής μέχρι του 1900*. Αθήνα: Βιβλιοθήκη της εν Αθήναις Αρχαιολογικής Εταιρείας

Καλπαξής, Θ. 1990. *Αρχαιολογία και Πολιτική Ι*: Σαμιακά Αρχαιολογικά 1850-1914. Κρήτη:Πανεπιστημιακές Εκδόσεις Κρήτης

Καλτσάς, Ν. 2006. Διαχείριση μουσείων. Επισημάνσεις, προβλήματα, προτάσεις, στο *Αξιοποίηση κα Ανάδειξη της Πολιτιστικής Κληρονομιάς,* πρακτικά σεμιναρίου στο πλαίσιο της Ελληνικής προεδρίας της Ευρωπαϊκής Ένωσης υπό την αιγίδα του Υπουργείου Πολιτισμού. Αθήνα – Δελφοί 17-19 2003:239-242. Ταμείο Αρχαιολογικών Πόρων και Απαλλοτριώσεων.

Καπελώνη, Σ. και Π. Καλαμαρά, 2008. Εισαγωγή, στο *Αρχαιολογικά Μουσεία και Συλλογές στην Ελλάδα*:6-8. Αθήνα: ΥΠΠΟ-Διεύθυνση Μουσείων, Εκθέσεων και Εκπαιδευτικών Προγραμμάτων.

Κιτρομηλίδης Π.Μ. 1996. *Νεοελληνικός Διαφωτισμός.* Αθήνα:ΜΙΕΤ

Κόκκου Α. 1977. (2009). *Η μέριμνα για τις αρχαιότητες στην Ελλάδα και τα πρώτα μουσεία.* Αθήνα:Ερμής.

Κουρκουτίδου-Νικολαίδου, Ε. 1994. *Μουσείο Βυζαντινού Πολιτισμού,* No. 1. Υπουργείο Πολιτισμού-9[η] Εφορεία Βυζαντινών Αρχαιοτήτων (translated in English and French)

Κυριακίδου-Νέστορος, Α. 1978. *Η Θεωρία της Ελληνικής Λαογραφίας.* Αθήνα

Κωνστάντιος, Δ. 2003. *Η Πόλη, το Μουσείο, το Μνημείο. Δοκίμια πολιτιστικής Διαχείρισης.* Athens

Κωνστάντιος, Δ. 2002. Η Πρόκληση των Μουσείων στον 21° αιώνα στο *Το Μέλλον του Παρελθόντος μας. Ανιχνεύοντας τις προοπτικές της Αρχαιολογικής Υπηρεσίας και της Ελληνικής Αρχαιολογίας,* Πρακτικά 4[ου] Συνεδρίου 24-26 Νοεμβρίου 2000:174-176. Αθήνα:Ένωση Ελλήνων Αρχαιολόγων. [4th Conference Proceedings of the Archaeological Society of Greece 2000, Athens]

Κωνστάντιος, Δ. 2006. Ας μιλήσουμε για Μουσεία στο Ν. Ζαφειροπούλου (επιμ.) *Αξιοποίηση και Ανάδειξη της Πολιτιστικής Κληρονομιάς*: 189-191. Πρακτικά

Σεμιναρίου στα Πλαίσια της Ελληνικής Προεδρίας της Ευρωπαικής Ένωσης υπό την αιγίδα του Υπουργείου Πολιτισμού, Αθήνα-Δελφοί 17-19 Μαρτίου 2003. Αθήνα: Ταμείο Αρχαιολογικών Πόρων και Απαλλοτριώσεων.

Κωτσάκης, Κ. 2001. Από το Έκθεμα στο Νόημα. Η ερμηνεία στη σύγχρονη θεωρία της αρχαιολογίας στο Μ. Σκαλτσά (επιμ.), *Η Μουσειολογία στον 21ο αιώνα: Θεωρία και πράξη* :196-200. Πρακτικά Διεθνούς επιστημονικού Συμποσίου, 21-24 Νοεμβρίου 1997. Θεσσαλονίκη: Εντευκτήριο.

Κωτσάκης, Κ. 1997. Η Μαύρη Αθηνά. Αφηγήσεις στο κενό, *Σύγχρονα Θέματα* 64:37-41

Μακαρόνας, Χ. 1941-1952. *Μακεδονικά* 2: 560-677

Μαρθάρη, Μ. 2002. Εκθέσεις Μουσείων και ο Ρόλος του Αρχαιολόγου της Ελληνικής Αρχαιολογικής Υπηρεσίας: το Παράδειγμα Παρουσίασης του Πρωτοκυκλαδικού Κόσμου, στο *Το Μέλλον του Παρελθόντος μας. Ανιχνεύοντας τις προοπτικές της Αρχαιολογικής Υπηρεσίας και της Ελληνικής Αρχαιολογίας,* Πρακτικά 4ου Συνεδρίου 24-26 Νοεμβρίου 2000: 167-173. Αθήνα:Ένωση Ελλήνων Αρχαιολόγων. [4th Conference Proceedings of the Archaeological Society of Greece 2000, Athens]

Μαρωνίτης, Δ. 2002 Η Αρχαία κληρονομιά: Γέφυρες πραγματικές, στημένες, κομμένες, στο *Οι Χρήσεις της Αρχαιότητας από το Νέο Ελληνισμό*, Επιστημονικό Συμπόσιο 14-15 Απριλίου 2000: 13-24. Αθήνα: Εταιρεία Σπουδών Νεοελληνικού Πολιτισμού και Γενικής παιδείας (Σχολή Μωραΐτη)

Μαστραντώνης, Π. 2008. *Διαχείρηση Αρχαιολογικών Έργων. Θεωρητικό Πλαίσο και Ανάπτυξη Εξειδικευμένων Εργαλείων.* Αθήνα: Ινστιτούτο βιβλίου-Καρδαμίτσα

Μπούρας, Χ. 1996. Μνημεία της Αρχαιότητας. Τα Όρια των Αποκαταστάσεων, στο *Οι Ελληνικές Αναστηλώσεις*: 24-34. Αθήνα: Βιβλιοθήκη της εν Αθήναις Αρχαιολογικής Εταιρείας no 154

Πάλλας, Δ. 1987. Εναρκτήρια ομιλία του Προέδρου της Οργανωτικής Επιτροπής, στο Πρακτικά *Α' Συνάντησης Μουσειολογίας*, Αθήνα, 29-31 Οκτωβρίου 1984:17-21. Αθήνα:ICOM

Παπάγγελος, Ι. και Σ. Παλιομπέης. 2006. Προχριστιανικές Αρχαιότητες στον Άθω στο Σ. Αθανασιάδης και Χ. Χειλάς (επιμ.) *Άγιον Όρος και Προχριστιανική Αρχαιότητα.* Θεσσαλονίκη: ΚΕΔΑΚ-ΥΜΑΘ

Παπαδόπουλος Σ. 2003. Ανθρωπολογικά μουσεία. Μικρά μελετήματα. Πολιτιστικό Ίδρυμα Ομίλου Πειραιώς. Αθήνα

Παπαθανασίου, Ε. 2002. Ο Ρόλος του αρχαιολόγου στην 'ανάπτυξη' της περιφέρειας. Η ανάκτηση της τοπικής μνήμης μέσα από την κατάδειξη του ιστορικού τοπίου, στο *Το Μέλλον του Παρελθόντος μας. Ανιχνεύοντας τις προοπτικές της Αρχαιολογικής Υπηρεσίας και της Ελληνικής Αρχαιολογίας,* Πρακτικά 4ου Συνεδρίου 24-26 Νοεμβρίου 2000:324-333. Αθήνα:Ένωση Ελλήνων Αρχαιολόγων. [4th Conference Proceedings of the Archaeological Society of Greece 2000, Athens]

Παπαπετρόπουλος, Δ. 2006. Νόμος 3028/2002. *Για την Προστασία των Αρχαιοτήτων και εν γένει της Πολιτιστικής Κληρονομιάς.* Αθήνα-Θεσσαλονίκη: Σάκκουλας

Πετράκος, Β. 1982. *Δοκίμιο για την Αρχαιολογική Νομοθεσία.* Αθήνα: ΥΠΠΟ-ΤΑΠ.

Πετράκος, Β. 1987. *Η εν Αθήναις Αρχαιολογική Εταιρεία. Η Ιστορία των 150 χρόνων της (1837-1987).* Αθήνα: Βιβλιοθήκη της εν Αθήναις Αρχαιολογικής Εταιρείας

Περιοδικό της Εν Αθήναις Αρχαιολογικής Εταιρείας.1992. *Ο Μέντωρ*, 20

Πρωτοψάλτης, Ε. 1967. *Ιστορικά Έγγραφα περί αρχαιοτήτων και λοιπών μνημείων της ιστορίας κατά τους χρόνους της επαναστάσεως και του Καποδίστρια.* Αθήνα: Βιβλιοθήκη της εν Αθήναις Αρχαιολογικής Εταιρείας, αρ. 59.

Σακελλαράκης, Γ. 2003. *Η Ποιητική της Ανασκαφής*. Αθήνα: Ίκαρος.

Σακελλαρίου, Μ. (επιμ.) 1982. *Μακεδονία: 4000 χρόνια Ελληνικής Ιστορίας και Πολιτισμού*. Αθήνα

Σισμανίδης, Κ. 1993-1994-1995 … (άρθρα που αφορούν στην ανασκαφή των Αρχαίων Σταγείρων), στο *Αρχαιολογικό Έργο στη Μακεδονία και Θράκη*. ΥΠΠΟ και Αριστοτέλειο Πανεπιστήμιο Θεσσαλονίκης

Στεφανή, Λ. 2006. 5.000, 15.000, 200.000 Χρόνια πριν… μια Έκθεση για τη Ζωή στην Προϊστορική Μακεδονία. Η Νέα Μόνιμη Έκθεση για την προϊστορία της Μακεδονίας στο Αρχαιολογικό Μουσείο Θεσσαλονίκης, *Το Αρχαιολογικό Έργο στη Μακεδονία και Θράκη,*20:391-398

Τροβά Ε. (επιμ.) 2004. *Η Πολιτιστική Κληρονομιά και το Δίκαιο*. Αθήνα-Θεσσαλονίκη: Σάκκουλα

Φιλιππίδης, Δ. 1984. *Νεοελληνική Αρχιτεκτονική*. Αθήνα: Μέλισσα

Φιλιποπούλου-Μιχαϊλίδου, Έ. 1999. Μουσεία σε Κρίση Ταυτότητας, *Επτάκυκλος* 52:47-58

Χουρμουζιάδης, Γ.1980. Μουσείο: Σχολείο ή ναός, *Θέματα χώρου και τεχνών* 11:38

Χουρμουζιάδης, Γ. 1990. Η Ελληνική Αρχαιολογία ανάμεσα στο Μονόδρομο του Παρελθόντος και στο Λαβύρινθο του Μέλλοντος: Μια σύντομη αλλά Απαισιόδοξη Κριτική, στο *Πόλις και Χώρα στην Αρχαία Μακεδονία και Θράκη*. Πρακτικά συνεδρίου, 1986: 719-725. Αθήνα: ΥΠΠΟ και Ecole Francaise d' Athènes

Χουρμουζιάδης Γ. 2001. Δισπηλιό Καστοριάς. Για μια νέα Μουσειολογία, στο Μ. Σκαλτσά (επιμ.), *Η Μουσειολογία στον 21ο αιώνα: Θεωρία και πράξη*:233-236. Πρακτικά Διεθνούς επιστημονικού Συμποσίου, 21-24 Νοεμβρίου 1997. Θεσσαλονίκη: Εντευκτήριο.

Χουρμουζιάδης Γ. 1995. Σχόλια στην Ελληνική Μουσειολογία, *Αναλογίες*:205-206. Θεσσαλονίκη: Βάνιας

Χουρμουζιάδης Γ. 2002. Εμείς και οι Αρχαίοι, στο *Οι Χρήσεις της Αρχαιότητας από τον Ελληνισμό*, Επιστημονικό Συμπόσιο 14-15 Απριλίου 2000:159-168. Αθήνα. Εταιρεία Σπουδών Νεολληνικού Πολιτισμού και Γενικής παιδείας (Σχολή Μωραίτη)

Χουρμουζιάδης Γ. 1999. *Λόγια από Χώμα*. Σκόπελος: Νησίδες

Χουρμουζιάδη, Α. 2002. Το πρόγραμμα της αναπαράστασης, στο Γ. Χουρμουζιάδης (επιστ. επιμ.), *Δισπηλιό, 7500 Χρόνια μετά:* 331-348. Θεσσαλονίκη: University Press.

Χουρμουζιάδη, Α. 2006. *Το Ελληνικό Αρχαιολογικό Μουσείο. Ο Εκθέτης το Έκθεμα ο Επισκέπτης*. Θεσσαλονίκη: Βάνιας.

Χριστοφιλόπουλος, Δ. *Προστασία πολιτιστικών αγαθών*, Σάκκουλας, Αθήνα 2005.

Χριστόπουλος, Γ., Μπαστιάς, Ι., Σιμόπουλος, Κ. και Κ. Δασκαλοπούλου. (eds.) 1970. *Ιστορία του Ελληνικού Έθνους*. Αθήνα

www.ingramcontent.com/pod-product-compliance
Lightning Source LLC
LaVergne TN
LVHW052353100826
845147LV00013B/827

* 9 7 8 1 8 6 3 3 5 1 8 4 3 *